P9-CKA-031

Date Due

DE 1 8 '84 DE 2 05			
MY 3 91			
AP 29 '94			
MY 7 '97			
NO 30 00			
DE '02			
EE 9 '06			

John Donne and the
seventeenth-cen-
tury metaphysical
poets

Riverside City College Library
4800 Magnolia Avenue
Riverside, California 92506

DE   '86

DEMCO

John Donne and the Seventeenth-Century Metaphysical Poets

Modern Critical Views

Henry Adams
Edward Albee
A. R. Ammons
Matthew Arnold
John Ashbery
W. H. Auden
Jane Austen
James Baldwin
Charles Baudelaire
Samuel Beckett
Saul Bellow
The Bible
Elizabeth Bishop
William Blake
Jorge Luis Borges
Elizabeth Bowen
Bertolt Brecht
The Brontës
Robert Browning
Anthony Burgess
George Gordon, Lord
    Byron
Thomas Carlyle
Lewis Carroll
Willa Cather
Cervantes
Geoffrey Chaucer
Kate Chopin
Samuel Taylor Coleridge
Joseph Conrad
Contemporary Poets
Hart Crane
Stephen Crane
Dante
Charles Dickens
Emily Dickinson
John Donne & the Seven-
    teenth-Century Meta-
    physical Poets
Elizabethan Dramatists
Theodore Dreiser
John Dryden
George Eliot
T. S. Eliot
Ralph Ellison
Ralph Waldo Emerson
William Faulkner
Henry Fielding
F. Scott Fitzgerald
Gustave Flaubert
E. M. Forster
Sigmund Freud
Robert Frost

Robert Graves
Graham Greene
Thomas Hardy
Nathaniel Hawthorne
William Hazlitt
Seamus Heaney
Ernest Hemingway
Geoffrey Hill
Friedrich Hölderlin
Homer
Gerard Manley Hopkins
William Dean Howells
Zora Neale Hurston
Henry James
Samuel Johnson and
    James Boswell
Ben Jonson
James Joyce
Franz Kafka
John Keats
Rudyard Kipling
D. H. Lawrence
John Le Carré
Ursula K. Le Guin
Doris Lessing
Sinclair Lewis
Robert Lowell
Norman Mailer
Bernard Malamud
Thomas Mann
Christopher Marlowe
Carson McCullers
Herman Melville
James Merrill
Arthur Miller
John Milton
Eugenio Montale
Marianne Moore
Iris Murdoch
Vladimir Nabokov
Joyce Carol Oates
Sean O'Casey
Flannery O'Connor
Eugene O'Neill
George Orwell
Cynthia Ozick
Walter Pater
Walker Percy
Harold Pinter
Plato
Edgar Allan Poe
Poets of Sensibility & the
    Sublime

Alexander Pope
Katherine Ann Porter
Ezra Pound
Pre-Raphaelite Poets
Marcel Proust
Thomas Pynchon
Arthur Rimbaud
Theodore Roethke
Philip Roth
John Ruskin
J. D. Salinger
Gershom Scholem
William Shakespeare
    (3 vols.)
    Histories & Poems
    Comedies
    Tragedies
George Bernard Shaw
Mary Wollstonecraft
    Shelley
Percy Bysshe Shelley
Edmund Spenser
Gertrude Stein
John Steinbeck
Laurence Sterne
Wallace Stevens
Tom Stoppard
Jonathan Swift
Alfred, Lord Tennyson
William Makepeace
    Thackeray
Henry David Thoreau
Leo Tolstoi
Anthony Trollope
Mark Twain
John Updike
Gore Vidal
Virgil
Robert Penn Warren
Evelyn Waugh
Eudora Welty
Nathanael West
Edith Wharton
Walt Whitman
Oscar Wilde
Tennessee Williams
William Carlos Williams
Thomas Wolfe
Virginia Woolf
William Wordsworth
Richard Wright
William Butler Yeats

These and other titles in preparation

Modern Critical Views

John Donne and the Seventeenth-Century Metaphysical Poets

Edited and with an introduction by
Harold Bloom
Sterling Professor of the Humanities
Yale University

CHELSEA HOUSE PUBLISHERS ◇ 1986
New York ◇ New Haven ◇ Philadelphia

Riverside Community College
Library
4800 Magnolia Avenue
Riverside, CA 92506

PR545.M4 J55 1986
John Donne and the
seventeenth-century
metaphysical poets

Copyright © 1986 by Chelsea House Publishers, a division of Chelsea
House Educational Communications, Inc.
133 Christopher Street, New York, NY 10014
345 Whitney Avenue, New Haven, CT 06511
5014 West Chester Pike, Edgemont, PA 19028

Introduction copyright © 1986 by Harold Bloom

All rights reserved. No part of this publication may be reproduced or
transmitted, in any form or by any means, without the written
permission of the publisher.

Printed and bound in the United States of America

Library of Congress Cataloging-in-Publication Data
John Donne and the seventeenth-century metaphysical poets.
   (Modern critical views)
   Bibliography: p. 249
   Includes index.
   1. English poetry—Early modern, 1500-1700—History and criticism.
2. Donne, John, 1572-1631—Criticism and interpretation. 3. Marvell,
Andrew, 1621-1678—Criticism and interpretation. I. Bloom, Harold.
II. Series.
[PR545.M4J55 1986]   821'.3'09   86-4208
ISBN 0-87754-677-0

Contents

Editor's Note

This book gathers together a representative selection of the best criticism available upon the principal seventeenth-century English poets, with the exception of John Milton, to whom a separate volume in this series is devoted. Four essays are given to John Donne, three to Andrew Marvell, two to George Herbert, and one each to Robert Herrick, Richard Crashaw, Henry Vaughan and Thomas Traherne. The editor is grateful to Douglas Smith for his erudition and judgment in helping to locate and select these essays.

My introduction centers upon Dr. Samuel Johnson's critique of the Metaphysical poets, and also upon his skepticism as to the possibilities of devotional poetry. I share both Johnsonian reservations, and attempt to clarify them here. Four remarkable essays upon the poetry of Donne then follow, starting with John Freccero's learned and brilliant exegesis of the psychic cosmology of the "Valediction: Forbidding Mourning." John Hollander's advanced and witty analysis of Donne's metric transcends its own formalism by showing us that, in Donne's mode, "the truest tenderness is the most feigning."

The essay by William Kerrigan is an original exploration of Donne's highly individual theological daring in the use of anthropomorphic metaphors throughout his devotional poems. Related to such daring is Donne's mastery of "the imaging of the logical conceit," which is Claudia Brodsky's concern in her subtle essay on the persuasive or positive aspect of Donne's tropes in its interplay with the critical or negative aspect, which deconstructs imagery from its apparent sense.

Two very different critics of George Herbert, Stanley E. Fish, who emphasizes the role of the reader's response, and Helen Vendler, a more formalistic close reader, are juxtaposed in this book. Fish attempts to convince us that, in Herbert's poetry, "ambiguity . . . is the true literalism," because for Herbert Christ is everything, and in comparison we are nothing.

In sharp contrast, Helen Vendler praises the provisional quality of Herbert's poetry, which allowed him to see himself alternately as in a filial relation to Christ, and as an originating ego in his own right.

Thomas R. Whitaker, in the best essay I have read on Robert Herrick, finds a fruitful way of describing Herrick's symbolism, which mediates between art as "momentary imaginative transcendence of the temporal" and the world of natural flux. Herrick's dialectical opposite is Richard Crashaw, whose "dawn of Christian time" is celebrated by A. R. Cirillo in a strong reading of the hymn "In the Glorious Epiphanie of Our Lord God."

Louis Martz, our most eminent critic of the meditative and Metaphysical modes is represented here by his superb overview of Henry Vaughan's poetry. Martz's emphasis upon Vaughan's "paradise within" is a useful prelude to the far more complex visions of paradise as being without, within, betwixt, between—of the great and enigmatic poet, Andrew Marvell, whose work is examined here by three of our finest critics of seventeenth-century poetry. Ruth Nevo analyzes Marvell's contraries of pastoral innocence and the sting of experience, while Harry Berger, Jr. provides a complex and truly adequate interpretation of the marvelous "Upon Appleton House." An even more intricate exegesis is given in Geoffrey Hartman's sinuous reading of the astonishingly subtle "The Nymph Complaining for the Death of Her Faun."

This book concludes with Barbara K. Lewalski's essay upon the ecstatic Thomas Traherne, which recognizes his limitations when compared with Donne, Herbert, and Vaughan, and yet sturdily argues the case for his still valid achievement. By indicating that Traherne moved too far towards a philosophical abstractness in his verse, Lewalski reminds us that the true achievement of the school of Donne was to balance argument with trope, devotional intensity with worldly wit.

Introduction

I

Abraham Cowley is a poet remembered today only by scholars, and I doubt that he has a dozen readers a year among them, whether in America or in Britain. In the later seventeenth century he was regarded as a canonical poet, hugely influential, very much the Ezra Pound of his era. Though faded by Johnson's day, he was still famous enough to lead off the *Lives of the Poets*, where he, rather than Donne, is regarded as the founder and chief ornament (rather dimmed) of the Metaphysical school or line of wit, the bad old way superseded by Dryden and Pope.

Literary history, particularly the history of criticism, has a habit of making ludicrous many of a period's firm judgments. When I was young, Shelley was ignored or deprecated in literary and academic circles, and Donne was considered the paradigm of poetry. In the age of Eliot (or the Pound Era, if you prefer), you were dismissed as barbaric or eccentric if you believed that *Song of Myself* was the central American poem, or that Hart Crane was a permanent poet, and W. H. Auden perhaps something less than that.

Johnson himself thought his *Life of Cowley* the best of the *Lives*, since his discussion of the Metaphysical poets (he took his name for them from Dryden) was a pioneer venture. It may be unfashionable to believe this, but Johnson's discussion of the school of Donne seems to me still the most adequate we possess, despite the perpetual Donne revivals which go on continuously, from Coleridge through Arthur Symons in the nineteenth century, and endlessly in our own.

Johnson, whatever his blindnesses and flaws, remains the most fecund and suggestive literary critic in the language, with only Hazlitt and Ruskin as his near rivals. It could hardly be expected that he should have preferred John Donne to Alexander Pope; I do not, and in any case Johnson's analysis of Metaphysical poetry still seems to me more just than any of the modern

1

defenses, down to the persuasive attempt by Louis Martz to substitute "the meditative poem" for "the metaphysical poem" as a category. Martz gives a very useful account of both terms, and of their complex interaction:

> Meditation points toward poetry, in its use of images, in its technique of arousing the passionate affections of the will . . .
>
> For critical and historical purposes we should, I believe, attempt to distinguish between the "metaphysical" and the "meditative" qualities in this poetry . . .
>
> ["Metaphysical"] poems tend to begin abruptly, in the midst of an occasion; and the meaning of the occasion is explored and grasped through a peculiar use of metaphor. The old Renaissance "conceit," the ingenious comparison, is developed into a device by which the extremes of abstraction and concreteness, the extremes of unlikeness, may be woven together into a fabric of argument unified by the prevailing force of "wit."

This is responsible and lucid, though a long way from the fierce verve of Johnson on the same matter:

> Wit, like all other things subject by their nature to the choice of man, has its changes and fashions, and at different times takes different forms. About the beginning of the seventeenth century appeared a race of writers that may be termed the metaphysical poets . . .
>
> The metaphysical poets were men of learning, and to shew their learning was their whole endeavour . . .
>
> If the father of criticism has rightly denominated poetry . . . *an imitative art*, these writers will, without great wrong, lose their right to the name of poets; for they cannot be said to have imitated any thing; they neither copied nature nor life; neither painted the forms of matter, nor represented the operations of intellect.
>
> Those however who deny them to be poets, allow them to be wits. Dryden confesses of himself and his contemporaries, that they fall below Donne in wit, but maintains that they surpass him in poetry.
>
> If Wit be well described by Pope, as being "that which has been often thought, but was never before so well expressed," they certainly never attained, nor ever sought it; for they endeavoured to be singular in their thoughts, and were careless of their diction. But Pope's account of wit is undoubtedly erroneous: he depresses

it below its natural dignity, and reduces it from strength of thought to happiness of language.

If by a more noble and more adequate conception that be considered as Wit, which is at once natural and new, that which, though not obvious, is, upon its first production, acknowledged to be just; if it be that, which he that never found it, wonders how he missed; to wit of this kind the metaphysical poets have seldom risen. Their thoughts are often new, but seldom natural; they are not obvious, but neither are they just; and the reader, far from wondering that he missed them, wonders more frequently by what perverseness of industry they were ever found.

But Wit, abstracted from its effects upon the hearer, may be more rigorously and philosophically considered as a kind of *discordia concors*; a combination of dissimilar images, or discovery of occult resemblances in things apparently unlike. Of wit, thus defined, they have more than enough. The most heterogeneous ideas are yoked by violence together; nature and art are ransacked for illustrations, comparisons, and allusions; their learning instructs, and their subtilty surprises; but the reader commonly thinks his improvement dearly bought, and though he sometimes admires is seldom pleased.

Wit is, for Johnson, as he says: "strength of thought" and not mere "happiness of language." Though he went on to deny Donne and his followers a share either in "the pathetick" or "the sublime," Johnson gave them what was, for him, a measure of true praise:

Yet great labour, directed by great abilities, is never wholly lost: if they frequently threw away their wit upon false conceits, they likewise sometimes struck out unexpected truth: if their conceits were far-fetched, they were often worth the carriage. To write on their plan, it was at least necessary to read and think. No man cold be born a metaphysical poet, nor assume the dignity of a writer, by descriptions copied from descriptions, by imitations borrowed from imitations, by traditional imagery, and hereditary similies, by readiness of rhyme, and volubility of syllables.

In perusing the works of this race of authours, the mind is exercised either by recollection or inquiry; either something already learned is to be retrieved, or something new is to be examined. If their greatness seldom elevates, their acuteness often surprises; if the imagination is not always gratified, at least the powers of reflection and comparison are employed; and in the mass of materials which ingenious absurdity has thrown together, genuine wit and useful knowledge may be sometimes found, buried perhaps in grossness of expression, but useful to those who know their value; and such as, when they are expanded to perspicuity, and polished to elegance, may give lustre to works which have more propriety, though less copiousness of sentiment.

Reading and thinking are activities Johnson always recommended to poets, particularly at his own moment, yet these paragraphs of praise are qualified by the absence of Johnson's deepest veneration, which is for wisdom and its poetic refinement through elaborate invention. Johnson is careful to deny Cowley (and Donne, his master) invention, the essence of poetry, though his care is uneasily qualified by an implicit realization that is made explicit in *The Rambler* No. 125:

Definitions have been no less difficult or uncertain in criticism than in law. Imagination, a licentious and vagrant faculty, unsusceptible of limitations, and impatient of restraint, has always endeavoured to baffle the logician, to perplex the confines of distinction, and burst the enclosures of regularity. There is therefore scarcely any species of writing, of which we can tell what is its essence, and what are its constituents; every new genius produces some innovation which, when invented and approved, subverts the rules which the practice of foregoing authors had established.

We cannot fault Johnson for not seeing Donne as such a new genius of innovation, and not merely because we would excuse the critic's blindness as a product of the vagaries of taste. Towards Donne, Johnson is both puzzled and respectful. His Donne is "a man of very extensive and various knowledge," "abstruse and profound," "indelicate," whose work, when improper, "is produced by a voluntary deviation from nature in pursuit of something new or strange." But this Donne troubles Johnson, as Cowley does not. What Donne calls into question is Johnson's criteria of the general or the universal, and the natural, and to have provoked the great critic in regard to those criteria is to have manifested indubitable poetic strength.

II

Johnson had a great distrust of devotional verse, which I suspect was a hidden element in his ambivalence towards the Metaphysical poets. Even in the *Life of Cowley*, the distrust is evidenced, when Johnson discusses Cowley's frigid religious epic, the *Davideis*:

> Sacred History has been always read with submissive reverence, and an imagination over-awed and controlled. We have been accustomed to acquiesce in the nakedness and simplicity of the authentick narrative, and to repose on its veracity with such humble confidence, as suppresses curiosity. We go with the historian as he goes, and stop with him when he stops. All amplification is frivolous and vain; all addition to that which is already sufficient for the purposes of religion, seems not only useless, but in some degree profane.
>
> Such events as were produced by the visible interposition of Divine Power are above the power of human genius to dignify. The miracle of Creation, however it may teem with images, is best described with little diffusion of language: *He spake the word, and they were made.*

Two very diverse judgments, moral and aesthetic, uneasily mingle here. "Submissive reverence," with one's imagination "over-awed and controlled," is hardly a proper stance for any critic, let alone the strongest critic in Western literary tradition. This moral position is curiously reinforced by Johnson's keen aesthetic apprehension of the sublime economy of style manifested by the Authorized Version of the Holy Bible, much of it the work of the preternaturally eloquent William Tyndale and of Miles Coverdale. Poor Cowley has little hope of sustaining close comparison to Tyndale, but that is his Johnsonian punishment for daring to provoke a great critic into "submissive reverence." At that, Cowley fared better than the unfortunate Edmund Waller, whose Sacred Poems stimulated Johnson to the most powerful strictures against religious verse ever written:

> Contemplative piety, or the intercourse between God and the human soul, cannot be poetical. Man admitted to implore the mercy of his Creator, and plead the merits of his Redeemer, is already in a higher state than poetry can confer.
>
> The essence of poetry is invention; such invention as, by producing something unexpected, surprises and delights. The topicks of devotion are few, and being few are universally known; but few as they are, they can be made no more; they can receive no grace from novelty of sentiment, and very little from novelty of expression.

Poetry pleases by exhibiting an idea more grateful to the mind than things themselves afford. This effect proceeds from the display of those parts of nature which attract, and the concealment of those which repel the imagination: but religion must be shewn as it is; suppression and addition equally corrupt it; and such as it is, it is known already.

From poetry the reader justly expects, and from good poetry always obtains, the enlargement of his comprehension and elevation of his fancy; but this is rarely to be hoped by Christians from metrical devotion. Whatever is great, desireable, or tremendous, is comprised in the name of the Supreme Being. Omnipotence cannot be exalted; Infinity cannot be amplified; Perfection cannot be improved.

The employments of pious meditation are Faith, Thanksgiving, Repentance, and Supplication. Faith, invariably uniform, cannot be invested by fancy with decorations. Thanksgiving, the most joyful of all holy effusions, yet addressed to a Being without passions, is confined to a few modes, and is to be felt rather than expressed. Repentance, trembling in the presence of the Judge, is not at leisure for cadences and epithets. Supplication of man to man may diffuse itself through many topicks of persuasion; but supplication to God can only cry for mercy.

Of sentiments purely religious, it will be found that the most simple expression is the most sublime. Poetry loses its lustre and its power, because it is applied to the decoration of something more excellent than itself. All that verse can do is to help the memory, and delight the ear, and for these purposes it may be very useful; but it supplies nothing to the mind. The ideas of Christian Theology are too simple for eloquence, too sacred for fiction, and too majestick for ornament; to recommend them by tropes and figures, is to magnify by a concave mirror the sidereal hemisphere.

How well do Donne's devotional poems, or Herbert's, or those of Crashaw, Vaughan, Traherne withstand this formidable theoretical assault? Do the meditative poems of the Metaphysical school escape the indictment that their tropes merely "magnify by a concave mirror the sidereal hemisphere"?

Perhaps Johnson could be accused of overstating the aesthetic risk of devotional verse, yet he is refreshingly original and all but unique among critics in addressing himself to this difficult, and for him painful matter. It should be noted that Johnson's exalted praise of Milton, extraordinary in a critic who opposed Milton in politics, religion, and cultural vision, is founded upon the critic's conviction that Milton almost uniquely overcomes the limitations of a religious poetry:

> Pleasure and terrour are indeed the genuine sources of poetry; but poetical pleasure must be such as human imagination can at least conceive, and poetical terrour such as human strength and fortitude may combat. The good and evil of Eternity are too ponderous for the wings of wit; the mind sinks under them in passive helplessness, content with calm belief and humble adoration.
>
> Known truths, however, may take a different appearance, and be conveyed to the mind by a new train of intermediate images. This Milton has undertaken, and performed with pregnancy and vigour of mind peculiar to himself. Whoever considers the few radical positions which the Scriptures afforded him, will wonder by what energetick operation he expanded them to such extent, and ramified them to so much variety, restrained as he was by religious reverence from licentiousness of fiction.

It is by the standard of *Paradise Lost* as a Christian poem that Johnson found the meditative poetry of the school of Donne unpersuasive and uninteresting. As readers of Donne's sublime hymns, or Herbert's *The Temple,* we rightly are convinced that Johnson's sensibility was surprisingly narrow when he read the Metaphysicals. On the basis of his quotations from Donne in the *Life of Cowley,* Johnson seems to have shied away from Donne's divine poems, and he avoids quoting from Herbert. What seems an overwhelming virtue of Metaphysical devotional verse, its detailed imagery and highly individualized figurations, must have offended Johnson's Horatian passion for the universal. Certainly he had little patience for the minute particulars of the Metaphysical trope:

> The fault of Cowley, and perhaps of all the writers of the metaphysical race, is that of pursuing his thoughts to their last ramifications, by which he loses the grandeur of generality; for of the greatest things the parts are little; what is little can be but pretty, and by claiming dignity becomes ridiculous. Thus all the power of description is destroyed by a scrupulous enumeration; and the force of metaphors is lost, when the mind by the mention

of particulars is turned more upon the original than the
secondary sense, more upon that from which the illustration is
drawn than that to which it is applied.

III

Frank Kermode, a foremost contemporary critic of Donne, accurately
remarks: "It remains true that to write of the fortunes of Donne in the past
seventy years is, in effect, to write less about him than about the aesthetic
preoccupations of that epoch." I would amplify Kermode's observation,
fifteen years later, by suggesting that the years 1915-1955 had very different
"aesthetic preoccupations" than the years 1955-1985, or than the years
remaining to this century are likely to have. Eliot, as Kermode says, sought
to associate his own poetry with the mode of Donne, but Eliot's poetry, as
Kermode does not say, in fact derives from Tennyson and Whitman. *The
Waste Land* has far more in common with "Maud" and "When Lilacs Last
in the Dooryard Bloom'd" than it does with *The Second Anniversarie* or
"A Nocturnall upon S. Lucies Day." Kermode associates the restoration of
Donne "to his place among the English poets" with the restoration of "wit
to its place in poetry." Johnson associated wit with poetry and Pope. I myself
find more wit in the Shelley of *The Triumph of Life* than in Donne, but
then I am of a different critical generation from that of Kermode.

I doubt that future defenses of Donne and of his school will organize
themselves as Modernist celebrations of a Metaphysical agility in wit. Donne
seems now as archaic as Spenser, and as specialized as Ben Jonson. The
Eliotic vogue for him is now over, and with it is gone the New Critical notion
that every good short poem must follow the paradigm of a Donne lyric or
meditation. Johnson's powerful critique of the Metaphysicals may not be
the last word, but it has recovered a good part of its force during the past
thirty years. The recent essays reprinted in this volume manifest a serious
attempt to appreciate the school of Donne on a basis very different from
the one that extends from Eliot to Kermode. Donne and Herbert do not seem
to me poets of the eminence of Spenser and Milton, and a critical epoch
that preferred them to Spenser and Milton was certain to pass away as an
almost grotesque interlude in the history of taste. But they are the principal
devotional poets in the language, hardly equalled by Hopkins or by the Eliot
of the *Quartets* or the later Auden. Whatever Johnson thought, the sacred
Milton was anything but a devotional poet. A sect of one, Milton
persuasively redefined Christianity almost as drastically as William Blake

did. Curiously enough, it was rather Donne and Herbert, and their fellows, who merited Johnson's praise. For them, the good and evil of Eternity were not "too ponderous for the wings of wit."

JOHN FRECCERO

Donne's Compass Image

In the twelfth chapter of Dante's *Vita nuova*, Love appears to the poet in the form of an angel and gives himself a mystic definition: "I am as the center of a circle, to which all parts of the circumference stand in equal relation; *you, however, are not so.*" For Dante, as for most thinkers of his time, the spatial and temporal perfection represented by the circle precluded its use as a symbol for anything human. The perfect circularity of the *Paradiso* was a gift awaiting the man who had been through Hell; it could never be considered a birthright, for perfect circles transcend the human just as the heavens transcend the earth. So great was the gap between perfection and humanity that it could be spanned only by the Incarnation.

Dante and the early Florentine humanists were the last Italians for several centuries to take Love's admonition very seriously. Later thinkers of the quattrocento would not accept any such limitation and with their rhetoric attempted to set man free from the great chain which bound him to the angels above and to the beasts below. By attributing to the human soul an angelic perfection, they attempted to divorce it from its body, which they were prepared to leave to the protective custody of Lorenzo de' Medici. While they claimed for the soul eternity's symbol, the infinite circle, they surrendered to *Il Magnifico* the more limited space around the Square of the *Signoria*, thus making of God's circular hieroglyph not only an emblem of man's dignity, but also of his solipsism. This metamorphosis of the circle from the transcendent to the mundane, recently and brilliantly traced by Georges Poulet, was historically coincident, at least in Italy, with the metamorphosis of the human soul from incarnate reality, to angelic

From *ELH* 30, no. 4 (December 1963). ©1963 by The Johns Hopkins University Press.

abstraction, to poetic fiction. The beast which was left behind, however, remained substantially unchanged.

Among English poets who underwent the influence of Italian love poetry of the Renaissance, John Donne stands out as one who sought to reconcile the errant soul to its body once more. This meant rescuing human love from both the angelic mysticism and the erotic formalism of the Italian tradition and restoring it to its proper domain: humanity. Donne was primarily concerned neither with the angel nor with the beast, but rather with the battlefield separating them, long since vacated by the Italians; insofar as he defended that middle ground in the question of human love, his poetry marked a return to a more "medieval" sensibility. It is the thesis of this paper that his most famous image, that of the compass in "A Valediction: Forbidding Mourning," protests, precisely in the name of incarnation, against the neo-Petrarchan and Neoplatonic dehumanization of love. It makes substantially the same point made by Love to the young Dante three hundred years before: angelic love is a perfect circle, while beasts move directly and insatiably to the center; *tu autem non sic.*

Human love is neither because it is both; it pulsates between the eternal perfection of circularity and the linear extension of space and time. The compass which Donne uses to symbolize it, therefore, traces not merely a circle but a dynamic process, the "swerving serpentine" of Donne's poetry and of his thought. This is the essence of the love celebrated in the "Valediction: Forbidding Mourning," a vortical reconciliation of body and soul. At the end of its gyre, on the summit where time and eternity meet, stands the lovers' Truth: "hee that will/ Reach her, about must, and about must goe . . . " (Satyre III, 80-1). Because Love's truth is incarnate, however, its celestial apex is at the same time the profound center of an interior cosmos which is governed by its own laws and bounded by the lovers' embrace. For such lovers there can be no breach between the macrocosm of space and time and the microcosm of Love because all of reality is circumscribed by the point upon which their love is centered. With its whirling motion, Love's compass describes the expansion of the lovers' spirit from eternity to time and back again.

This motion is the archetypal pattern of Love's universe, the principle of coherence joining matter and spirit throughout all levels of reality. This study will show that this is the motion traced by the compass. We shall see that the principle of motion in Love's universe is patterned upon what was considered the principle of motion in all reality. . . .

In his sermons, Donne expresses the incarnate dynamism of humanity with the figure of married love: "As farre as man is immortall, he is a married man still, still in posession of a soule, and a body too." "Death," he tells us, "is the Divorce of body and soule; Resurrection is the Re-union. . . ." It is from this exegetical commonplace that the argument of the "Valediction: Forbidding Mourning" derives its force. If incarnation is not simply an abstraction, but rather the informing principle of reality, then the terms of the analogy are reversible and the union of body and soul may serve as a figure for the love of husband and wife. Donne the preacher wrote of death and resurrection in figurative terms of the separation and reunion of husband and wife; as a lover, in the poem we are about to discuss, he had written to his beloved of their separation and eventual reunion in figurative terms of death and resurrection: "As virtuous men passe mildly away . . . so let us melt. . . ." The poem reversed a traditional figure and gave to the neo-Petrarchan dialectic of presence and absence a new metaphysical meaning. As the soul is indissolubly linked to the body, so the husband is linked to his faithful wife. The "Valediction" is a *congé d'amour* which precludes grief in the same way that the death of a virtuous man *forbids mourning*; that is, the simile with which the poem begins glosses the poem's title by hinting that, just as the righteous soul will at the Last Judgment return to its glorified body, so the voyager will return to his beloved.

The ironic reversal of a traditional theme is not mere flippancy. Donne characteristically pushes the analogy to a fine philosophical point. If the union of husband and wife, their love, is like the union of body and soul, then it too is a "hylomorphic" entity which cannot be simply reduced to the carnality or to the spirituality of which it is nevertheless composed. It is Love incarnate, possessed of a single soul ("Our two soules . . . which are one") and, in its perfection, of a single body: Adam and Eve cleave unto each other and are one flesh (Gen. 2:24). The doctrine of the Resurrection can be of little comfort to lovers whom death parts, since there is no marriage in heaven. In the case of these lovers, however, who part only temporarily, the Resurrection lends considerable force to the poetic statement of their inseparability because, by inverting the whole theological structure and balancing it on a personification—the body and soul of Love—Donne gives the entire weight of Revelation to his promise to return. Love dies a physical death when the lovers part, for their bodies "elemented" its body. Its soul lives on, however, in the comfort of the Resurrection, when husband and wife, the components of Love's body, will cleave together once more. It is because their Love is like a just man that it can "passe mildly away," "care lesse" (but like the lovers still *care*) to miss its body, knowing that it will end where it began, reconciled to the flesh once more.

The beginning of the poem states the relationship of the lover to his beloved in terms of the union of body and soul. The ending of the poem traces the emblem of that union, the geometric image of a soul that cannot be perfect while it remains disembodied and therefore cannot be represented in the same way that Dante represented angelic love. In other words, the "circle" which ends the poem is no circle in the ordinary sense, but is rather a circle joined to the rectilinear "otherness" distinguishing man from the angels. This explains the apparent inconsistency in Donne's image, a poetic inconsistency, it would seem, compounding the obscurity of the final verses. Two different movements are executed by the compass:

> And though it in the center sit,
> > Yet when the other far doth rome,
> It leanes and hearkens after it,
> > And growes erect, as that comes home.

These verses clearly decribe motion along a radius, from a center to a circumference and back to the center again. On the other hand, the last stanza of the poem clearly decribes circular motion:

> Such wilt thou be to mee, who must
> > Like th'other foot, obliquely runne;
> Thy firmnes drawes my circle just,
> > And makes me end, where I begunne.

Together, these two movements comprise the dynamism of humanity. With its whirling motion, the compass synthesizes the linear extension of time and space with the circularity of eternity.

The metaphysical importance of the geometrical problem presented by these verses becomes apparent when we examine a passage from the sermons in which Donne distiguishes between the circle of eternity and the human circle which is in the making: "This life is a Circle, made with a Compasse, that passes from point to point; That life is a Circle stamped with a print, endlesse, and perfect Circle, as soone as it begins." We are not told what the radius of eternity's circle is, for the stamp is merely intended to convey its simultaneity, not its dimensions. No finite circle can express the all-encompassing dimensions of eternity, nor can any localized center give a hint of its omnipresence. Like the God of the mystics, eternity is an infinite circle whose center is everywhere, circumference nowhere. In terms of earthly coordinates, it can be represented only by the dimensionless point which is both a center and a circumference. The human circle, on the other hand, has its limits. Both its radius and its sweep are measured by time and space.

Nevertheless, it tends toward eternity as its goal. Geometrically speaking, then, it moves toward the circular perfection of the center; when the circle is finally closed, its radius will no longer have finite extension but will coincide with the limitless point of eternity. The compass of the human soul opens with time and closes toward eternity all the while that it whirls around the central point which is both its beginning and its end.

The epigrammatic quality of the last verse suggests that the harmonization of the circle and the line is indeed complete and that both motions end at their point of departure. Like Plato's star-soul, the soul of Love ends with the perfect circularity with which it began. Its movement is therefore a pulsation, a contraction following an expansion ("Our two soules . . . endure not yet/ A breach, but an expansion"), a synthesis of two distinct motions: circular, but with an ever-increasing radius until a maximum circumference is decribed, whereupon the radius decreases and the circle contracts, approaching the point as its limit ("Thy firmness drawes my circle just"). The word "just" certainly refers to circular perfection; at the same time, however, it recalls the virtuous men of the first stanza and therefore underscores the analogy between the soul of Love and the soul of a "just" man. The dimensionless *point* of dying coincides with the central point of return, the transition between a "just" life and the infinite circle of glory. Thus, like the Aristotelian circle, Donne's has no beginning or end along its circumference, but is rather contracted and expanded along its radius, so that the beginning and end of its pulsation coincide at the center. Were it otherwise, we would have difficulty applying the resultant image to the two lovers who part and are reunited. If we were to take "end" to mean some point on the circumference, then the feet of the compass would remain equidistant throughout such an image, whereas the meaning is that the lover begins from the center, beside his beloved, is separated from her and finally will return. No matter how far he "romes," however, his thoughts revolve about her. Such a movement is at once linear and circular.

In antiquity, the spiral was considered to be the harmonization of rectilinear motion with circularity. Chalcidius, in his commentary on the *Timaeus*, decribes spiral motion precisely in terms of the twofold movement of a compass: radial, from the center to circumference, and circular, around the circumference. This passage is probably the ultimate source of Donne's compass image:

> We usually call "spiral" that genus of circle which is described
> when one foot of a compass is fixed and the compass is either
> stretched out or closed up, either by chance or intentionally, so

that circles are decribed such that not only does the extremity
of the circular line not return to its place of origin but is even
deflected a given amount either above or below the previous
circular line so as to make either wider or narrower circles.

The spiral is therefore a kind of circle whose outline is unfixed until outward
motion ceases and inward motion begins, retracing the same gyre in the
opposite direction toward the central point of origin. When we consider
the figure, our attention is directed toward the center as beginning and end
of all movement, while the periphery remains undefined and vague. So in
the poem, our attention is directed not toward Donne's destination abroad
but rather toward his wife, to whom he will return, no matter how far he
roams.

A similar focus is characteristic of most of the *lemmata* that were
illustrated in Donne's day with the emblem of the compass. *Donec ad idem*,
for instance, stands for a meditation on death and its accompanying compass
image serves to illustrate God's condemnation of Adam, that he will end
where he began: *donec revertaris in terram* (Gen. 3:19). The poet or
preacher's promise to return to his central theme is pictorially represented
with the compass and the *lemma: non vagus vagor*. Even the Jesuit
missionary's obedience to his superior can be similarly illustrated: *si jusseris,
ibit in orbem*. Most of the similes in love poetry of the sixteenth century
which are based on the compass also stress central constancy in spite of
circumstantial vicissitudes. So the explicit compass image from Guarini's
madrigal: "un piede in voi quasi mio centro mi fermo,/l'altro patisce di
fortuna i giri," or the submerged compass image of Maurice Sceve, of which
we shall have more to say later: "ma pensée, à peu pres s'y transmue, Bien
que ma foy, sans suyvre mon project, Çà et là tourne, et point ne se remue."
Insofar as these compasses have their origin in the tradition of Chalcidius'
image, they trace spirals, whether their authors knew it or not.

We can however be sure that John Donne knew it. The word "rome"
in the verse, "Yet when the other far doth rome," cannot refer to circular
motion, anymore than can the finite verb *vagor* in the emblem books, for
a circle does not wander. Donne used the compass image in precisely the
same way that Chalcidius used it in the passage we have quoted; that is,
to describe a wandering path which is nevertheless rooted in circular
regularity. The exemplar of all such orbits is the path described by the
planets, or "wandering" stars.

Plato used the movements of the heavenly bodies in order to "spatialize"
his conception of intellectual process; it was in this way that he managed

to give to his idea of *paideia* a symbolically dynamic dimension. In his microcosmic analogy, the perfect circling of the fixed stars represented the perfect movement of the speculative reason, whereas the rectilinear motion characteristic of the elements represented the lowest human faculties. Between these upper and lower limits of human potentiality there lay the human composite itself, a synthesis of both circle and line. Like the planets, the human soul partakes of the movements of both the outermost sphere, rationality, and of the sublunary world of matter.

Planetary movement was considered to be spiral because it seemed to be composed of at least two opposing movements. Like the sun and moon, the planets rise and set each day, moving from east to west. At the same time, they move along the Zodiac from west to east. The resolution of these two motions, from the perspective of the earth, described a slow-moving spiral from one tropic to the other. In other words, from what we know to be the earth's rotation and revolution, the sun, moon and planets seem to follow a spiral course. Chalcidius continues the passage containing the compass image as follows:

> [Plato] has correctly called them [the planets] errant stars, rotating in a spiral, because of the inconstant and unequal circular movement. If, for example, the star of Venus is in the sign of Aries and then is rapt by the course of the universe so that it is carried further and further away from its previous progression, there will certainly be some declination away from Aries; and as many more turnings as it makes, so much the more will it descend from Aries to Pisces, the next sign, and from there it will be impelled to Aquarius. On the other hand, if it were rapt the other way it would proceed from Aries to Taurus and thence to Gemini and Cancer, its gyre becoming ever smaller in due measure; which gyre the Greeks call *helix* . . .

In most of the redactions of Chalcidius' commentary, this passage is accompanied by a diagram of Venus' orbit, viewed from the pole and projected onto the plane of the ecliptic.

The word "rome" suggests the planetary, or at least "wandering," character of the lover's journey away from his beloved. We shall see that several other words in Donne's last verses prove that the imagery is basically astronomical. For the moment, our suggestion seems confirmed by the phrase in the second verse of the last stanza, "obliquely runne." This phrase not only describes planetary motion quite accurately, but also points toward the Platonic analogy which we have been discussing and hence to the significance of the spiral form. In the first place, the word "oblique" is still used as a substantive in English to denote the ecliptic, the imaginary line which runs along the center of the Zodiac and traces the path of the planets, sun and moon. In the Middle Ages, Dante used a form of the word as an adjective to describe the ecliptic: "l'oblico cerchio che i pianeti porta," while in the Renaissance Théophile de Viau speaks of the sun's path as an "oblique tour," thereby giving to the word the meaning of "spiral," at least implicitly. Of particular interest to us, however, is that Donne here uses an adverbial form, "obliquely," which indicates not a path or a line but a *kind* of motion, the motion which in the Latin Neoplatonic tradition was referred to as the *motus obliquus*.

Plato's geometric analogy for the three "motions" of soul, circular (divine), spiral (human) and rectilinear (animal), from which he derived his theory of microcosm and macrocosm, enjoyed a great vogue in subsequent Neoplatonic writings. According to the pseudo-Dionysius, for instance, the three "conversions" were characteristic not only of the heavens and of the human soul, but also of the angels. The highest order of angels moves circularly around God and the lowest order moves directly toward man. Between these, the middle order rotates around God while at the same time pursuing its terrestrial missions. In like manner, the human soul can turn directly to God by divine intuition (*supra nos*, St. Bonaventure was later to say), or to the outside world (*extra nos*); but since the "unitive" way is given to few men, most must proceed to God with a combination of those two movements (*intra nos*). This last movement, the spiral, is emblematic of the soul incarnate, of the soul whose inner life is a continual contemplation of God in spite of worldly vicissitudes.

In the Latin translations of the Dionysian corpus, from the ninth to the fifteenth centuries, the translation usually offered to describe the "spiral motion" of the human soul is the Latin adverb "oblique." Marsilio Ficino comments upon the three movements of the soul under the rubric, "De motu angeli et animae triplici, id est, circulari, recto, obliquo." Elsewhere, he uses the same words to describe celestial movement. The planets, he tells us, move "sinuosa quadam obliquitate, velut in spiram." It seems most likely that this tradition, at once astronomical and mystical, underlies Donne's use of the words "obliquely runne." If this is the case, then Donne himself alludes to the geometrical solution of the problem presented by his own lines. A compass can lean or grow erect *at the same time* that it describes a circle only if that "circle" is in fact a spiral. The next to the last line of the poem does indeed indicate diurnal, circular motion, the fixity of love, while the last refers to a dyastolic and systolic pulsation, the "zodiacal" exigencies of life, for these two patterns are combined in the figure that "obliquely" runs.

To return to our summary of the strategy of the poem, with which we began this paper, we said that the "body" of Love dies when the lovers part and is "resurrected" when they are reunited. The compass image manages to span these two moments and thus provides us with an emblem of duration, a fixity of being (in so far as it is a single image) in the process of becoming (in so far as it moves). That duration is literally the time of the lovers' separation from each other and figuratively the history of the disembodied soul of Love, awaiting its glorification at the end of time. In the universe of Love, the time measured by the compass' whirling is the *marking* of time between one moment of eternity and the next, between the creation of time and its dissolution. It cannot be a circle for it is as yet incomplete, as the soul is incomplete without its body, as the lover is incomplete without his beloved. When the restoral is finally achieved, however, the lovers will be reunited, the soul of Love will be reconciled to the body of Love and the planets will end their wandering at their points of origin.

To a modern reader, planetary imagery may seem gratuitous in a poem which is primarily concerned with the relationship of body and soul as a figure for the relationship of two lovers. To thinkers of the Renaissance, however, there seemed to be an intimate connection between the life of the cosmos and the life of man. The exile of the soul from its body was thought to last precisely as long as the exile of the planet from its home. According to the doctrine of "universal restoral," which is Platonic in origin, the life of the entire universe is measured by the Cosmic Year. All of the heavenly bodies will return to precisely the same positions from which they began at the end of 36,000 solar years. Ausonius is one among many in antiquity who describe this *apocatastasis*; his verses call to mind the *lemma* of Death's compass, *donec ad idem*:

> donec consumpto, magnus qui dicitur, anno,
> rursus in anticum veniant vaga sidera cursum,
> qualia dispositi steterunt ab origine mundi.

By an association which seemed to Christian astrologers inevitable, in spite of the protestations of critics such as Pico della Mirandola, the *apocatastasis* of the ancients was taken to be coincident with the Christian Apocalypse and hence with the resurrection of the body. Thus when the human soul ends where it began, the planets, *vaga sidera*, will return to the positions they occupied at the Creation. Marsilio Ficino, characteristically, defends the religious doctrine with the astrological "fact" in order to bolster his own somewhat shaky belief in the Resurrection:

> Nor should it appear absurd that souls, after they have left their natural state, should return again to the same place, for indeed the planets leave their natural homes [*domicilia*] and seek them again. Further, particles of elements which are expelled from their natural place return again to it. Nor is it difficult for the infinite virtue of God, which is everywhere present, which created everything *ex nihilo*, to bring together those elements of a body which had once been dissolved.

The homes of the planets, their *domicilia* or *klairoi* in the celestial sphere, mark the beginning and end of planetary motion. Donne the lover, metamorphosed into a planet wandering from his beloved, also begins and ends at "home" (line 4, stanza 8). The poet has once more reversed a traditional argument, reversing signifier and thing signified and interposing a concrete image increasing the distance between them. As the soul will return to the body, so the soul of Love (the lovers' two souls) will return to its body (the lovers' two bodies), as the planets come "home."

If our contention that the compass image has primarily astronomical reference is correct, then there are a series of words in the next-to-last stanza that still require interpretation. The stanza says of "Thy soule the fixt foot":

> And though it in the center sit,
> > Yet when the other far doth rome,
> It leanes, and hearkens after it,
> > And growes erect, as that comes home.

We have suggested that "rome" characterizes the motion of the wandering stars and that "home" designates their *klairoi* or *domicilia*. Another position which astrologers felt obliged to determine was the planetary *exaltatio*, or as the word is still translated, the "erect" position. Vittoria Colonna, for example, describing the auspicious moment of her lover's birth, says that the planets were in that position:

> > Gli almi pianeti in propria sede *eretti*
> > Mostravan lieti quei benigni aspetti,
> > Che instillan le virtù nei cor più rari

In the history of astrology there was considerable disagreement about how the "homes" and the "exaltations" of the planets were measured. According to Pliny in the passage which is the *locus classicus* for the discussion of the *exaltatio* of the planets, the critical point on the Zodiac was reached by the planet when its orbital arc was at its highest elevation from the center of the earth. Using this criterion, he provided a catalogue of planetary domiciles: "Igitur a terrae centro apsides [i.e., planetary arcs] altissimae sunt Saturno in scorpione, Iovi in vergine, Marti in leone . . . (etc.)." Later thinkers, and especially the Arabs, disagreed, and insisted that the measurement of the *altitudo* was to be taken not from the earth but from the center of the Zodiac to the zodiacal sign. From this new form of calculation they put together a totally different catalogue of "exaltations." For our purposes, however, it should be noted that the measurements themselves, according to a probably spurious passage in the text of Pliny, were taken precisely by means of the compass: "Omnia autem haec constant *ratione circini* semper indubitata." The point on the Zodiac diametrically opposed to a planet's *exaltatio* is the point of *deiectio*; if the former be described in terms of a compass which is tracing a spiral and is at its maximum erection, then the *deiectio* will be the point of the compass' maximum depression. It is at this point that the compass "leanes," when the moving foot is at its greatest distance from the foot fixed in the orbit's center. In the context of the "Valediction," the suspicious lines "It leanes, and hearkens after it,/ And growes erect as that come home" are primarily a geometric indication that, at the end of the exile of Love's soul, the planets will be exalted in their homes awaiting the final consummation and the lovers' eternity.

A word must be said here about the literal meaning of the phrase, "It leanes . . . and growes erect" as it applies to the woman, in order to lay to rest the erotic interpretation sometimes given it. Whatever else the poem may be, it obviously constitutes a song of praise to the woman. In the Middle Ages, the most famous of such *encomia* was the praise of the virtuous wife taken from Proverbs 31:10-31: "Who can find a virtuous woman . . . for her price is far above rubies." The verses in the original form an acrostic, each verse beginning with a letter of the alphabet in order from Aleph to Sin. Verse 20 reads: "She stretcheth out her hand to the poor." Albertus Magnus in his *De Muliere forti* notes that the verse begins with the letter Caph (כ) which he interprets *inclinatio*, referring to the compassion which inclines the hardness of the heart. Verse 24, "She maketh fine linen," is introduced by the letter Samech (ס), which he interprets *erectio*, the hope which raises us up. Donne may have been using the words "lean" and "erect" as similar compliments to his faithful beloved; this would explain why he uses the words with respect to her in spite of the fact that the purely literal meaning of the words is necessarily applicable to both legs of the compass. More interesting, however, is the fact that the Hebrew letters standing for the words *inclinatio* and *erectio* constitute ingenious hieroglyphs for separation and reunion. Caph, the broken circle (כ), marks the separation of the feet of the compass, whereas Samech brings them together and closes the circle (ס) as the compass becomes erect. This interpretation of the words has the advantage of doing violence neither to the poem nor to its context and, if it strains our credulity about how much Donne could put into a single line, it at least avoids the physiological naiveté required for an erotic interpetation of the words.

We have seen that the souls of the lover and the beloved together constitute the soul of Love, tracing humanity's emblem in a spiral course around the center which is their common possession, much like a planetary orbit around the axis of the universe. It happens that the gyre of the planetary soul is the archetype of motion in the human soul as well. The compass stands for a principal of motion that is common to humanity and to the heavens. It is this analogy which relates the beginning of the poem to its ending, for if the soul of Love moves like a planet, it also moves like a *human* soul. Further, once we understand this movement, we shall also understand how a soul can be one and yet logically twofold ("Our two soules . . . which are one") in literal, as well as figurative terms. We shall have to discover why the compass is a perfect image of the soul.

In order to clarify the interrelationship of the cognitive and appetitive powers of the soul, Aristotle in the *De Anima* described its workings mechanistically in terms which recall "stiffe twin compasses." All movement consisted of three factors: 1) that which originates movement; 2) the means whereby it originates it; 3) that which is moved. In locomotion, the origin of movement is the soul, working through the heart (1). The means (2) are the vital spirits, pushing and pulling against a stationary point which provides thrust: the "fixt foot" (stanza 8 of the "Valediction"). The thing which is moved is the other foot. If we analyze the origin of motion, the heart, we find that it is where the beginning and end of motion coincide, the center of articulation, a joint between two extremities. Aristole compares it to a ball-and-socket joint (*gigglimus*), or to the elbow. This is because it is the mid-point between the alternate movements of pushing and pulling in the motions of an animal. When a human being walks, one side remains fixed while the other moves, the latter in turn becoming fixed while the former moves. An interesting poetic description of the first steps of Adam is given to us in the *Microcosme* of Maurice Scève, where the word for "measure," *compas*, is perhaps used as a pun:

> Dresseé sur piés branchus, une jambe en avant,
> L'autre restant, se vit à cheminer savant,
> Et se conduire droit en tous lieux pas à pas
> Mesurant son alleure avec grave compas.

According to Averroes, the pushing and pulling movements are not precisely straight because the vital spirits themselves, which are responsible for transmitting the heart's impulses to the limbs, move in a gyre: a *motus gyrativus* around the heart.

The movement of the soul is precisely analogous to the local motion of the body. It is the appetitive faculty, the will, which, like the left foot, provides thrust, while the reason steps out first, like the right foot. They are joined to each other by the faculty of choice itself, whose "highest" point came to be called the *apex mentis*. The link between all of these and the body is *pneuma* or *spiritus*, the mysterious substance which is the locus of contact between body and soul. If the *apex mentis* is like the heart, the joint of a compass, then the will is its fixed foot while the reason is the other. The *pneuma* which joins them traces its gyre on the plane of human action.

In the compass of the human soul, it is the will which remains fixed in its constancy while the reason moves out. So in Scève's submerged compass image, the lover's "pensée" may be diverted, but "ma foy, sans suyvre mon project,/ Çà et là tourne, et point ne se remue." So too, the Plantin device serves as an image of constancy in action: *Labore et constantia*. To this is doubtless related Cesare Ripa's use of the compass as an emblem for "pratica," by which he probably means the practical reason. Donne chose to compliment his beloved on her constancy, her faith, with this emblem. At the same time he consoled her by suggesting that they were as the will and reason respectively of a single soul, "inter-assured" of the apex of the mind. For all of its dazzling virtuosity, the conceit is analogous to an ancient exegetical commonplace. As Adam represents *ratio*, or the highest faculty of the soul, so Eve represents *appetitus*, which is in direct contact with the body. Together, they are one.

We have so far been concerned with establishing the principle which governs the movement of the poem, symbolized by the compass image. It is this universal principle which gives the "Valediction" its coherence upon so many analogical levels of reality. . . . Something must also be said of the poem's relationship to the literary tradition from which it takes its point of departure. It will be seen that Donne's originality here, as so often, consists in the startlingly new form that he bestows upon time-worn banalities. Thematically, the "Valediction: Forbidding Mourning" resembles the medieval *congé d'amour*, wherein a lover takes leave of his lady and consoles her by claiming that they are not really two individuals, but rather affirms that they are one, or that he has left with her his heart. In Renaissance treatments of the presence-absence antithesis, elements of the *congé* are combined with Petrarchan and stilnovistic themes and often expressed in terms of Plotinian theories of ecstasy, as has been pointed out recently by Merritt Hughes. Among the *trattati d'amore* of the cinquecento, Sperone Speroni's is almost exclusively concerned with the antithesis of presence and absence, although he does not mention the Resurrection, as does Marsilio Ficino in a similar context. Nor is the consolation of a reunion at the end of a cosmic year entirely original; Giordano Bruno, in a rare fabulist mood, pokes fun at the idea of "universal restoral" and Plotinian ecstasy with a bizarre *congé d' amour* of his own, written thirty years before Donne's poem:

> The flea, which had been educated according to the dogma of the divine Plato, was consoling the bedbug with loving words from the height of the roof, while a cruel fate was dividing the two companions: the chamber-boy, shaking the mattress, was already at the point of casting them down and throwing them off to diverse fates, for he was rolling up the sleeve of his shirt from his naked arm. The bedbug's face was lined with tears as it said: "Not my fate, not my cruel fate bothers me, that this my spirit should abandon these ugly and miserable members, but rather does that violent separation disturb me because you, dear Flea, are forced by iniquitous fates to leave me, fates which tear me away and cannot give you back to me." The flea answered, "Do not torment yourself, for this your torment transfixes me, consumes me and makes me unhappy. My spirit and yours are not twin, o bedbug of one soul with me, for you are more intimate to me than I am to myself; wherefore my worry for you bothers me while I have no worry for myself. Therefore, even if thundering Jove himself separate these our two bodies iniquitously, nevertheless, only when he makes me leave my very self can he cause my spirit to leave you, my fate, my death, once my life and my hope. But even making me forgetful of myself, I find it difficult to believe that he can make me forgetful of you. Weep not, my life's blood, I know certainly that our two bodies

will one day be together again. I should like to say more, but
already we are torn apart. Ahi! ahi! Now farewell sweet love! After
two times, three times, one hundred thousand years, added to
which two other times three and two times three hundred
thousand (which I hope will come to pass auspiciously and
happily), you will look for me a second time and I myself will
see you a second time.

It is however the Resurrection, not the cosmic year, that Donne offers to
his wife as a consolation forbidding mourning. This is not simply an
attempt to adapt a Platonic banality to the Christian revelation, but rather
has the effect of transposing the theme of "restoration" from the universe
of space and time to an interior dimension. The criticism of Bruno, which
is to say the criticism of the "layetie" who do not understand that the entire
universe and its mystery are recapitulated in the microcosm of Love, is
groundless here; the "Valediction" establishes a *symbolic* cosmology, Love's
universe, where time begins at the lovers' parting and ends at their reunion.
The poem and the duration it spans seems at first to be a breach of eternity's
circle; as we read, however, we come to realize that the time is eternity's
moving image—its end is its beginning—and the 36,000 years of its reign
(measured in Donne's 36 verses) constitutes merely a pause for lovers who
are eternally one. Similarly, space is transcended in Love's symbolic cosmos
by the assurance that, thanks to the constancy of Love's faith, the
centrifugality of any separation will be overcome by the centripetal force
that binds all of reality to the same Center.

The neo-Petrarchan antithesis of presence and absence underlies the
simile of the dying man with which the poem begins, but its banality is
here transcended by what Albert Béguin has called love's "chemin vers
l'intérieur." As each of the lovers is the life of the other, separation is
tantamount to the death of their superficial identity. The absence of his
beloved forces the lover into himself to begin the spiral descent toward the
void where his life once was. At the center of his being, he discovers, not
his heart, nor even the heart of his beloved, but rather the "heart" of the
entire universe, the Center about which all of reality revolves. It is here, in
the depths of his subjectivity, that death is transcended and the whole
universe interiorized around the pole-star of Love. Upon this transcendence,
the death *intra nos* that ultimately leads *supra nos*, a new, more authentic
identity is established. The miracle of Love's *askesis* is that in thought, by
participation in the "mind" which transcends them, man and woman are

joined together and transmuted above the sphere of the moon, "refin'd" to await their glorious reunion. All of the heavens are embraced by the soul of their love, for at Love's center is the point which is in fact a cosmic circumference.

JOHN HOLLANDER

Donne and the Limits of Lyric

So much has been written about Donne's metrical roughness that a comprehensive survey of commentary upon what the poet himself called "my words masculine perswasive force" would parallel the whole course of his reputation. Aside from the disagreements of his contemporaries about his metrical style—the strictures of a Jonson, the complex praise of a Carew—we can trace even in the revived but canonical twentieth-century phase of Donne's career a shift from an acceptance of Jonson's famous "not keeping of accent" to the commendation of it as a positive and unique virtue. Even though Jonson may have been complaining to Drummond of Hawthornden about the slightly more than fashionably irregular verse of the satires and even as, in twentieth-century criticism, a Browningesque rather than a Tennysonian sense of verbal music in verse began to be praised, Grierson, writing before 1912, would find it necessary to apologize for "a poetry, not perfect in form, rugged of line and careless in rhyme" as being yet "a poetry of an extraordinary arresting and haunting quality, passionate, thoughtful, and with a deep melody of its own." That "deep melody" of speech has since almost become a cliché of Donne criticism; it is used with force and clarity by the editor of a recent college text edition:

> To begin with, despite the absence of any facile smoothness of versification, the lines have a strange and original music, derived largely from an imitation of the accents of emotionally heightened conversation. . . . Donne's metrical control is of an astounding virtuosity, although that virtuosity is generally in the service of drama rather than of song.

From *Vision and Resonance: Two Senses of Poetic Form*, 2d ed. ©1985 by Yale University. Yale University Press, 1985.

Coleridge, in some notes on Donne made in Lamb's copy of the poet in 1811, put the matter almost perfectly in observing that *"all* Donne's poems are equally *metrical* (misprints allowed for) though smoothness (i.e. the metre necessitating the proper reading) be deemed appropriate to *songs*; but in poems where the writer *thinks,* and expects the reader to do so, the sense must be understood in order to ascertain the metre." This might just as well be about Browning. Whether they "imitate" or, in fact, embody, and whether they emulate "the accents of emotionally heightened conversation" or, as I shall try to show, are partly a necessary consequence of a speaker's trying to make himself understood—in any event, Donne's jagged rhythms, when considered against the smoothness usually demanded of strophic song texts, remain highly problematic, even when highly praised. "Donne," says Arnold Stein, "is a conscious master of harshness," and he is speaking for the literary temper of Modernism, for an age which approves of strong lines not for their wit, their "tension" alone, but for the rhythmic insistence upon domination over the meter and its schemata which would place them in a line stemming from Catullus and Villon—the lyric of insistent talk, rather than the lyric of written flow (Horace and Ronsard). The Modernist sense of that tradition which makes of the speaking voice the most authentic singing has been one that has found the irregularity of Wyatt's experimental pentameters valuable per se. It has found thinness and smoothness in what its Victorian forebears had thought of as lyrical language. And still largely unacquainted or unimpressed with Browning, it has made the rhythms of the *Songs and Sonnets* into touchstones for revision of prosodic theory.

In these second thoughts on the nature of the unmusicality of Donne's lyrics, I should like to consider their roughness in a literally, rather than figuratively, "musical" context, and to inspect certain features of his rhythmic style, strophic patterning and rhetorical tonality which make the "songs" of their title so hard to take with an older, Elizabethan literalness. Some of these problems need no new discussion. Certainly the rhythmic variations within the versification of metrically identical strophes is not a problem peculiar to Donne. Composers of monodic airs like Dowland who set a great variety of texts would always work out a setting for the initial stanza and cheerfully ignore the lack of fit in subsequent ones, whether or not the performance of those following stanzas could be made possible with a little melismatic assistance. In the case of a rhythmically active line like the opening one of the great, anonymous peddler's song from Dowland's 1600 *Book of Airs*:

Fine knacks for ladies, cheape, choice, brave and new

the equivalent line of the third strophe gets a weaker setting, requiring
displaced word stress on the line's only two disyllables. Thus

Fine Knacks for   la - dies   cheape choise brave— and new
With - in this packe pinnes   points   la - ces ——— and gloves

That is, in both cases the iambic norm is stretched by the rhythm of the
text, but the *ad hoc* accentual underlining of one which a musical setting
provides will not fit the cadences of another. With Donne, this situation
is frequent and strongly marked. Let us consider one of the most interesting
of the seven settings of Donne lyrics by seventeenth-century composers edited
by André Souris and Jean Jacquot, the version of "The Expiration" by
Alfonso Ferrabosco from his 1609 book of airs. Here again, the setting cannot
possibly hope to accommodate the second strophe in its rhythmic setting
of the first one: "Any so cheape a death as saying goe." The terminal line
of the second strophe, for example, must be sung to this rhythm:

Being   dou - ble dead   go - ing——— and bid - ding goe

It is interesting to note that although the final imperative "Go!" is meant
in both lines, it should be in inverted commas in the first instance—"saying,
'Go!'" as a quick, easy death—whereas in the second, it is a direct but
conditional command of the singer-lover. No matter how "expressive," by
early-baroque or Modern standards, the setting is to be, it must surely
comprehend the *sense* of the text. For example, the music in a good setting
should punctuate the final two lines of the song, with its own rhythms, so
as to do something like this:

> Except it be too late to kill me so,
> (being double-dead—going and bidding), Go!

Now Ferrabosco's setting realizes neither the speech-rhythm of the
phrase "saying, 'Go!'" in the first strophe, nor that of the complex syntax
of the second. But at the crudest level of rhythmic fitting of musical downbeat
to normal word stress (let alone to phrase stress among monosyllabic groups,
or stress maxima in an iambic context) the second strophe will not work.
It is rewarding to contrast Ferrabosco's setting of just these lines with another
one, from an anonymous musical manuscript of about the same time.

A - ny   so   cheape   a death ———— as   say - ing goe

Here, at least the "saying, 'Go!'" phrase is plausibly treated; the syntax, and, hence, the rhetoric of speech is recognizable in the melodic interpretation of it. I mention syntax only because so much recent discussion of Donne's metrics has concentrated on declamatory and emotional effects of apparently aberrant stress-positioning in Donne's iambic lines, without appeal to the basic complex relations between phrase-stress patterns and syntactic structure in English. But if the anonymous setting handles the terminal line of the first stanza well, its reciprocal is even more distorted than in Ferrabosco's version. It demands two sorts of accentual deformation:

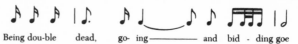

the first, on "going," exacerbated by the long tied note value on the second syllable; the second, making the phrase "bidding go" syntactically equivalent—through rhythmic identity—to "saying go." But "bidding" is, as we have seen, part of another, complex parenthetical phrase, the very syntactical existence of which dissolves in song. Or, at any rate, this song.

In other words, Donne's rhythmic modulation of language is such that even the most musicianly attention to word stress (and this, indeed, is not always Ferrabosco's strongest point) will frequently not suffice to accentuate correctly the textual syntax. In view of the increased attention, in early seventeenth-century monody, given to freeing the text from polyphonic labyrinths, in view of the growing influences outside of Italy of the *stile espressivo* of recitative, the unique problems of English prosody remained a stumbling block in the way of properly "committing short and long," not only in strophic settings but in through-composed ones as well.

One of these problems is that posed by contrastive stress. Even in the case of another poet, one who took pride—or at least believed himself undeserving of hanging—in keeping of accent, the accentual properties of English phrase structure posed a difficulty for musical setting. Ben Jonson's friend and collaborator Ferrabosco was, again, the victim; this time, the text in question is the final couplet of the famous seduction song from *Volpone*, out of Catullus, later included in *The Forrest* in 1616. "'Tis no sinne loves fruits to steale,/ But the sweet theft to reveale."

While the purely melodic effect is lovely and sophisticated—a stylistically forward-looking evaded cadence on the chord of the sixth at "beene," heralding the repetition of the words in a final phrase, etc.—it is almost as if the text laid under it were a fairly clever verse translation of that for which the music was composed. The sense of the couplet becomes clear only when we underline the emphatic stress:

> To be *taken,* to be *seene,*
> *These* have crimes *accounted* been

"Crimes" needs no added stress, since it refers back to, rather than contrasts with, the "sinne" of the previous couplet. *"These"* (i.e. getting caught, not adultery itself), or, more subtly, "accounted" (morality is mere fashion) are the words which take an implicit contrastive stress in speech. According to the setting, the preceding lines of the text would have had to suggest that these were blessings, and "crimes" was then given emphatic development.

Ben Jonson's lyric culminates in the moral arguments of seduction which are frequently rhetorically contrastive. But we have only to turn to a far less schematic example, again from Ferrabosco's treatment of Donne's "The Expiration," to see how fundamental this problem is. Consider the third line of the first strophe:

Turne thou (ghost!) *that* way, and let *me* turne *this*

This has been italicized and repunctuated to gloss its meaning in the context of the stanza ("So, so, breake off this last lamenting kisse,/ Which sucks two soules and vapours both away,/ Turne thou ghost that way, and let me turne this"). We may observe that, as in so many of Donne's lines, the "roughness" comes about as a result of ambiguities in reading the metrical disposition of stresses. "Let *me* turne *this*" falls perfectly into iambic position because of the contrast with the preceding "Turne *thou* (ghost) *that* way." It also allows "kisse" and "this" to rhyme with greater reason, whereas if "this" were enjambed, for example (as in, say," . . . and let me turne this/ As yet unbloodied dagger from my heart"), any coherent musical setting would have to avoid a rhythmic ictus on "this." Similarly, another syntactic version of the line "Turne thou ghost that way which faces East" would call for a musical downbeat on "way" to make sense of it. But to emphasize "way" in the setting of Donne's line would be something like the way certain Romance foreign accents mis-stress English words. Here, then, is Ferrabosco's setting

| Turne | thou | (ghost!) | *that* way. | and let | *me* turne | *this* |

which commits just that fault, totally missing, in its rhythmic generations, the point of the line. The other, anonymous setting cited before, incidentally, manages this problem better:

Turne —   thou ghost that way   and let me   turne   this

The contrastive stress is pointed up in the setting, and at least gross syntactic grouping—aside from any nuances of expression which might grace that grossness—has been satisfied. But as we might expect, the consequences for the reciprocal line in the second strophe are more disastrous than merely a matter of musical rhythm wrecking word stress.

O———   if it   have let   my word worke on   thee

Here, the gasping rest after the poorly treated "if it have, let . . ." is grotesque and irrelevant.

The setting of any poem to music recapitulates, in a strange way, the very process of metrical composition in a language; this is especially true in the case of English iambic verse. A particular line will make manifest certain possibilities implicit in the iambic schema (allowable reversals, promotions, or demotions in trisyllabic words, heightening of syllabic prominence by means other than stress, such as rhyme, assonance, alliteration, etc.). Just so will a musical setting of that line go one step further and resolve ambiguities that may remain yet exist in the fulfilled rhythmic line. For example, we know that line 21 from "A Valediction: Of Weeping,"

> Weepe me not dead, in thine armes, but forbeare

is not dactylic only because of our knowledge of its context of versification, of the metrical convention of the poem itself. For if the line had been preceded by a different one, the rhythmic possibilities would have gone the other way, as in, say,

> Swéete though tŏ drówne iň the tídes ǒf thy háire,
> Weepe me not dead in thine armes but forbeare . . . etc.

A good musical setting, like a proper scansion in the act of reading, or an actual oral performance of the line by a speaker, will resolve the ambiguity. But let us take this back one step further: we know how frequently Donne's lines which look "rough" (or, in the precisely defined terms of a recent prosodic theory, "unmetrical"), turn out not to be so if the proper attention is paid to contrastive stress.

A startling case of this occurs in "A Nocturnall upon S. Lucies Day," in such a way as to suggest an alternative reading of syntax and, thus, of the nature of the image therein embodied. The mourning poet says of the alchemist Love

> He ruin'd mee, and I am re-begot
> Of absence, darknesse, death; things which are not.

In order that the rhyme may function at all, let alone not set off what Milton called "wretched matter and lame Metre," the final syllable must be stressed; in order that Donne may not really deserve hanging, the semantic phrase stress must allow that to happen. Now assume for a moment that the phrase "things which are not" means "things which aren't, which don't exist." The rhythmic phrasal paradigm would be that of the phrases from Jeremiah 5:21, "which have eyes and see not." "Things which are not" would in any case give either a truncated predicative, or else a totally existential meaning of the copula. We should then expect, in the first instance, a completion of prediction in a *contre-rejet* in a following line (as, say, ". . . things which are not/ Present, brighte, alive. . . ." But the stress on "not" suggests another reading, with a different paradigm of syntax and scansion; "things which are hot," for example, would take an iambic stress on the final adjective, "hot" (unless specifically stressed contrastively, of course, viz. "things which *are* hot"—as opposed to things which *aren't*). If Donne's phrase is modeled on this one, we must take "*not*" as adjectival, rather than as a negative particle, a nonce term meaning "not x, x being any predicate whatsoever." The ontological joke about reifying nothing is even stronger in this reading, and Love's alchemy far more impressive—the "quintessence . . . of nothingnesse" would certainly be, if nothing else, "not."

Recent theories of prosody have interested themselves in Donne's emphatic stress for a variety of reasons. The *Songs and Sonnets* and the *Elegies* seem encrusted with examples of lines which become fairly regular iambic pentameter when the purely contrastive stress is recognized:

> by that remorse,
>
> Which *my* words masculine perswasive force
> Begot in *thee*, and by the memory
>   ("On His Mistresse," 3-5)

is a self-illustrating case. Pairs of pronouns frequently contrast in Donne; this is basic to the texture of his rhetoric. Phrases like "my words," normally stressed [· ́], are shifted to [́·]. With the normal iambic option for trisyllables, "masculine" can be either [́··] or [·· ́], and with the latter choice, the line becomes regularized, rather than "sprung" as in older ways

of scanning Donne ("Whích my wórds másculiñe pérswásive fóŕce," for example). If the line is indeed as potent as the language it describes, then it is at least normally erect.

A few more examples, perhaps: line 20 of the "The Anniversarie"

> When bodies *to* their graves, soules *from their* graves remove.

falls into its Alexandrine role more adroitly when the double contrasts of "to-from" and "their-their" are realized. Line 24 of the same poem

> but wee
> Can be such Kings, nor, *of* such, subjects mee;
> [punctuation mine]

depends upon a contrastive elevation of "of." A particularly delicate effect is gained in "The Primrose," where, in line 8

> Í wálke tó fiñde à tŕue Lóve; añd Í seé

the iambic irregularity obtained by reversal of stress in positions 7 and 8 rushes on toward an enjambment of "see"; this differs sharply from the situation in line 13

> For shoúld my tŕue-Lóve lesśe then woman bee . . .

in the stressing of the compound. In the first instance, "true Love" with a plus-juncture, a spondaic accent, the stress pattern of Christian-name-plus-surname, or however an informal prosodic descriptive vocabulary would want to put it, is the usual adjective-noun pair. In the second instance, the name of the flower, the stress has regressed to the first syllable of the compound, and the four or six petals of the false floral emblem of love are matched by a skewed stress pattern on the words of its name as well.

It is just these contrasts which in English are far from being mere nuances, but engage fundamental grammatical relationships. To a French or Italian ear, particularly that of a musician, they might die away; and since the rhythmic generations of melodic lines were constantly being influenced by Continental music, the ability of English composers of the seventeenth century to embody and enhance in their settings the basic rhetorical stuff, the compelling speech-music of strong lines, markedly decreased. Smoother, post-Jonsonian lyric traditions, moving toward the thinness of Augustan song texts, provided easier materials for song settings than could poetic language rhythmically exciting in itself. Expressive formulae took precedence over rhetorical complexity, which, fortunately, texts began to abandon. Can we tell, for example, from John Hilton's (1599-1657) setting of "A Hymne to God the Father" whether, in the rhythmic realization of

♩ ♪ ♪ ♩ | ♪ ♪ ♪ ♪ ♩ ♩ | ♩··   ♪ | o

When thou hast done,   thou hast not done,   [for   I   have more]

the composer has "set" the pun on the poet's name? At least he has not reduced the paradox to the more trivial one by implying with musical ictus a speech rhythm of "When thou hast done, thou hast not done."

No matter what the genres of the *Songs and Sonnets* lyrics are considered to be—and they embrace dramatic monologue, emblem verse, implicit dramatic scene (as when the insect is successfully threatened and killed in the white space between successive strophes in "The Flea"), argument, or whatever—the modulation of personal speech makes the sounds of sense, and makes sense of the sound patternings of the meter. It is not the diversity of genres per se which makes so many of the songs un-songlike. Many a Jacobean composer, "his art and voice to show," would set and sing all manner of texts; William Byrd in his 1589 and 1611 books of madrigals set four passages from Geoffrey Whitney's emblem book, and, in an earlier volume, a quantitative translation of a group of lines from Ovid's *Heroides*. Musical and textual quotations from street cries and well-known tunes work their way into art songs by John Daniel and Thomas Campion. The latter could insist on the similarity of lyrics and epigrams:

> Short Ayres, if they be skilfully frame, and naturally exprest, are like quicke and good Epigrammes in Poesie, many of them shewing as much artifice, and breeding as great difficultie as a large Poeme.

It is ultimately a matter of modality that marks the metaphysical lyric from a musical point of view, a mixture of basic tonalities within a particular song. Whether polyphonic or monodic, the song is at a loss to handle the dialectic between lyric modes, the simultaneous presence of contrary impulses which even the formal musical dialogue (an increasingly popular seventeenth-century form) could only trivialize. This is particularly true in the case of the most complex kinds of post-Petrarchan love poetry. The Petrarchan poem will develop a mode and an emotional tonality of its own, and while it may turn against that tonality (particularly in the sestet of a sonnet) a sequential musical shift could represent it in a setting.

For example, in Thomas Campion's 1601 book of airs, there is a conventionally Petrarchan lyric whose first strophe goes as follows:

> Mistris, since you so much desire
> To know the place of Cupid's fire,
> In your faire shrine that flame doth rest,
> Yet never harbourd in your brest.
> It bides not in your lips so sweete,
> Nor where the rose and lillies meete,
> But a little higher, but a little higher;
> There, there, O there lies Cupids fire.

The lady's eyes, a source of a higher, purer love than is her mouth, are here celebrated in the language of the sonneteers, and the air of sanctity, the forswearing of mere passion ("So meanely triumphs not my blisse," goes a line in the second strophe) are all familiar enough. But in his fourth book of airs, published ca. 1618, Campion parodied his earlier song in some now-fashionable anti-Petrarchan second thoughts. The first strophe:

> Beauty, since you so much desire
> To know the place of *Cupids* fire,
> About you somwhere it doth rest,
> Yet never harbour'd in your brest,
> Nor gout-like in your heele or toe;
> What foole would seeke Loves flame so low?
> But a little higher, but a little higher,
> There, there, o there lyes *Cupids* fire.

This is a satiric reduction, a literal lowering: here love starts, as Donne suggests that it should in "Loves Progresse," from below, that it may find its home in sex, at the body's center. Campion's setting for the second song is more chromatic in melodic line than is the first, and the lute part bawdily points up the repeatedly ascending "But a little higher" with contrapuntal nudging.

These two songs represent two conflicting modalities. The major tradition of European song would have to differentiate between those modalities in setting them. Many of Donne's major lyrics embody a constant process of dialectic between modalities, conducted by an ingenuity masked as a reality principle, juggling hyperbole and abuse, insisting that the truest tenderness is the most feigning, that the most faithful caresses are those of wit and will combined. Art song could not begin to treat such complexity musically until Schumann began to set Heine *Lieder*. The poet of the *Songs and Sonnets*, double fool—perhaps even exponential fool—as he was, seldom ran the real risk of being a triple one.

WILLIAM   KERRIGAN

The Fearful Accommodations
of John Donne

Critics of John Donne have marked a peculiar violence in his sensibility
not to be dissociated from the "boldness" and "daring" of his conceits.
Among readers of the divine poems in particular this intemperate
temperament has become an object of controversy. Qualities that made
Donne a love poet of sublime egotism also, for some critics, damaged his
religious verse irreparably; "The 'Holy Sonnets' and the 'Hymns,'" argues
a suspicious Douglas Bush, "are focused, like the love poems, on a particular
moment and situation, on John Donne, and the rest of life and the world
is blacked out, does not exist." Moreover, the agoraphobic playfulness and
unrelieved ingenuity so appealing in the context of human love have seemed
less suitable to the doctrines of the Christian faith. It is one thing to run
circles of wit about the straight-line orthodoxy of Petrarchan love poets,
quite another to bend the cherished corners of dogma. Poems such as "Batter
my heart" and "Show me deare Christ" may appear desperately inventive,
the work of a histrionic convert who "has to stimulate his awareness of God
by dwelling on the awfulness of God." Like other Renaissance poets whose
devotional verse has been assailed, Donne has been defended by scholars
assuming (however implicitly) that negative evaluations are directed,
whether by ignorance or design, against the religion itself. Louis Martz and
Helen Gardner, locating a tradition of formal meditation intended to
achieve sensual immediacy, interior drama, and intense emotion, have
disarmed objections by subtly disarming the poems, revealing those
idiosyncratic, "tasteless" moments in the religious verse as the respectable,

From *English Literary Renaissance* 4, no. 3 (Autumn 1974). ©1974 by *English
Literary Renaissance*.

if passionate, consequences of devout contemplation. Still, many readers—all those, in fact, who find in the tastelessness of Donne either the sure measure of his limitation or the problematic force of his greatness—will sympathize with the hesitations of Frank Kermode, who writes of "Show me deare Christ": "Perhaps we dislike this metaphor (Christ as *mari complaisant*) because the image of the Church as the Bride is no longer absolutely commonplace; but having accepted the image we are still unwilling to accept its development, even though we see that the main point is the *glorious* difference of this from a merely human marriage. Something is asked of us we can no longer easily give. Many of the Holy Sonnets have this perilous balance; their wit is always likely to seem indelicate as well as passionate." The "we" of this passage is more just than it might first appear, for the great ambivalent power of Donne's sonnet depends on how, as the marital conceit develops toward holy adultery, the "me" of the first line becomes the "our sights" and "most men" of the sestet, thus implicating readers in the express desire to woo the spouse of Christ. The poem has been designed to force "us" to participate in the alarming extension of a traditional metaphor. Drawn into uneasy complicity with the speaker, readers may find the "*glorious* difference" less compelling than the inglorious similarity.

The Ignatian exercises evoked to explain these violations of taste are in reality one minor consequence of the major theological problem of anthropomorphism. As we cannot conceive of God except in terms conceivable to a human mind, our apprehension of a timeless, infinite, unsearchably wise deity must be anthropomorphic to one degree or another—as, arguably, must all our apprehensions. On the one hand, anthropomorphism would seem to be a fundamental human instinct to make this world comfortable, familiar, explicable, and responsive, appropriate in nature to be the object of both our feelings and our thoughts. Such a postulate might account, to choose a trivial example, for the acceptably "normal" behavior permitted the pet owner in our civilized culture, who may name, fondle, dress, and bury his beast, even engage the brute in imaginary conversation ("That's a good boy!") without fear of seeming insane: behind him stands an unbroken tradition of rational beasts in myth, folklore, romance, fairy tale, and the modern cartoon. Considered generically, as permissible expressions of our abiding loneliness, there is an unsettling brotherhood between the pet owner projecting his humanity downward in the hierarchy of being to his dog and the religious man projecting his humanity upward to his God, addressing his deity as his "father" or "king." Yet we would err in assuming that this brotherhood is anything but universal. Anthropomorphism, though involved with the unique needs of individuals, may represent the inherent condition of perception itself. Men have so often found, even in the most precise endeavors of the mind, that they gaze in a mirror while supposing themselves to observe the world. A case in point from the early decades of this century would be the conviction of molecular physicists such as Eddington and Pauli that the indeterminate position of an electron had solved definitively the ancient debate between free will and determinism; their confusion between the "choice" of quantum orbits and the ethical "choice" of human beings was, as Cassirer realized immediately, based on the imputation of a gross anthropomorphism to an electron. Despite the exposure of this and similar misconceptions, the human intellect cannot be expected to ward off forever the specter of its own operations. Thinkers seep into their own thoughts and we are, sometimes unknowingly, the objects of our own intelligence. Egotism, as skeptics both ancient and modern have always hoped to remind us with their array of stunning fallacies, is an attribute of knowing: we must believe what we know and much of what we know is essentially solipsistic. The Nobel physicist P. W. Bridgeman, considering the apparatus of perception, has drawn the radically skeptical conclusion that progress in molecular physics will soon be at an end, since the human mind is not so constituted that it may think accurately about the physical world. So perhaps we are blind in the very act of seeing.

Christian theologians debated similar issues, distinguishing anthropomorphism as the emotional need of individual believers from anthropomorphism as the necessary condition of theological knowledge. Recognizing the two directions implied by this discrimination, we may draw a useful line between those rational beings who keep always before them the difference between God as he is known and God as he is, and those more passionate for whom, in the ecstasies of devotion, the difference between a heavenly father and an earthly father tends to disappear. It is precisely the trespass of this fine line that complicates our response to "Show me deare Christ." For what disturbs Kermode, and what has disturbed critics of "Batter my heart," is Donne's eagerness to display the most anthropomorphic consequences of anthropomorphism—in short, to imagine with some detail the sexuality of God. Approving the theological tenor, we suspect the anthropomorphic vehicle. Perhaps the Ignatian exercises, with their extraordinary reliance on the power of corporeal images, promoted unsettling formulations of this kind. But these impressive poems appropriately raise the larger question of how and why Donne thought of man while thinking of God.

By outlining the history of Christian accomodation and attending to its psychological implications, I hope to appreciate the strategy of these two sonnets, clarifying both the logic which informs them and the ambivalence which they inspire. . . .

TWO HOLY SONNETS

Joan Webber has shown that Donne, in common with other Renaissance theologians, understood the verses of the Bible as "enfolding" significance. In preaching manuals the word "opening" referred to the division and interpretation of the text; the preacher merely exposed or dilated meanings assumed to be already present, though compressed, in the Bible itself. A sacred metaphor, like a seed bearing a tree, contained the full extension of its vehicle and the consequences of that extension for its tenor. Perhaps this conception may help to describe that special way with conceits which we designate "metaphysical wit," indicating how Jack Donne became Dr. Donne without changing his habits of mind. For the way Donne presented the conventional metaphors of love poetry was exactly analogous to the way he "unraveled" or "opened" the sacred conceits of his sermons. In "The Broken Heart," for example, Donne constructed an elaborate metaphor to describe his failure with a certain cold lady. His scorned heart shivers like glass. But where is it now? She has refused the heart, so its pieces must still reside in his breast: as a broken mirror shows many little faces instead of one large face, so his heart cannot love anymore, but only reflect lesser images in liking, wishing, and adoring. The poem unravels, unfolds, discloses, and displays what already exists, compressed in the hoary cliché "You broke my heart." Donne reinvigorated this dead trope by assuming its literal truth and proceeding to complicate the tenor (his relationship with the lady) to fit the extended vehicle (the broken mirror). In a sense, the witty developments of the poem pre-exist in the initial cliché, folded up in the weave of convention and waiting there for a curious expositor. Donne did not open the vehicle to include, or the tenor to respond to, the sweeping of shards, seven years bad luck, or the purchase of a new glass—but there was nothing in his method, no restraint in theory, to prevent him from doing so.

Similarly, the disturbing rape in the last line of "Batter my heart" should be understood as implicit in the ancient theological conceit of the righteous soul's marriage to God. If the good man weds God, then the sinful man weds God's "enemie," and if God would claim this recalcitrant soul, then he must grant divorce and possess her by force. Given Donne's conception of sacred metaphor, the accommodated marriage would enfold infidelity, divorce, and even imprisonment. It would compress all the things which attend earthly marriages, the only ones we know and the only ones our language can properly signify. More specifically, it may be appropriate to mention, but absurd to continue mentioning, that Donne was in fact imprisoned by the father of his bride and that this poem resembles, with interesting shifts of identity and reattributions of virtue, the drama of his own marriage:

> Batter my heart, three person'd God; for, you
> As yet but knocke, breathe, shine, and seeke to mend;
> That I may rise, and stand, o'erthrow mee, 'and bend
> Your force, to breake, blowe, burn and make me new.
> I, like an usurpt towne, t'another due,
> Labour to'admit you, but Oh, to no end,
> Reason your viceroy in mee, mee should defend,
> But is captiv'd, and proves weake or untrue,
> Yet dearely'I love you, and would be lov'd faine,
> But am bethroth'd unto your enemie,
> Divorce mee,'untie, or breake that knot againe,
> Take mee to you, imprison mee, for I
> Except you'enthrall mee, never shall be free,
> nor ever chast, except you ravish mee.

To be sure, the poem is not so daring as it might have been. The phrase "three person'd God," for example, identifies the male lover addressed in Trinitarian terms, themselves derived by accommodation from the earthly family. I suppose that John Donne, in certain mood, might have considered naming the holy lover as the "father" of this hapless bride and played out the grotesque results in allusions to incest—but Donne, thankfully, was not Crashaw. Nevertheless, "Batter my heart" does suggest by implication the details of its final phrase.

Though often described as a poem with three conceits of equal importance developed in successive quatrains, really the poem evolves from and toward a single metaphor. For the bride addressing her lover, equated to the soul addressing God, is the implicit situation throughout—unless we are to believe that suddenly and ridiculously, with the phrase "Yet dearely'I love you," our speaker changes sex. Revealed with increasing clarity from line 9 to line 14, the figurative terms of this address are assumed in the "heart" of the opening line and continue to be assumed in the formal simile of the second quatrain. Thus the actual tenor of "Batter my heart" and "like an usurpt towne" is not, as in the usual reading, an experience of conversion. These subsidiary conceits have primary reference to the love relationship, itself an accommodated vehicle for the spiritual life of the soul, and during most of the poem the true sense of this crucial primary reference is left unsettled.

So clear as vehicle and so loose as tenor, the language of the first two tropes is purposefully dislocated. This speaker would have her heart reformed by the tinker's tools. But what exactly is she inviting from "three person'd God" when the terms of tinkering are translated to the terms of love? It will not suffice to recall the emblem tradition, where muscular arms wielding various tools reached from the clouds to batter or burn the miraculously suspended heart of the Christian Everyman, for the heart of this poem belongs to a misguided bride: the "emblem," if such it is, must be reshaped within the figures of another and controlling "emblem." The simile of the "usurpt towne" would appear to be clearer, at least in its reference to the interior betrayal of "weake or untrue" reason, since these words provide a semantic link between political intrigue and amorous infidelity. But "Labour to'admit you" implies that "three person'd God" is there at the gates, besieging the "usurpt towne" in the person of a monarch reclaiming his territory. We must contend once again with the activity desired of the lover who is, in this second subsidiary trope, a warfaring king. What do the propositions of the second quatrain mean when transferred, as they must be transferred, to the love relationship? The language hovers, referentially uncertain, until fixed upon the desired event of the final line. There drama and definition coincide. "That I may rise, and stand, o'erthrow mee," "breake, blowe, burn and make me new," and "Labour to'admit you"—the drifting metaphors of the poem strike anchor in that ravishment which would make the speaker newly "chaste."

The root problem in interpreting this sonnet is not whether its tripartite development conceals some allusion to the Trinity. Probably it does. What readers must confront, as fearlessly or fearfully as the poem itself, is the way Donne has unbalanced his central equation by choosing to detail the physical violation. Though metaphors be equations, we do not understand them as such: one term of this conceit must have linguistic, philosophical, and psychological priority and be, as we say, the theme, subject, or motive of the poem. Because of the personified "Reason," because "three person'd God" is named as the lover, we recognize that sexual rape is here a metaphor for the forcible entrance of the deity into an otherwise impenetrable soul. But the design of the poem grants extraordinary emphasis to the penetration of a tight body. Insofar as the tropes reach out of local context to describe the climactic invitation, that sexual event acquires the force of a tenor. The intercourse of the speaker and God becomes virtually a "real" presence in the poem, a final repository of reference—the shore on which the gathering wave of implication finally breaks. Donne has turned his anthropomorphic conceit toward actual event, generating what might be termed a "cumulative metaphor." As the tinkering and the besieging express a desire for renewal and reclamation, looking forward to the ravishment, so do the very instruments and objects of attack progress logically toward the sexual. A paradigm of this linguistic mobility, the opening phrase undergoes successive redefinitions. "Batter my heart" is addressed first to God the tinker, then becomes doubly applicable to the warrior God of lines 5 and 6. She would "admit" the just ruler, but to "no end": by inference she wishes the monarch to reclaim his city with some "battering" engine of war, most likely a battering ram. Finally she "would be lov'd faine," though her heart is hard and her gates are closed, and the initial phrase becomes synonymous with the plea for ravishment, *heart* being not uncommon as a slang word for *vagina* during this period. The commands of the poem proceed through a series of transformations in assaulter and thing assaulted. The vehicles of her wishes flow together. The battered heart becomes the attacked city which becomes the ravished vagina. The tinker's tools become the monarch's engine which becomes, indeed, the penis of God. Donne's accumulation of assaults and batteries rests precisely there. We have the effect, in psychoanalytical terms, of moving from sublimation to cathexis or, in theological terms, of moving from relatively "safe" accommodations—God the tinker, God the king—to a "dangerous" accommodation made all the more evocative by the scheme of the movement itself. Donne has contrived a most "awful discrimination" of the human from the divine. Though all of sexuality, even prostatitis and moniliasis, may in theory lie folded within the ancient metaphor of spiritual marriage, Donne has opened a suggestiveness near to crude anthropomorphism. And crude anthropomorphism is another name for outright blasphemy.

Recognizing how overtly this poem dares the forbidden, we can appreciate the uncommon power of its closing paradox. The equation of ravishment and chastity deflects the perilous situation reached through the unraveling of accommodated love; having painted himself into a corner, Donne extricated himself by switching colors. We should eschew all interpretations that diminish the mystery of chaste ravishing. The word "chaste" here does not denote Spenserian chastity, the sancification of sexuality in lawful marriage. More to the point, if we must have analogues, are the legends of the hagiographical tradition, which often represent the

restoration of innocence to fallen female saints, or the discussion early in
The City of God of the ravished martyrs who retained their physical purity.
For as "make me new" would suggest, "nor ever chaste" concerns the
recovery of virginity. Donne created this paradox by applying the traditional
logic of accommodation. In Milton's formulation, we may participate
without error in accommodated speech so long as "weakness when viewed
in reference to ourselves" is understood as "most complete and excellent
when imputed to God." What does it mean when, in the unfolding of
anthropomorphic metaphors, the God we believe to be perfect would appear
to be irregular? When God himself takes on those qualities he would
suppress in us? With the conviction that God is the author of goodness alone,
one can only say that human imperfection has obscured divine perfection.
But how can we understand divine perfection? Since we know only human
perfection, we can indicate our recognition of the failure of accommodation
by conflating earthly weakness with earthly virtue: we can reaccommodate
the failed accommodation. Therefore the rape of "Batter my heart" must
preserve, rather than destroy, chastity. The God who violently ravishes must
be the God who honorably abstains, the possessed soul a virgin soul. To
escape from an irregular anthropomorphism, Donne introduces a
"complete and excellent" anthropomorphism, equating the imputed
human vice to the appropriate and opposite human virtue. Anthropomorphism twice applied eludes anthropomorphism altogether. God, unlike any
man, can be at once lustful and honorable. The soul unlike any body, can
be at once ravished and chaste. Beautifully calculated, the final line of "Batter
my heart" presents the word "chaste" before "ravish me," relaxing anxieties
an instant before the revelation that focuses them. As we read the last phrase,
the human act we comprehend has already been diverted to a superhuman
paradox. All at once we see the base and the miraculous.

The strategy of "Batter my heart"—approaching the forbidden,
reaching a moment of dangerous anthropomorphism, deflecting that
danger, just before the moment appears, with an equation between carnality
and virtue—also informs "Show me deare Christ." Here the passionate
speaker desires to enjoy the true church promised in the Bible, ending the
miserable schisms of history. In the accommodated terms of the poem, this
desire becomes the eager sexuality of the "amorous soule":

> Show me deare Christ, thy spouse, so bright and cleare.
> What, is it she, which on the other shore
> Goes richly painted? or which rob'd and tore
> Laments and mournes in Germany and here?
> Sleepes she a thousand, then peepes up one yeare?

Is she selfe truth and errs? now new, now outwore?
Doth she, 'and did she, and shall she evermore
On one, on seaven, or on no hill appeare?
Dwells she with us, or like adventuring knights
First travaile we to seeke and then make love?
Betray kind husband thy spouse to our sights,
And let myne amorous soule court thy mild Dove,
Who is most trew, and pleasing to thee, then
When she'is embrac'd and open to most men.

Until the final three lines the revelation sought is only distantly sexual. The speaker wishes to view the "bright and cleare" spouse in her radiant nakedness, not to possess her. Donne might have discontinued the unfolding of his conceit at the provocative but inexplicit "Betray . . . to our sights," since the word "betray" carries a sexual implication neatly subordinate to its primary meaning as a synonym for "Show" in line 1. Moreover, the activity of seeing was itself invested with sexual significance in the classical optics Donne inherited. The word "propagation" referred to the multiplication of the visual image in the spatial continuum between the object and the eye—seeing was making love to the world. "Making babies" in Elizabethan slang denoted the mutual gaze of lovers. And certainly the Italianate love poetry of the sixteenth century had established gazing, glancing, glimpsing, peering, peeking, and peeping as a kind of sexual activity, a foreplaying near in effect to a consummation, electric as lightning and magnetic as the lodestone, sufficient to cause both orgasmic ecstasy and postvisual depression: Cupid's poets appreciated the many arrows in the quiver of an eye. However, as "make love" in line 10 foreshadows, the poem shifts from subdued implication to overt proposition. Much resembling the sweep towards ravishment in "Batter my heart," there is a sense of inexorable progression in these lines, an unveiling of desire to match the unveiling desired.

The conceit of "Show me deare Christ" extends beyond the tradition of its origin. In the common formulation the church is the bride of Christ, and by joining the church a man becomes metaphorically a woman; he becomes a "member" of the earthly body of the bride. Whereas Donne accepted a figurative womanhood in "Batter my heart," here he has made the marriage of the church a triangular affair by insisting on his actual, rather than symbolic, sexuality. Given this fundamental revision, the argument unfolds with pseudo-logical exactitude. Because the church triumphant has yet to appear, Christ must be guarding his bride from other men; and because such jealousy is contrary to the true nature of Christ, he can be wooed into compliance with human wishes. So Christ is asked to become at last a "kind husband," generously betraying his wife to his friends. She will please him "most" when she is "embrac'd and open to most men." Reminiscent of many of the *Songs and Sonnets,* the wit of the concluding passage depends upon our ability to deduce the fallacious argument which must have preceded the statement before us. The doors of a church remain open; the more men who enter, the more pleased Christ is. Moving freely from object to concept and tenor to vehicle, the speaker offers a proposition admirable as religious desire but startling as sexual desire.

The bride of "Batter my heart" wished to be penetrated by an eager male. The eager male of "Show me deare Christ" wishes to possess an "open" bride and he assumes the collective voice of "most men," convincing the husband to permit this betrayal in the interests of his own pleasure. With "a reverentiall feare" we again confront "an awful discrimination of Divine things from Civill." And again there is the balm of paradox. The bride is "most trew" when most unfaithful: she is at one time "selfe truth" and yet "errs." The husband finds her "most . . . pleasing" when human cuckolds find their wives most abhorrent: in her openness she will please him as a "most trew" spouse. Just at the moment of its definition, twisted adultery, in accord with the principles of accommodated speech, becomes equated with exemplary fidelity.

The reversal from vice to virtue differs ever so subtly from that of "Batter my heart," yet the difference is telling. For virginity and ravishment are forever incompatible on this earth. The conclusion of the earlier sonnet, anthropomorphically nonanthropomorphic, translates readers from the familiar life of the body to the inexpressible life of the soul. We approximate transcendence with the aid of a marvelous proportion: as ravishment is to the body, so chastity is to the soul. Similarly, no wife imaginable can be at once "most trew" and "open to most men." Yet this wife has been imagined, to our exquisite amazement, and she seems worthy to be the wife of Christ. However, the second reversal of "Show me deare Christ" does not escape from human categories. It is indeed possible for a human husband to consider his spouse "most . . . pleasing" when most untrue, and not only in the Darien, Connecticut, of modern America. Augustine put this case to his interlocutor in the dialogue *On Free Choice of the Will*:

> Evodius. I know that adultery is an evil because I myself would
> be unwilling to allow adultery in the case of my wife. And
> whoever does to another what he does not wish done to
> himself, does evil.
> Augustine. What if someone's lust is so great that he offers his

own wife to another and willingly allows her to be seduced
by the man with whose wife he in turn wants to have equal
license? Don't you think that he does evil?

Evodius. Yes, the worst evil!

Augustine. By the rule you mentioned such a man does not sin,
for he does nothing that he would not endure. You must
find some other reason by which to prove that adultery is
evil.

Donne must find some other reason by which to prove that cuckoldry is
miraculous. The Christ of the closing passage does not elude a recognizable
and unhealthy human attitude. Donne has generated a paradox in the sense
of "a proposition contrary to orthodoxy"— for husbands pleased by
infidelity are rare—but not a paradox in the sense of "a proposition true
but impossible." We are left with an awful similarity rather than an awesome
discrimination; the fine balance of danger and relief at the conclusion of
"Batter my heart" does not recur. I feel that this difficulty accounts for the
lingering dissatisfaction of Frank Kermode and accounts indirectly for the
popularity of Helen Gardner's interpretation of the sonnet, which turns
attention away from the problems of lines 10-14 to concentrate instead upon
the theological and topical significance of lines 1-9. The last passage,
beautiful as it is, nearly crumbles. Donne almost loses control of his reader's
imagination and therefore of his intentional meaning. The lame paradox
of "and pleasing to thee, then" threatens to undermine the triumphant
"most trew," for if we can imagine a human *mari complaisant*, we can also
imagine his willing wife. This activity pushes "most trew" away from "most
faithful" toward "most true to your desires." By now the poem is close, too
close, to the tactless exercises in accommodated devotion we find in Crashaw,
daring with no sense of danger, creating neither mystery nor wit, but leaving
us aghast at the combination of great verbal power, unquestioned faith,
neurosis, and stupidity. We finish "Show me deare Christ" with a twinge
of the wrong sort of "reverentiall feare."

SOME CONCLUSIONS, SOME SPECULATIONS

Human terms were the only ones he had. Donne could not conceive of God
without discovering, somewhere in the folds of his conception, human vice.
It may be objected that the two poems I have discussed do not unravel
metaphors inherent in Christian theology; one may dismiss the religious
implications of these fearful accommodations by supposing that Donne,
acting out some private compulsion, deliberately generated the inessential

images of God the rapist and Christ the willing cuckold. But consequences of anthropomorphism as grotesque as these lie coiled in the most central Christian doctrines. The *De ecclesiastica rhetorica* of Valerio, a popular manual for preachers, alerted its readers to this contingency by forbidding the wanton, though logical, "opening" of doctrines such as the redemption:

> There are, however, many warnings which the orator must heed in the use of metaphors. First that they be not taken from remote things. . . . Finally that they do not originate from anything unseemly, as when someone would call God the killer of Christ; for he commanded that he should die for the sins of men so that he satisfy by that death divine justice and open the gates of Heaven to believing men. He ought not for that reason to be called killer; and, in short, easy metaphors, taken from beautiful things and applied with judgment, which wise men have called the essence of prudence, illuminate the sermon.

As a "father" God raises his "son" to a position of full equality. But as a "father" God also requires the sacrificial murder of his "son" to atone for our disobedience. Of course, to the extent that God the Father appears sadistic, to that extent he is not to be apprehended as a human being. When the metaphor turns perverse, God vacates the metaphor. Yet again, without the metaphor—and it is one sanctioned by the Bible, the exegetical tradition, the liturgy, and the prayers of many generations—we cannot think of God at all. It may be "the essence of prudence" to confine oneself to "easy metaphors." But there is, as Valerio realized, a dreadful logic to be avoided as we expound the most comforting doctrine of the Christian faith.

Donne was the one great poet of the English Renaissance to exploit the fearful consequences of accommodation in his devotional verse. Spenser, Herbert, Milton, and Marvell were careful to avoid imputing vice to God. When they unfolded anthropomorphic metaphors, they did so with evident caution. The Christ of Herbert's "The Sacrifice" exhibits an inhuman sense of humor, but in comprehending his ironies we admire without qualification the intelligence and self-possession they imply. In the devotional lyrics of Herbert accommodated vice never remains, at the end of the poem, to trouble our conception of the God addressed, since by then all blasphemies have redounded upon the speaker. More comparable to Donne in this regard was Ben Jonson, whose lyric "To Heaven" addresses God as an accommodated "judge" dispensing something less than justice. But Jonson did not, in the manner of his contemporary, emphasize the distance between true and false human judgment. Donne alone explored

the difference between God as we know him and God as we must believe
him to be, compelling us to recognize the conjunction of vice and virtue
as the necessary condition of our knowledge of the deity. Accommodation
for Donne was both our gift and our curse. He wrote of the two faces of
God in his brilliant Holy Sonnet XIII, superimposing the compassionate
Son upon the vengeful Father:

> Marke in my heart, O Soule, where thou dost dwell,
> The picture of Christ crucified, and tell
> Whether that countenance can thee affright,
> Teares in his eye quench the amasing light,
> Blood fills his frownes, which from his pierc'd head fell,
> And can that tongue adjudge thee unto hell,
> Which pray'd forgiveness for his foes fierce spight?

Tears extinguish the fearful light, blood hides the frowns, the tongue of
judgment prays for mercy—it is a lovely definition of the Atonement, the
cancellation of Old Testament wrath by New Testament love. Christ
incarnate perfected the accommodated speech of the Bible, embodying God
in human form and leaving an example of unambiguous virtue in this life.
Yet for Donne that other face remained, hidden rather than vanquished, and
while a "beauteous forme" could not "affright," the contorted visage of a
wrathful God was there to be imagined behind the face of compassion. The
paradoxes of "Batter my heart" and "Show me deare Christ" reenact, within
the particular terms of their anthropomorphism, this concealment: behind
chastity is violation, behind fidelity is adultery. Mysteriously, our love for
God is linguistically and psychologically inextricable from our lust.

   Within the context of Christian time the fearful accommodation of God
to man presupposes a mythic history. The primal likeness between God and
man was genuinely harmonious. There was no grotesquerie to complicate
our prelapsarian knowledge of the deity, because there was no human evil—
no rape, adultery, or murder. Adam in his garden, the unfallen image of
God, could understand his divine "father" or "friend" without fear of
unraveling an "awful discrimination" from these metaphors. That first
disobedience, defacing man, inevitably defaced his image of God:

> No more of talk where God or angel Guest
> With Man, as with his Friend, familiar us'd
> To sit indulgent, and with him partake
> Rural repast, permitting him the while
> Venial discourse unblam'd: I now must change
> These Notes to Tragic.

So Milton began Book IX of his epic, announcing both the historical loss of "Venial discourse unblam'd" and the loss within his own poem of unambivalent celebration. When the Fall turned all notes to tragic, harmonious likeness became fearful likeness. Because we know God in our own image and because that image, being corrupt, will at some time turn perverse when fitted to God, God must remain an object of dread for those unwilling to abjure the ancient privileges of analogy. It is true that God is fearful because he is incomprehensible. It is equally true that God is fearful because we can and do understand him. The creator, in this important sense, fell with the creature.

John Donne dramatized with special clarity the problems of all Christian devotion. Surely Aquinas was correct in his belief that a man with religious emotions ought to assume a divine "personality" appropriate to receive them. The issue was where that assuming must halt. Sober men such as Calvin endeavored to avoid the embarrassments of anthropomorphism by sealing up the Scriptures against unrestrained imaginations. Theologically this was doubtless the genteel position. But with insistent wit Donne, like other believers before and after him, made the old metaphors reveal their hidden grotesquerie. Such effects should be considered as neither the pathological impositions of a terror-struck convert nor the doctrinal expositions of a stolid conformist. Rather, the temperament and the religion unveiled each other. Donne arrived at these moments by permitting the traditional language of devotion to mean what it does mean and opening that language until, having proposed a fallen God, he raised his healing paradox. Behind the merciful face of God lay another face twisted in wrath and capable of the most fearsome acts. Finally, both faces belonged to man. For whenever his accommodated metaphors spoiled, his humanity had failed, not his God: in deference to this failure he conjured the image of man rectified. At such moments Donne worshipped human evil with the difficult faith that evil was, when predicated of God, perfection. "The love of God begins in fear, and the fear of God ends in love; and that love can never end, for God is love."

CLAUDIA   BRODSKY

Donne: The Imaging
of the Logical Conceit

This essay will attempt to indicate alternating conceptions of the problem of poetic wit or conceit in Donne's erotic poetry, and to investigate an instance in the religious poetry in which that problem and the range of its versions are suspended: Donne's exhortation to "true religion," Satire 3. At the outset I should state that the long-standing dispute as to whether Donne's extraordinary displays of figuration prove him a member of the Petrarchan and self-consciously rhetorical traditions in poetry, or the master of a purely personal style, is one that Donne's poetry in particular, and poetry of less obvious linguistic sophistication in general, appears to me to prove moot. In her seminal study of the image patterning of Elizabethan and Metaphysical poetry, Rosemund Tuve redresses the singular emphasis of "modern criticism" upon the poet's personal experience by demonstrating the salience of logical and rhetorical concerns in the poetic practices and theoretical poetics of the English Renaissance. Her insistence, that an exclusive focus upon individual sensory perceptions is not only particularly unsuited to the study of the poets of Donne's time (who were routinely trained in formal argument) but would also be hard pressed to account for the poetry of our own era, comes closest to the view held in this investigation of the unfruitful, if not foolish, dissociation of poetry, shaped by any single "sensibility," from its traditionally recognized "sister arts":

In much modern criticism which assumes that Metaphysical

From *ELH* 49, no. 4 (Winter 1982). ©1982 by The Johns Hopkins University Press.

images are intended to direct out attention to the quality rather than to the meaning of experience—especially to any generalized "truth"— there is considerable emphasis upon images as being conditioned not by the poet's logic but by his sensibility. I shall assume at the outset that these two are never really divorced in any poem, that no poem has ever been born out of logic by immaculate conception, and that, alternatively, no poem ever entirely lacks logical meaning. I shall thus avoid inserting constant reminders that the Elizabethans (and even myself) have no notion that "poem" and "logical discourse" are to be identified, even though they do not set the two in opposition.

Of course, all images *do* convey the poets's perception of the quality of his experience. All poetic with which I am acquainted accepts this, as a given; the task here is to look for some indications that the early seventeenth century erected it into a sufficient criterion. Much modern criticism does; modern poems which do are rather harder to find.

Consonant with her investigation of the logical conditions upon which the structure and semantics of poetic imagery rest, Tuve defines the Metaphysical conceits as an image combining a complex number of formal categories, or "places," in the construction of its meaning. The differing effects of Elizabethan and Metaphysical conceits may be traced, she suggests, to "differences between extended pursuit of a simple logical parallel and extended pursuit of a likeness by basing it on several logical parallels." Figures of the latter kind, whose "effect" is that of "sharp wit," "cannot be framed without the use of multiple predicaments and are usually found from more than one of the places of invention." The dual capability of the Metaphysical conceit would thus be its power to condense many logically consistent meanings within the scope of a single image or word, and conversely, its power to expand the semantic field of an image into a multiple range of possible meanings.

Recommending Tuve's definition for its own critical coherency, we may ask if the imagery whose complex patterning she indicates represents the tension of that complexity within its scope. Does the metaphysical conceit conceive in turn of the logical "predicamants" it presents? As Tuve helpfully recalls from a historical perspective, Donne, the master of the Metaphysical conceit, was himself fully familiar with the seventeenth-century Ramist school of logic, whose speculations included a concern with the relation of dialectical or logical argument to poetic forms. Yet in pointing to and aligning the many sides of the poet, Tuve does not indicate that, *as* poet, Donne may have imaged the logical implications of linguistic extravagance or wit; i.e., that the poet's imagery may reflect upon the problem it engages of making both figurative and logical sense. Responding to Tuve's important illumination of the underlying logical structure of image patterns, we may question the status of logic as it is brought to light by the use of imagery, turning first to the figures offered in the poems of the means by which sense is constructed or conceived.

Such images would refer both to the poet's experience of explicit circumstances and to the transformation of experience in poetic discourse, by acting as an analogical or metaphoric link between the two. As Tuve states of the signifying function of metaphor generally, the figure effects a transference of the sense commonly associated with a familiar "concrete situation" to another situation whose meaning does not ordinarily derive from that relation. In the erotic poetry, certain images make radical claims for their own meaning by representing an exclusion (and signifying an inclusion) of all other relations. Sensual experience is imaged as itself and as the sum of all experiences; the lovers' isolation is propounded in metaphor to be the world. These metaphors, themselves hyperboles, carry the criteria of the poem's own internal coherency, along with our conception of the subject it figures, to purposeful excess, as the totality of visible phenomena is forcefully equated with an imaged erotic realm. The problem of possible inconsistencies of meaning is eclipsed by a circumscription of all possible meanings within an emphatically specified, logical, as well as literal, "place." In sonnets such as "The Good Morrow" and "The Sun Rising," the lover's sexual bond is substituted for all human intercourse: a movement of absolute inversion is effected by which the poem demands both that its dominant image be, and that it can *only* be, exhaustively understood. The outstanding metaphors of this globalization of signification are, most obviously, those of "the world," a "sphere," "an every where":

> And now good morrow to our waking souls,
>   Which watch not one another out of fear;
> For love, all love of other sights controls,
>   And makes one little room, an every where.
>   ("The Good Morrow," 8-11)

> Thou sun art half as happy as we,
>   In that the world's contracted thus;
> Thine age asks ease, and since thy duties be

> To warm the world, that's done in warming us.
> Shine here to us, and thou art everywhere;
> This bed thy centre is, these walls, thy sphere.
>   ("The Sun Rising," 25-30)

Image patterns focused upon hyperbolic conceptions induce a "centre" and sufficiency of vision by command. They elude the classical question of the objective adequacy of their diction by admitting no external objects of comparison. At the same time, however, by figuring on a level indicative of everything, these images necessarily portray the particularities of nothing. The transformation of "one little room" into "an every where" and the transference of the predicament of human mortality to the sun ("Thine age asks ease") extend and immortalize the lovers by effective default, just as the least qualified and most striking of Donne's hyperboles, "Nothing else is" ("The Sun Rising, " 22), enforces the lovers' ontological status as fact by precluding any understanding of its mode. Metaphors intending to global dimensions can by their own claims neither make distinctions in the matter they signify, nor, therefore, render it recognizable. Imaged signification that defies logical examination denies itself in turn as an access to knowledge.

An alternative to figures whose successful totalization of meaning depends upon a principle of nondiscrimination is a more selective visual metaphor, that of the portrait or "picture." The signifying potential of pictorial images is specifically thematized in Elegy 5 and the sonnet, "Witchcraft by a Picture." The subject of the portraits referred to in both poems is identified as the poet. In Elegy 5 a comparison is played out between the poet's verbal portrayal of his future appearance ("When weather-beaten I come back" [5-10]) and the literal picture of himself that he leaves behind upon departing: "So foul, and course, as oh, I may seem then,/ This shall say what I was" (12-13). In "Witchcraft by a Picture," the image of the portrait is from inception a compound conceit, its appearance represented by a teardrop in which the poet sees himself reflected. The "art" of this doubly imaged "picture" is thus made to disappear by his departure:

> But now I have drunk thy sweet salt tears,
> And though thou pour more I'll depart;
> My picture vanished, vanish fears
> That I can be endamaged by that art
>   (8-11)

Implying in conclusion that his absence in this case will be permanent, the poet evokes the replacement of the present teardrop portrait by "One picture more . . . /Being in thine own heart, from all malice free" (13-14).

Particularized pictorial images, as the differing arguments of these poems demonstrate, seem to grant universal grounds for comparative cognition. In proffering portraits of varying figural dimensions to the lover from whom he takes leave, the poet suggests as much; in composing the image of the portrait into their dominant theme, the figural patterns of the poems seem to indicate the same.

Understood as a reflective mimetic form, the picture would perform the double role described above: that of supplying the means both of a consistent understanding of experience and of the coherent construction of imagery within a poem. Yet at the moment they achieve their formal mediative function, the pictures imaged in the poems are themselves referentially invalid. They attain logical efficacy when representing what no longer is: an appearance whose impermanence is engraved in the very purpose of portraiture, as is made explicit by the stated departure of the subject it depicts. The meaning of each picture can only be derived in comparison with a substitute image (the poet's radically dissimilar figure upon return; the picture he may not return to see, nor could, since it is in his lover's "heart") to which it bears no resemblance. The specifically logical significance of the image as portrait depends upon its divergence, upon analysis, from the appearance and associated experience it reflects. Thus the image of the picture acts as the critical wedge of the poetry, poised between the consequential understanding of its figural pattern and the claim of fidelity to the referent the figure portrays.

If we move from conceits whose matacritical dimension is visually or externally bound, to conceits that comment upon their own internal basis— the infinite capability, within language, to substitute and combine—the problems posed for the criterion of logical coherency as arbiter of the "truth or untruth" of poetic imagery become more clear. In an attempt to convince his lover to undress (Elegy 19, "To His Mistress Going to Bed"), the poet compares the clothed body to a picture but further specifies that visual image as being like the "covering" of a book. The conceptual force added to his argument by the second conceit is that a book cover, unlike a picture, derives its meaning from a content within. While the removal of a picture reveals nothing more than additional space, a book cover turned aside displays the purpose of its appearance, the text it announces, protects, or adorns. The movement of figural transformations, from picture to covering to book, is intensified by a change in poetic diction from the stated comparison ("like," 39) of simile to the abrupt copula ("are," 41) of metaphor:

> Like pictures, or like books' gay coverings made
> For laymen, are all women thus arrayed;

Themselves are mystic books, which only we
(Whom their imputed grace will dignify)
Must see revealed.

(39-43)

Initiating the same verse paragraph is a linguistically less complex, and logically less persuasive, manipulator's sleight of hand: "As souls unbodied, bodies unclothed must be,/ To taste whole joys" (34-35). A moment's reflection reveals the insubstantial argument of this relatively uncomplicated conceit: by blasphemously comparing "bodies" with "souls," the poet elevates what is more or less conventional and dispensable (clothing) to the level of that which is mortally indispensable (the body), thereby forming a pseudocorrelation between the essential ("unbodied") quality of the soul and some equally essential quality of the body "unclothed." The latter, however, within the terms of the analogy constructed, could only be its starting point, the soul. Ending where it began, figuration here, rather than completing a transference of meaning, breaks down into deductive circularity. As a rhetorical and logical means of persuasion, however, the image of "mystic books" works far more successfully; for it is understood within the conceit of the written text (in distinction from that of "bodies" or "pictures") that the object it refers to contains its own coherency, the meaning by which its printed surface is defined.

Yet the significance that the image convincingly conveys, through a perfect coordination of its structure and its referent, does not rest within the poem at the purpose of revelation. "To see revealed" is finally not the organizing motive of the poem's figural movement, nor the final intention of the poet speaking as lover. Once removed to render visible the "mystic" text beneath it, the "gay covering" of this imaged "book" will be replaced by another of far greater externality. The conceit of the disclosed text only proves itself truly effective when concealed by a further "covering" that bears no intrinsic relation to its content: the body of the lover made seducer by that fact. The poem concludes by reversing the relevance of its major figure: "To teach thee, I am naked first, why then/ What needst thou have more covering than a man" (47-48). The image of the book, of language made into meaningful, coherent form, shows itself persuasive for its own appearance of depth, yet persuades—as the lover's playful but persistent argument makes evident—to a submission of depth to superficies, of revelation to eroticism: a textual *and* referential event whose experience runs contrary to the meaning the image evokes.

The conceit of the "revealed" text arises in a related context at the end of "The Ecstasy." The intention and tone of the voice in the poem do not appear, as in Elegy 19, to be directly motivated by erotic designs. The image of the body as book is introduced to represent the necessary end of love, rather than to serve as a discursive means of seduction. Furthermore, the tension of the figural pattern in which it participates lies not between the cover and content of the book itself, but between the book as a finite corporeal phenomenon and the continual growth of "Love's mysteries in souls":

> To our bodies turn we then, that so
>   Weak men on love revealed may look;
> Love's mysteries in souls do grow,
>   But yet the body is his book.
>
>   (69-72)

"Book" here is not equated with "souls," but understood to be a bodily translation of their distinct, though unspecified, power of animation. "Bodies" articulate, but are not identical to "mysteries," which "grow"; as such they effect an inevitable, while perhaps only minimal, difference in their meaning, an observable but "small change":

> And if some lover, such as we,
>   Have heard this dialogue of one,
> Let him still mark us, he shall see
>   Small change, when we're to bodies gone.
>
>   (73-76)

The bodily text, the poet asserts, displays and maintains (at least most of) an underlying discourse of love: "this dialogue of one." Yet if the image of coherent imagery, the "book," is assured significance by its subservience to the always partially invisible subtext of "souls," the image of the potency for imaging, "language," offers no such certainty of correspondence or control. In introducing the image of language, the poet indicates the possibility of coherent patterns of meaning that, while true to their own internal logic of grammar and syntax, may be devoid of the truth of their semantic sense.

The "language" to which I refer might best be initially distinguished as phenomenal in nature; it is linked, in Elegy 7, to the visual and tactile senses. The poet reminds an unacknowledging lover that she owes her literacy in this mode of signification to him:

> Nature's lay idiot, I taught thee to love,

> And in that sophistry, oh, thou dost prove
> Too subtle: Fool, thou didst not understand
> The mystic language of the eye or hand
>
>   (1-4)

In "The Ecstasy" the poet refers to a language contrastively free of all phenomenal appearance, the "soul's language," intelligible to "any, so by love refined" (21-22). Prior in the poem to its argument for sexual union ("But O alas, so long, so far/ Our bodies why do we forbear?" [49-50]), the image of "soul's language" suggests a means of communication without bodies and without books, a language absolved equally of phenomenal referent and phenomenal manifestation: a language, in short, which takes no shape. This hypothetical mode of meaning, relying upon no images of its own (letters, characters, or signs of any kind), nor supplying sense through the images it composes (whether understood as literal denotations or figural substitutions), would be a language lacking the properties by which language is defined. The logical paradox spelled out by "language" here is perhaps not so prominent, but, upon inspection, equally as problematic, as the comparison of the body with the soul in Elegy 19. The second part of the poet's analogy is again deficient in its final term: the "language" named cannot be considered a metaphor (or must be considered an inherently failed one) for something else. A wholly nonphenomenal or noumenal "language" is not a language. To designate it as such is not even to effect a catachresis, since in this case, as opposed to that of an apparent object without a proper name, no objective or phenomenally based assertion can be made that this unarticulated medium exists. Indeed, before the understanding of "soul's language" could be hypothesized, the lovers' bodies, in making "sense" appear, "first" made their love apparent to one another—a fact for which the poet turns to them with gratitude:

> We owe them thanks, because they thus,
>   Did us, to us, at first convey,
> Yielded their forces, sense, to us,
>   Nor are dross to us, but allay.
>
>   (53-56)

Ingratitude for instruction given in the art of conveying sense is the ground of the poet's complaint in Elegy 7. Having "taught thee to love," he reproaches a mistress (who was evidently once his own as well as "Nature's lay idiot"), he should be awarded the sexual fidelity which is his due. yet just as faithfulness here implies exclusive rights to a wife's adultery, so "love" is itself an image for a learned erotic skill. Similarly, the term "mystic" is equated with and substituted for "sophistry" in describing the "language" acquired. That "language" performs the function in the poem of a highly effective and, as defined by Tuve, properly Metaphysical conceit. Its significance combines the logic of different individual semiotic modes, ranging from the faculties of physical emotion ("the air of sighs"; "the eye's water" [5-7] to calculations of gesture and aesthetic effect ("the alphabet of flowers . . . devisely being set" [9-10], with that of their model, "words" (13,25). The grievance of a jealous lover and teacher makes its reference clear:

> Remember since all thy words used to be
> To every suitor, *Ay, if my friends agree;*
> Since, household charms, thy husband's name to teach,
> Were all the love-tricks, that they wit could reach;
> And since, an hour's discourse could scarce have made
> One answer in thee, and that ill arrayed
> In broken proverbs, and torn sentences.
> Thou art not by so many duties his
> That from the world's common having severed thee,
> Inlaid thee, neither to be seen, nor see,
> As mine: who have with amorous delicacies
> Refined thee into a blissful paradise.
> Thy graces and good words my creatures be;
> I planted knowledge and life's tree in thee,
> Which oh, shall strangers taste?
>
>   (13-27)

The formal claims to possession enumerated by the speaker only serve to heighten the side-effects of the linguistic forms he has taught. For proficiency in the logic of "love," like fluency in any "language," entails an aptitude that, once learned, exceeds sexual and pedagogic dominion. To gain as lover one who was "severed" from "the world's common" through an education in the semiotics of eroticism may be to transform her into a "blissful paradise," but it is also, inevitably, to lose her to the "common," or community in which that semiotics circulates. For a knowing "paradise" differs from an "idiot" of "Nature" only in so far as it is more difficultly dominated, improbably "inlaid." Future scenes of sequestration will always be disrupted by "strangers" who share the same linguistic ability. The reader of Elegy 7 may respond to the speaker's frustration with the satisfaction of finding he has recieved his just deserts, or further recognize the possibility

that as poet he may be parodying his own demands as lover. Yet an additional
aspect of this "sincere" or implicity self-conscious complaint renders it
disturbing on another level. That dimension is made most strikingly
apparent in the peom's final substitutions for "sophistry" and "language":
"knowledge and life's tree." What we have accepted to mean a learned
licentiousness is here equated with both the desire to discern truth and the
symbolic origin of organic nature as figured in Genesis 2:3. The figural use
of the verb "to love" to describe the ability he has engendered was
immediately offset by the doubles entendres of the poet's opening, less than
loving, address: "Nature's lay idiot." The sense of the ineffable
conventionally accorded to "mystic" was similarly countered by the further
qualification of its object, "language," as being "of the eye [or] hand." But
the reference to "knowledge and life's tree," while opposed in gravity of
meaning by the mock-serious stance taken throughout the poem, returns
to reflect upon the logic of its opening conceits. To equate "sophistry"—
the skill of persuading to apparent truth through an antonymical
manipulation of the articulation of appearances, "language"—with
"knowledge" may be considered a fitting and itself perfectly logical
hyperbole, since the power to persuade might just as well be called
"knowledge" with respect to a subject who formerly could be called an
idiot." But in additionally claiming to have "planted" "life's tree" in that
subject, the poet indicates that "language" has endowed with living nature
her who had been its uncomprehending adjunct. If "sophistry" was opposed
to "Nature" in the initial patterning of the lover's complaint, "knowledge,"
a substitutive figure for "sophistry," is allied to an image of nature as that
pattern proceeds. Furthermore, this image of the origin of nature is
introduced as inhering within the successful student, rather than as a
personified and external universe in whose obedience her ignorance was
unbroken or maintained. What should be, and is thematized throughout
the poem as, an acquired second nature is made to appear more indigenous,
more natural to the subject it inhabits than a "Nature" without significance,
or from which one cannot learn.

As a reflection upon the relation between linguistic meaning and
linguistic logic, the development of the conceit of language within the poem
coherently questions its own signification. "Language," equated with
"sophistry," is condemned for its functional ability to confuse appearance
with truth. Yet the equation of "language" with "knowledge and life's tree"
posits it as the means of a specifically human "nature" to discern correctly
between the two. Unlike the images of the picture or book, the image of
language offers no mimetic point of reference or underpinning in "love's
mysteries." Instead, figured as the medium necessary to the progress of erotic

pursuits and being the matter of which books are made, it undermines the meaning of the latter image as a mere vehicle or faithful translation of those "mysteries." The image of the disclosed, or figuratively disclothed, book in Elegy 17 revealed the purpose of providing another "covering." The image of language in Elegy 7 reveals that "love" or erotic virtuosity, truth or appealing appearances, may with equal coherence be the meaning it is used to convey; that the "knowledge" that should lie behind or beneath its use may instead be co-extensive with its surface; that "language" may conceal a depth of meaning or may not be concealing at all. Nor can the problem of logical signification raised by the poem's organizing figure be dismissed from a supposed position of poetic mastery: the bitter lover of Elegy 7 has already made that discovery; his newly literate mistress is bound to. To lack "language," on the other hand, is to be excluded from the very endeavor of deriving meaning from logical competence: to be an "idiot"—that is to say, incapable of recognizing even a single side of the paradox from which the activity of imaging devolves.

The shift in Donne's poetry from erotic to religious concerns is not accompanied by an abandonment of the conceit for less extravagant poetic forms. Frank Kermode has argued that the strength of Metaphysical wordplay made it particularly apt to the task of "preaching the Word," itself discernible only through Biblical figurations. He further suggests that Donne's Christian belief underlay his "understanding" of poetic wit:

> How did "strong lines" go with the preaching of the Word? First: their cultivation did not mean that the Word was neglected. It was stated, divided, illuminated, fantastically explicated. . . . Secondly: the Word itself gives warrant for all the devices of the learned preacher. The style of the Scriptures is "artificial"; indeed, the Psalms are poems. . . .
>
> Donne's wit, of course, depends on the assumption that a joke can be a serious matter. Wit, as he understood it, was born of the preaching of the Word, whether employed in profane or in religious expression.

Kermode describes the Satires as a cycle of poems sharing the characteristics of their genre but not particularly distinguished for their conceits:

> they have the usual energy, a richness of contemporary observation rather splenetic, of course, in character, Pope thought them worth much trouble, but it is doubtful if, except for [Satire 3], they play much part in anybody's thinking about Donne.

Kermode identifies Satire 3 as the poem in which the style of the erotic verse
and the subject of religious devotion earliest met, "show[ing] that even in
his youth Donne considered the language of passionate exploration and
rebuke appropriate to religious themes," but also notes a discrepancy
between the unsettled affective tone of the poem and the seriousness of its
purpose: "What makes the poem odd is the brusk impatience of its manner,
an exasperated harshness proper to satire but strange in a deliberate poem
about religion." Indeed, the tension in the poem that Kermode indicates
becomes more fundamentally apparent when its terms are reversed. We may
ask why "a deliberate poem" should evoke a sense of "impatience" with
regard to its own patterning, or why the persuasion to "true religion," an
enterprise Donne would be the last to satirize, designates satire as the genre
within which its imagery is to be understood.

The salient earnestness of Satire 3, unconventional by generic
definition, also marks it as an unusual moment within the canon of poems
particularly appreciated for the significance of their figurations. While
offering no precise explanation of his praise, Coleridge singled out the poem
for its "force and meaning" and suggested its value as an exercise in the
teaching of reading—one whose mastery would make the reading of Milton
appear light:

> If you would teach a scholar in the highest form how to *read,*
> take Donne, and of Donne . . . [Satire 3]. When he has learnt
> to read Donne, with all the force and meaning which are involved
> in the words, then send him to Milton, and he will stalk on like
> a master *enjoying* his walk.

The poem has also been paid specific attention by J.B. Leishman, who
argues that its singular effect rests in the rare balance struck by Donne
between an interest in his own imagery and in the subject he portrays. The
brilliance of logical invention is further invested in the poem with the poet's
intention of articulating truth:

> We often feel that Donne is far more concerned with the working
> out of his ingenious similes than with the subject (whatever it
> may be) which they profess to be illustrating and illuminating.
> However, in his Third Satire, on the search for true religion,
> Donne *is* inspired by his subject in itself, and his wit and his
> similes never get out of hand. . . . The rough lines of this satire
> are penetrated by an intense eagerness for truth, for what to the
> young Donne, no less than to Spenser, was saving truth.

The "eagerness for truth" to which the critic refers is presented clearly in the poem as the purpose of its argument. At the opening of the second verse paragraph, the Satire's first full pause, the poet states directly and with outstanding dramatic effect: "Seek true religion" (43). The persuasive power of this literal command is heightened by the extended image patterns that precede it. As concise a semantic and syntactic unit as can be found in Donne's poetry, it unequivocally affirms the significance of the subject it invokes, just as "Nothing else is" denied the possibility of being, and therein of meaning, to any subject other than the lovers for which it stands. "True religion" emerges as the single alternative to endeavors described figuratively, and defined appositely, as false. Both the "easy ways" lacking the "merit of strict life" (14–15), and the acts of courage imaged next in close succession (17–32), are paralleled in the second verse paragraph by alliances struck too simply with one, every, or no religious order (43–69). While the mundane pursuits imaged in the first verse paragraph are condemned for their improper investment of passion, the miniature narratives of the second verse paragraph portray the poor logic of witless sectarianism. Facile adoptions of religious doctrine remain as far from the truth as contests for merely material rewards. To be sought above them, and positioned in the poem between them, cannot be "religion" as such, but specifically, and exclusively, "true religion." The perceivable stress in the poem upon distinguishing truth is not only a stylistic effect of its imagery: it is conceived as the meaning that structures that imagery, introduced here in modifying rather than figural form.

Yet the form of devotional truth of a passionate link between logic and meaning, must finally be afforded its particular appearance in the poem, if its own logic is not to signify a thinly disguised facticity, its conceits fail to make comparative, conceptual sense. In order to achieve logical significance, the descriptions of mistaken pursuits must be completed, by analogy, in the imaged pursuit of truth. The figural pattern within the poem requires that "true," a quality describing a referent ("religion"), become "Truth," a formal image made meaningful by that pattern. The most significant of modifiers must be turned into a figure. Viewed thematically as an invocation to genuine religious devotion, or metacritically as a commentary upon the claim of poetic imagery to truth, the poem, in attaining its coherence, must image both true meaning and the form of its recognition. The theme and structure of Satire 3 preclude the poet from "covering," as persuasive lover, what he reveals, or asserting his rights over signification by complaint. Instead, if aiming to instruct the reader to "Truth," the poet must appear to set the art of persuasion aside.

His approach is in fact singularly free of marked conceits. A genealogical path to truth is first advised:

> ask thy father which is she,
> Let him ask his; though truth and falsehood be
> Near twins, yet truth a little elder is.
>
> (71–73)

The heuristic fiction of the precedence of "truth" over "falsehood" is presented here with precise and elegant effect. Logically, however, it implies a disturbing ratio of inquiry: knowledge of truth will increase in proportion to its distance from its present pursuit. The problem of deception, or at least, of inadequate definition, is also involved here, since whatever is offered as prior knowledge may appear, by the criterion of precedence, to be true. After proceeding to propose a course of unrelenting skepticism ("To adore, or scorn an image, or protest,/ May all be bad; doubt wisely" [76–77]), the poet pauses abruptly for a second time in the satire, replacing the notion that "image[s]" are most "wisely" viewed with "doubt," with the poem's own image of "Truth." A blank image named within a visual context, it appears with unexpected and decisive power within the poem, as if it itself were suddenly sighted by the satirist with surprise. The passage is one of the most moving in Donne's poetry:

> doubt wisely, in strange way
> To stand inquiring right, is not to stray;
> To sleep, or run wrong is. On a huge hill,
> Cragged, and steep, Truth stands, and he that will
> Reach her, about must, and about must go;
> And what the hill's suddenness resists, win so
>
> (77–82)

The imaging of "Truth" as an unqualified figure, poised upon a "huge," discretely figured "hill," combines the sense of a perfectly controlled poetic emblem with that of an overwhelming of poetic expression such as is most commonly associated with the Romantic sublime. The satire represents the ineffable in name alone, yet situates it in specifically modified, terrestrial terms. Departing radically from the formal complexities of the conceit, and from the factual referents figured throughout the poem (i.e., historical events and individuals; actual religious trends), the poet presents a highly persuasive portrait of truth while suspending the dilemma of logical persuasion. His convincing narrative of resistance overcome also provides, perhaps not entirely coincidentally, a perfect summation of the observations made by otherwise differing critics as to the difficulties involved in discerning his own poetry's significance. "Truth," the final term of the poem's structural analogy, and the final test of significance for the poetic conceit, is imaged without access to analogical comparisons and in the absence of even a modest display of Metaphysical wit.

The formidable effect of the passage is not reduced by the consideration that its directness and simplicity of diction are strikingly uncharacteristic of Donne. The lines are in fact, as Milgate's commentary indicates, an adaptation by Donne of familiar ancient topoi. In a special appendix to this section of the satire, on which Donne is reported to have "bestowed so much care in revision," Milgate outlines "the remote origins of the image" from Hesiod's *Works and Days*, through Xenophon's *Memorabilia*, to Kebes' *Tabula*, with other "possible sources" given as Lucretius' *De Rerum Natura* (later paraphrased in Bacon's "Of Truth" and *Device on the Queen's Day*) and St. Augustine's *Confessions*. Milgate states in conclusion: "By Donne's time, these images and ideas, often intertwined, had become commonplaces, and it is impossible to point to a precise source of the lines in the Satire." Whatever the degree of specific reference or influence to which it owes, Donne's representation of truth is primarily a rewriting of well-known, traditional images. The leading innovator in the development of the conceit returns to recognizable topoi in figuring for the poem's reader, or the inquirer of religion, the approach and appearance of meaning whose status is that of "Truth." Commonplace conceptions are substituted for the complex places of logical invention: the conceit does not, or cannot, represent the truth of its own coherency, the coincidence of its logic with its significance.

At a third and final pause in the poem, however, another extended conceit is introduced. The development of its logical structure and meaning display them in the process of breaking apart. The motor of that process, as designated by the conceit, is "power." The poem's rushing cadence is again brought to a sudden halt and an earthly scene presented, its figural status underscored by an explicit exposition of the conceit's basic simile:

> That thou mayest rightly obey power, her bounds know;
> Those past, her nature, and name is changed; to be
> Then humble to her is idolatry.
> As streams are, power is; those blessed flowers that dwell

> At the rough stream's calm head, thrive and prove well,
> But having left their roots, and themselves given
> To the stream's tyrannous rage, alas are driven
> Through mills, and rocks, and woods, and at last, almost
> Consumed in going, in the sea are lost:
> So perish souls, which more choose men's unjust
> Power from God claimed, than God himself to trust.
>
> (100-10)

Similar to the passage presenting "Truth," the imaging of "power" is preceded by advice to a skeptical stance in her regard. The effect of the scenes described by the simile also lies in their crossing of emblematic qualities with images of nature. (The polysyndeton of line 107 in particular almost reads as if written by Wordsworth.) The poet's argument here is comparably persuasive in its structure. Yet the logical patterning of its imagery entails a strange semantic turn. In figuring man's natural subservience to the proper source of power, "God himself," the poet invokes the image of "blessed flowers that dwell . . . thrive and prove well" (104-5). That image must be presented in a second version, however, if it is to encompass within its meaning the occasion of power's pursuit. Thus a natural image is forced, by the pattern upon which it is constructed, to perform in a most unnatural manner: "those blessed flowers" are next depicted as "having left their roots, and themselves given / To the stream's tyrannous rage," by which they "are driven through" a succession of unsubordinated natural objects. Although it remains unclear if these "flowers" are directly endowed with volition, they are at the very least disturbingly capable of motion—not a displacement of petals ascribable to other causes, but an independent leave-taking of "their roots." Some "souls" may "choose," the poet states, completing the conceit and concluding the poem, to "trust" "men's unjust / Power from God claimed" (109-10). In so doing, they may simply be said to sin, or perhaps to act against their nature. But to carry out the intention of its argument, i.e., to demonstrate that these actions may be logically and linguistically understood, the poem must contain them within the scope of its conceit, with the result that a coherent pattern of imagery refers to two opposing meanings: one of a natural state of power, the other of a nature with a power of its own. The logical structure of the conceit is consistent; the meanings of "power" that it structures cannot be. In persuading to the "power" of "true religion," Satire 3 images powers that diverge. Its final passage may be suggestive of the persuasive *and* critical capabilities of the poetic conceit: the power to structure imagery into apparent sense and the power to image in movement against that structure. The falsity, or failure, of the conceit would thus be tantamount to a forced, or weak, convergence of the two; its truth, which it cannot image or by logical argument "win," would lie in the tenacity of resistance between them.

THOMAS R. WHITAKER

Herrick and the Fruits of the Garden

Confronted with a poem of Herrick's, a critic has something of a problem. Although he can easily murmur about poetic gems, or say, with Masefield, that Herrick is "the one consummate singer of light, lovely, delicate lyrics . . . , whose art is perfectly spontaneous and light of heart," such comments are not completely satisfying. Perhaps for that reason Herrick's poems have not, in this century, received the attention they deserve. Too often they have been either accepted as conventionally important, and thus not discussed seriously, or else dismissed scornfully as trivial and sentimental. Thus in F. R. Leavis's account of seventeenth-century poetry, Herrick serves only as a foil to the "line of wit." Contrasting "The Funerall Rites of the Rose" with a passage from Marvell, Leavis asserts that:

> Herrick's game, Herrick's indulgence, in fact, is comparatively solemn; it does not refer us outside itself. "Let us," he virtually says, "be sweetly and deliciously sad," and we are to be absorbed in the game, the "solemn" rite. . . . What Marvell is doing is implicitly "placed"; not in the least solemn, he is much more serious.

It is possible, I think, to share many of Leavis's standards and yet disagree with this estimate. But properly to answer Leavis's charge, one must go beyond the conventional view of Herrick as a "consummate singer of light, lovely, delicate lyrics": one must show how Herrick's "game" is "placed," how it refers us outside itself, and what "seriousness" lies beneath its undeniably charming lyric surface. In *The Well Wrought Urn*, Cleanth Brooks has demonstrated this with regard to one poem, "Corinna's Going

From *ELH* 22, no. 1 (March 1955). ©1955 by The Johns Hopkins University Press.

a Maying"; and in *The Universe of Robert Herrick*, Sydney Musgrove has outlined (with, I think, some overstatement) the Christian bearing of the poetry. Here, following a somewhat different approach, I wish to deal with the imaginative world of *Hesperides*.

As "The Argument of His Book" tells us, this is a realm of nature, ritual, youth, love, perfumes, trans-shifting times, dainty myths, fairies, and religion. And the second poem in the volume, "To his Muses," places these elements in a pastoral world of assumed naiveté:

> . . . such lines as these
> May take the simple villages;
> But for the court, the country wit
> Is despicable unto it.

But this is pastoral irony; Herrick's world is decidedly complex and courtly. His "rustic" religion draws upon classical, Christian, and native English sources; his images drawn from nature are delicately symbolic; and his "love" is often the refined badinage of the Roman and Alexandrine poets. Indeed, Herrick colors all with a feeling for *art*—the subtle crafts of feminine adornment, poetry, and ritual. This last is especially important, for, as the opening verses make clear, this is above all a ceremonial poetry. It treats largely of "May-poles, Hock-carts, Wassails, Wakes" (The Argument of His Book), and also is itself a "holy incantation" suitable to a ceremonial occasion,

> When laurell spirts i'th'fire, and when the hearth
> Smiles to itself, and gilds the roof with mirth.
> ("When He Would Have His Verses Read")

As ceremonial poems, Herrick's "games" are already "placed" to some extent, related in a particular way to the every-day world. Of course, this alone would be insufficient "placing": a ceremony may also be an "indulgence," and admittedly Herrick's ceremonies do not always have Marvell's fine poise and urbane wit. But they have more poise and wit than Leavis implies, and their relative inferiority does not make them "trivial." As *Hesperides* now stands, the mediocre effusions Herrick might have spared us may overwhelm such poems as "The Funerall Rites of the Rose," and cause the volume as a whole to seem but refined self-indulgence. But a selected edition of some fifty poems would establish a very different context, one that would support such poems (as Herbert's *Temple* supports its individual poems) by expanding and deepening their symbolism, and occasionally by criticizing their weaker tendencies—by "placing" them as "The Argument of His Book" and "When He Would Have His Verses Read" do in an introductory fashion. For the best of Herrick's poetry outlines an imaginative realm of some scope, and indicates an awareness of its limitations, its dangers, and its proper uses. A series of excursions from the particular "ceremony" that Leavis deprecates may serve to introduce some of the ways in which this context operates.

> The Rose was sick, and smiling di'd;
> And (being to be sanctifi'd)
> About the Bed, there sighing stood
> The sweet, and flowrie Sisterhood.
> Some hung the head, while some did bring
> (To wash her) water from the Spring.
> Some laid her forth, while others wept,
> But all a solemne Fast there kept.
> The holy Sisters some among
> The sacred *Dirge* and *Trentall* sung.
> But ah! what sweets smelt every where,
> As Heaven had spent all perfumes there.
> At last, when prayers for the dead,
> And Rites were all accomplished;
> They, weeping, spread a Lawnie Loome,
> And closed her up as in a Tombe.

The personification of the "Sisterhood" is not merely decorative. As "Upon Julia's Recovery" tells us, the sisterhood of flowers includes not only those "ally'd in blood," but also those who have "sworn" allegiance—and the withered roses and the drooping Julia are at least sworn sisters. The sympathy between flowers and humans goes deep, and often explicitly engages Herrick, as in "To Daffodils":

> We have short time to stay, as you,
>   We have as short a Spring:
> As quick a growth to meet Decay,
>   As you, or any thing.
>   We die,
> As your hours doe, and drie
>   Away,
> Like to the Summers raine;
> Or as the pearles of Mornings dew
>   Ne'r to be found againe.

The "Sisterhood" is a religious order—again for good reason: it embodies an essentially religious concern for transcending the flux of life. In "To Daffodils" the poet shares with the flowers his sense of life's transient beauty, feels in himself the same creative force and potential death, and so calls after them:

> Stay, stay,
> Until the hasting day
> Has run
> But to the Even-song;
> And, having pray'd together, we
> Will goe with you along.

The theme is similar in "The Funerall Rites of the Rose." We see the eternal sickness of the rose that was later to prompt Blake's cry, the transience of beauty which dies in the very act of smiling. However, the flowery sisterhood, a religious order of ephemeral virgins, does not accept the fact of death, but seeks to transcend or transfigure it in the rites of sanctification:

> Some hung the head, while some did bring
> (To wash her) water from the Spring.
> Some laid her forth, while others wept,
> But all a solemne Fast there kept.

These lines offer some of the wit and complexity of reference Leavis finds lacking in Herrick's poetry. William Empson has pointed out the suggested pun on "Spring," and the assimilation of the implicit dew image that accompanies it to the tears in the next line. (Herrick, we may note, uses the same verbal play rather differently in "A Nuptiall Song," where "Shewers of Roses" punningly "drown" the bride with a "flowrie Spring.") Here, freshness of growth (with suggestion of a resurrection) and tears for decay are inseparable. The decay, of course, is still before our eyes in another witty phrase: "Some hung the head"—they follow the rose in the very act of mourning for her. The fusion of dew and tears is also lightly suggested in "To Daffodils," where the weeping, in the first line, reappears as the drying summer rain and the pearls of morning dew; it plays an important part, too, in "Corinna's Going A Maying"; and it is the symbolic base for "To Primroses fill'd with Morning-Dew":

> Why doe ye weep, sweet Babes? can Tears
> Speak griefe in you,
> Who were but borne

> Just as the modest Morne
> Teem'd her refreshing dew?

All things "Conceiv'd with grief are, and with teares brought forth." The
dew is both sad and refreshing: beauty is always mourning, yet the
generations of beauty are endless. So in "The Funerall Rites of the Rose,"
growth and decay are juxtaposed for mixed grief and consolation, and the
freshness of spring is an element in the sanctification of death.

Another element inseparable from transience—intensified by it and
sanctifying it—is its very beauty:

> But ah! what sweets smelt every where,
> As Heaven had spent all perfumes there.

The perfumery belongs to the element of art that frequently heightens the
natural world of *Hesperides*. Here it suggests a distillation of sensuous
beauty; but it is thoroughly harmonized with the dominant note of
transience by the word "spent," which not only intensifies by hyperbole but
also suggests the exhaustion or passing that is central here.

This use of perfumery, however, does relate to Herrick's frequent use
of art as a stabilizing element, and escape from the flux of nature. In "Upon
Julia's Recovery," Herrick uses conventional imagery with unusual aptness:

> Droop, droop no more, or hang the head
> Ye *Roses* almost withered;
> Now Strength, and newer Purple get,
> Each here declining *Violet*.
> O *Primroses*! let this day be
> A Resurrection unto ye;
> And to all flowers ally'd in blood,
> Or sworn to that sweet Sister-hood:
> For Health on *Julia's* cheek hath shed
> Clarret, and Creame commingled.
> And those her lips doe now appeare
> As beames of Corrall, but more cleare.

Upon recovery Julia emerges from the realm of drooping vegetation
imagery, her health is fixed in the final image of coral lips, and she
momentarily has the stability and permanence of an artifact. This
permanence is also suggested at the end of "The Funerall Rites of the Rose":

> At last, when prayers for the dead,
> And Rites were all accomplished;

> They, weeping, spread a Lawnie Loome,
> And clos'd her up, as in a Tombe.

Death is sanctified by art; the beauty of the rose is removed from the flux of nature to the static realm of art, as in another poem:

> You have beheld a smiling *Rose*
>   When Virgins hands have drawn
> O'r it a Cobweb-Lawne:
> And here, you see, this Lilly shows,
>   Tomb'd in a *Christal* stone,
> More faire in this transparent case,
>   Then when it grew alone;
> And had but single grace.
>   ("The Lilly in a Christal")

The transfiguration of death explicit here is implicit in "The Funerall Rites of the Rose." Thus Herrick dramatizes the concept of immortality through art in terms of his imaginative world—though he also uses the more traditional expressions of the concept, as in the conclusions of "To Live Merrily, and to Trust to Good Verses" and "To the Reverend Shade of His Religious Father."

The world of *Hesperides* offers opportunity for many treatments of this paradox of decay and fruition, death and transfiguration. It is applicable to, and conversely may be symbolized by, the loss of virginity:

> Strip her of Spring-time, tender-whimpring-maids,
> Now Autumne's come, when all those flowrie aids
>   Of her Delayes must end.
>   ("A Nuptiall Song")

The poem's attitude toward this is complex: the hearty pleasure in literal and symbolic deflowering is qualified by the maidens' sense of the lost spring and justified by the sacramental fruition of autumn already foreshadowed:

> Then come on, come on, and yeeld
> A savour like unto a blessed field,
>   When the bedabled Morne
> Washes the golden ears of corne.

Somewhat similar is the irony of "To Cherry-Blossomes," which may symbolize deflowering by death, or by a lover:

> Fruit, ye know, is comming on:

> Then Ah! Then, where is your grace,
> When as Cherries come in place?

But here the personification and the gentle warning operate to insist upon the irrevocable loss—annihilation—that accompanies fruition.

Another means of transcending this annihilation and attaining limited "immortality" also uses ceremony. The rites of the rose have their counterpart in the rites of salt and winding-sheet described in "To Perilla"; and so also does the flower-and-tear symbolism: "Let fall a *Primrose*, and with it a teare." But "weekly-strewings" must also be devoted to the poet's memory, that his ghost may

> not walk about, but keep
> Still in the coole, and silent shades of sleep.

Ritual not only sanctifies the time of death, but perpetuates the memory of life (while paradoxically preventing the ghost from walking) by a periodic celebration of death. Similarly, Herrick addresses another mistress:

> Dearest, bury me
> Under that *Holy-oke*, or *Gospel-tree*:
> Where (though thou see'st not) thou may'st think upon
> Me, when thou yeerly go'st Procession.
>
> ("To Anthea")

He shrewdly fuses the new ceremony with the old; his genius for eclectic ritual—"Part Pagan, part Papisticall," like that of the fairies ("The Temple")—is clearly not just the result of an eye for the picturesque. But the conclusion of "To Anthea" indicates dissatisfaction with this limited transcending of death:

> Or for mine honour, lay me in that Tombe
> In which thy sacred Reliques shall have roome:
> For my Embalming (Sweetest) there will be
> No Spices wanting, when I'm laid by thee.

He desires a union transcending Anthea's death as well; but the wit recognizes the impossibility of this demand, and, as a tribute to the joy of present union with Anthea, reaffirms that the values of *Hesperides* are firmly in this life. Hence, of course, the recurrent dissatisfaction with various forms of immortality:

> when or you or I are made
> A fable, song, or fleeting shade;

>All love, all liking, all delight
>Lies drown'd with us in endlesse night.

"The Funerall Rites of the Rose" is clearly more than a game, an "indulgence." It not only describes, but is a ceremony. The reader participates in it from time to time just as Perilla does her weekly strewings and Anthea her yearly processions. The poem periodically renews out awareness of death and sanctification of the rose—with all its delicately limned symbolic reference to our larger world. And, as ceremonial *art*, the poem itself embodies that sanctification: it *is* the tomb of the rose. If such ceremony is "escape," it is—like the ceremony of harvest-home—

>   like rain,
>   Not sent ye for to drowne your paine,
>   But for to make it spring againe.
>   ("The Hock-Cart")

And this last line is true whether we read "it" as impersonal and "spring" as a noun, or "paine" as the antecedent and "spring" as a verb. The ceremonial escape is artistic communion with the realm of death, transfiguration, and rebirth, in order to cause an analogous renewal within the spirit of the participator.

It is no accident, then, that in *Hesperides* the rites of death closely relate to the rites of fertility—that in "Corinna" the celebration of May ends in a vision of death, that in "A Nuptiall Song" the bride is stripped of springtime and laid in a winding-sheet, that in "The Funerall Rites of the Rose" the sisterhood brings "water from the Spring," and that in "The Hock-Cart" the harvest celebration exists "for to make it spring againe." Sir Simeon Steward's twelve days of Christmas will be, similarly, a winter "harvest" celebration, during which the plough and harrow "hang up resting" and

>   the fired Chesnuts leape
>   For joy, to see the fruits ye reape,
>   From the plumpe Challice, and the Cup,
>   That tempts till it be tossed up.

After this imagery that fuses ripeness and Dionysian ecstasy, Herrick appropriately advises,

>   Sit crown'd with Rose-buds, and carouse,
>   Till Liber Pater twirles the house
>   About your eares; and lay upon

> The yeare (your cares) that's fled and gon.
> ("A New-Yeares Gift Sent to Sir
> Simeon Steward")

And here we meet in person the god who looms close behind the dainty world of *Hesperides*: the English Lord of Misrule, Liber Pater, Dionysus. As Herrick claimed ("When He Would Have His Verses Read"), he wrote Dionysian enchantments, or holy incantations. But of course they are also peculiarly muted, refined, and Christianized—and this multiple qualification deserves some comment.

The basic paradox of Herrick's Dionysian world is that of "cleanly-wantonnesse" ("The Argument of His Book"), a phrase with various meanings. Often it suggests a refined sensuality like that of the Julia poems, where "wantonnesse," "transgression," and "wilde civility" are indirectly expressed by the seductive clothing that half-conceals and half-reveals. (See "Delight in Disorder," "On Julia's Clothes," "Julia's Petticoat," "Art above Nature," "To Anthea Lying in Bed," "The Lilly in a Christal," and "What Kind of Mistresse He Would Have.") Heightening desire by refining and distancing its object, clothing here performs one of the important functions of art in *Hesperides*; for Herrick, like Meredith's sentimentalist, frequently "fiddles harmonics on the sensual strings." Thus the flowery sisterhood of these rituals has a muted sexuality, which emerges clearly in other poems stressing the blood-sisterhood of Julia and the flowers. In some poems this refined sensuality may be what Leavis terms an "indulgence," as one of them, "A Vision," explicitly recognizes; but in the better poems the sensuous qualities are thoroughly *used*. Herrick's egocentric "love" for his mistresses is certainly not a means for exploring dramatic relations between two realized individuals. Rather, it intensifies the sense for beauty, for "Joy, whose hand is ever at his lips/ Bidding adieu." Herrick's world, like Keats's, exhibits the dangers of egoism, sensuality, and sentimentality; and where it approaches profundity it does so in a similar manner, if with more hesitation—through exploring the individual's awareness of the flux of the time world, and the counter-balancing stasis of art, of the ideal, of death.

However used, this refined sensuality is always in danger of going soft. The tendency appears in "A Song to the Maskers":

> Come down, and dance ye in the toyle
> Of pleasures, to a Heate;
> But if to moisture, Let the oyle
> Of Roses be your sweat.

The maskers are then urged to perfume the by-standers with "these sweets" as once the goddess Isis did. The pun here establishes an equation that is central to the mood of Dionysian revels; but Herrick characteristically deflects its force, stressing "sweet" where a Lawrence or a Giono (were he to use the combination) would, if anything, stress "sweat." A similar modulation occurs in "A Hymne to Bacchus," where Herrick renounces unstinted drinking, and promises, in order to placate the god, an offering of daffodils. Of course, this delicate offering has its place in Dionysian ceremony and in *Hesperides*: it points directly to the fertility-death symbolism we have noted. Nevertheless, the reduction of Dionysian ecstasy to an offering of flowers exemplifies the kind of refinement, and the correlative loss of vigor, that occur in much of the verse.

Frequently, however, Herrick chastens his Dionysus in a more vigorous manner, as in "When He Would Have His Verses Read." Rejecting "sober mornings" as a time for verse-reading, the poem builds to a Dionysian climax:

> When up the *Thyrse* is rais'd, and when the sound
> Of sacred *Orgies* flyes, A round, A round.
> When the Rose raignes, and locks with ointments shine,

—only to cap this with the controlling words:

> Let rigid *Cato* read these Lines of mine.

We have no longer an orgy of Dionysus dissolved in flowers, but rather one with overtones of Roman sternness and economy. And we recall the literary implications of Herrick's claim to be "a free-born Roman" ("His Returne to London"). Here "cleanly-wantonnesse" is a means of gaining, in imagination, the release and regeneration of Dionysian ecstasy while preserving the contrasting virtues of measure and decorum. This, which is no doubt possible only within the paradoxical realm of art, is precisely one of the functions of the anacreontic tradition Herrick uses: it is a literary, and hence highly qualified, participation in a realm that, in life, might be crude, dangerous, or immoral. This presence of a literary manner (thus the closing line of *Hesperides*: "Jocond his Muse was; but his Life was chast") is what lies behind our recurrent feeling of a distance between the poet and the delights celebrated. At its poorest, the verse is a merely "literary" toying with classical motifs; at its best, it creates an ideal realm which orders and fuses Horatian economy and Dionysian ecstasy.

One further qualification of this version of Dionysus is its Christian reference. This disputed aspect of the poetry I prefer to approach obliquely, by way of an examination of "His Winding-Sheet," a poem which reflects

Herrick's obsession with death and regeneration, and with the need and the danger of "escape."

> Come thou, who art the Wine, and wit
>   Of all I've writ:
> The Grace, the Glorie, and the best
>   Piece of the rest.
> Thou art of what I did intend
>   The All, and End.
> And what was made, was made to meet
>   Thee, thee my sheet.

The irony of these opening lines is especially powerful within the context of *Hesperides*. Death is addressed implicitly as mistress and as Liber Pater, as both ominous inspiration and beautiful subject of the poetry. The winding-sheet is the all and end in a double sense; and the irony extends to include two ways in which "what was made, was made to meet/ Thee": the poetry is an attempt to stave off death—but, like all art, it provides only brief immortality.

The following welcome brings out the implications lurking in those lines to mistress death:

> Come then, and be to my chast side
>   Both Bed, and Bride.
> We two (as Reliques left) will have
>   One Rest, one Grave.
> And, hugging close, we will not feare
>   Lust entring here:
> Where all Desires are dead, or cold
>   As is the mould:
> And all Affections are forgot,
>   Or trouble not.

The irony is intensified by our memory of the ideal of "cleanly-wantonnesse." This solution to the paradox is hinted at in several poems: the wedding custom in "A Nuptiall Song,"—"dispatch, and sowe/ Up in a sheet your Bride"; the shift of function in "To Perilla"—

> then wind me in that very sheet
> Which wrapt thy smooth limbs (when thou didst implore
> The Gods protection, but the night before)

—and such other fusions of death and sexual consummation as the conclusion of "To Anthea" and the couplet addressed to "The Rosemarie Branch":

> Grow for two ends, it matters not at all,
> Be't for my *Bridall*, or my *Buriall*.

(Taken another way, of course, this couplet belongs to Herrick's satires against marriage.)

The desire for "rest" in the opening lines of "His Winding-Sheet" suggests not only a function of periodic ceremonies, but also the more insidious temptation to use the imaginative world as mere escape. This is clear from the following lines, which suggest the catalogue of political evils opening "A New-Yeares Gift Sent to Sir Simeon Steward":

> Here, here the Slaves and Pris'ners be
> From Shackles free:
> And weeping Widowes long opprest
> Doe here find rest.
> The wronged Client ends his Lawes
> Here, and his Cause.
> Here those long suits of Chancery lie
> Quiet, or die:
> And all Star-chamber-Bils doe cease,
> Or hold their peace.

But the flicker of irony in the possible mere dormancy of the notorious legal processes hints at what is to follow:

> Here needs no Court for our Request,
> Where all are best;
> All wise; all equall; and all just
> Alike i'th' dust.

The irony turns on the word "just," which, because of the slight end-of-line pause, first appears parallel to "best," "wise," and "equall"—and then expands into a deflating parallel of another sort. Indeed, the element of escape and imaginative fulfillment has been so subjected to irony by the end of the poem that the winding-sheet is then no longer a welcome "All, and End," but is, like all of Herrick's escapes, temporary:

> In this securer place we'l keep,
> As lull'd asleep;
> Or for a little time we'l lye,
> As Robes laid by;

> To be another day reworn,
> > Turn'd but not torn.

Death too, is a time for sleep and renewal. But how can men thus transcend it? They will

> > for a while lye here conceal'd,
> > > To be reveal'd
> > Next, at that great Platonick yeere,
> > > And then meet here.

There is of course no literal belief in the Platonic doctrine invoked. Viewing Herrick as a Christian poet, one may consider the doctrine of recurrence as the vehicle for a belief in the resurrection on the Last Day. And yet the force of the series of metaphors is to insist upon a return to the life now known—not a translation to another life. This reflects the intensity of life-values throughout *Hesperides,* an intensity which lies behind the obsession with death, and which prevents that death, or any other mode of escape, from being a final solution. Viewed within the "pagan" context of *Hesperides,* then, this Platonic doctrine symbolizes a demand that death, like ceremony, be sent not

> > for to drowne your paine,
> But for to make it spring againe.

This Christian-Dionysian ambiguity runs through Herrick's symbolism. Thus the consolation "To the Lady Crew, upon the Death of Her Child":

> > Why, Madam, will ye longer weep,
> > When as your Baby's lull'd asleep?
> > And (pretty Child) feeles now no more
> > Those paines it lately felt before.
> > All now is silent; groanes are fled:
> > Your Child lyes still, yet is not dead:
> > But rather like a flower hid here
> > To spring againe another yeare.

And again in the poem "To His Dying Brother, Master William Herrick":

> > here Ile last, and walk (a harmless shade)
> > About this Urne, wherein thy Dust is laid,
> > To guard it so, as nothing here shall be
> > Heavy, to hurt those sacred seeds of thee.

For the Christian, the circle of generation *may* symbolize eternal regeneration; yet the vehicle carries its force, and it is significant that Herrick so consistently selects it. George Herbert, on the other hand, though using in "The Flower" seasonal imagery to dramatize the same sense of psychological renewal that Herrick often deals with, alters the metaphor when he suggests a Christian resurrection—moving beyond the cycles of generation to an unfading garden. In Herbert the corruptible puts on incorruption; in Herrick the corruptible springs again.

In these ambiguous metaphors Herrick resolves formally, with respect to an afterlife, what he cannot resolve logically: the tension between his Christian and Dionysian views. This is, however, only one way in which he deals with this problem. In "Corinna," as both Cleanth Brooks and Sydney Musgrove have noted, the pagan ceremony of spring "receives its due," while the Christian ceremonies which provide the implicit framework of the poem's world, temporarily retire into the background. But it will not do, I think, to maintain (as Musgrove does) that the relationship established here is generally true of Herrick's world—that is, that his universe is dominantly Christian and that the mass of secular poems express the "mind on a holiday," or merely "indicate a preference for certain kinds of social behaviour." The paganism goes deeper than this, as the previous analyses indicate. Herrick's verse moves in two worlds, which are imperfectly coordinated. Some poems bring into focus the ceremony of natural regeneration, the ceremony of Dionysus. There, as in "Corinna," Christianity may be in slight abeyance ("Few Beads are best, when once we goe a Maying"), it may sanctify the results of the natural process (as the priest does after the green-gowns have been given), or it may disappear entirely ("All love, all liking, all delight/ Lies drown'd with us in endlesse night"). In other poems the imagery may suggest to varying degrees a Christian transfiguration of the natural process—as in the references to the holy sisterhood of "The Funerall Rites of the Rose," or to praying and the "even-song" in "To Daffadills." Other poems, especially in *Noble Numbers*, focus upon Christian ceremony; and there one finds more narrowly Christian ways of coordinating the two realms, as in "The Transfiguration" or "The School or Perl of Putney," poems on which Musgrove relies heavily. In the large, *Noble Numbers* complements *Hesperides* just as the Christian imagery complements the pagan—and it is surely no accident that *Hesperides* is the better volume.

However the two realms may be related for Herrick the Anglican priest, they are not in fixed relation for Herrick the poet. Rather, the Christian and the qualified Dionysian are two perspectives upon a reality that transcends them both and so cannot be expressed by either symbolism alone.

Herrick is feeling for a harmonious middle realm, "Part Pagan, part Papisticall," that may present a variety of reactions to this complex and rather fluid world before him. To this end he attempts to create his own eclectic myth of the garden of the Hesperides, aided by what we presumptuously call a "modern" sense of myth's ability to order the facts and demands of the human situation. A gay poem "To Electra" is surprisingly relevant here, indicating his sense of myth's archetypal value:

> Ile come to thee in all those shapes
> As *Jove* did, when he made his rapes:

—but the myths are instrumental, not a substitute for life; in the end, the richness and intensity of life's activity will transcend all imaginative projections—

> And kissing, so as none may heare,
> We'll weary all the Fables there.

For that very reason, perhaps, Herrick did not find a central myth that would completely reconcile and exhaustively render his double perspective. Julia, however, may appropriately symbolize the object of his search:

> If thou wilt say, that I shall live with thee;
> Here shall my endless Tabernacle be:
> If not, (as banisht) I will live alone
> There, where no language ever yet was known.
> ("To Julia")

Julia presides over the dual realm of myth and language—for the myth provides the means of articulating his situation. She is thus, in another poem, the "Flaminica Dialis, or Queen-Priest," who petitions Love that they may escape death. And Herrick concludes: "Redemption comes by Thee." In this light fusion of divine and secular love, with Julia as Roman priestess and Virgin Mary, we see the ambiguous myth toward which Herrick was moving; a myth to embody his principal intuition, of a sacred world of transitory but continually regenerated delights, a world plagued not so much by moral evil as by time and death. "For if the sun breed maggots in a dead dog, being a god kissing carrion—Having you a daughter? . . . Let her not walk in the sun." Herrick is far from this view of the corrupting intercourse of life and death, good and evil. Rather, he sings "To Marygolds":

> Give way, and be ye ravisht by the Sun
> (And hang the head when as the Act is done)

> Spread as He spreads; wax lesse as He do's wane;
> And as He shuts, close up to Maids again.

Maidenhood and ravishment are enduring poles of the natural oscillation he celebrates.

Renewal is not always so simple as it is for the marigolds, to be sure, but nature's inevitable rhythms may still offer hope in time of political trouble:

> Fled are the Frosts, and now the Fields appeare
> Re-cloth'd in fresh and verdant Diaper.
> Thaw'd are the snowes, and now the lusty Spring
> Gives to each Mead a neat enameling.
> The Palms put forth their Gemmes, and every Tree
> Now swaggers in her Leavy gallantry.
> The while the *Daulian Minstrell* sweetly sings,
> With warbling Notes, her *Tyrrean* sufferings.
> What gentle Winds perspire? As if here
> Never had been the *Northern Plunderer*
> To strip the Trees, and Fields, to their distresse,
> Leaving them to a pittied nakednesse.
>   ("Farwell Frost, or Welcome the Spring")

And this is elaborated in a manner to evoke the entire imaginative world of *Hesperides*: the "lusty Spring" is also an artist, as, in their own ways, are the swaggering trees (blood sisters of the stately Julia) and Philomela, who fits in neatly as an archetype of the transmuting of suffering (through being ravished, as the marigolds) into the beauty of art and nature.

Of course, the individual may not endure through the entire process of ravishment and renewal—"Gather ye rosebuds while ye may"—and he consequently seeks to transcend death, and to escape from the temporal flux into the eternal realm of art or ceremony. But, as in "His Winding-Sheet," Herrick equates such permanent escape with death itself; he is close to Keats's recognition of the antimony of time and eternity. Man must choose between this realm, where men hear each other groan, where the rose is smiling and dying, and the realm of art, of the "cold pastoral," the tomb of the rose.

However, Herrick has found a way of mediating between these two realms. His symbolism crystallizes in art the situation of man: immersed in natural flux, yet realizing and so transcending that immersion, demanding an escape into the ideal realm of art. And as Dionysian ceremony, his verse then mediates between the symbolic art and its world of reference: it offers periodic communion both with the stasis of art, which it is, and with the heart of natural flux, which it dramatizes. It thus offers momentary imaginative transcendence of the temporal—that life may spring again. The escape of art leads back to the world of nature.

Of course, this is to delineate the ideal Herrick moved towards. His success was not uniform, nor need it have been— his quest was, in its diminutive way, Herculean. Julia, Corinna, and the rest, daughters of the Hesperides (the realm of the setting sun, of the dying rose), were means to an end. Through them he approached the golden apples, the natural fruit transmuted into artifact, the lily in the crystal. And he knew that the ecstasy of securing these apples is rightly but momentary. Athena, receiving the fruits of art dedicated to her, returns them once more to the garden, where they await the repeated quest.

STANLEY E. FISH

Letting Go: The Dialectic of the Self in Herbert's Poetry

THY WORD IS ALL

In the third stanza of "The Flower," George Herbert gives voice to an article of faith which is itself a description of the action taking place in many of his poems:

> We say amisse,
> This or that is:
> Thy word is all, if we could spell.
>
> (19-21)

The point of doctrine is, of course, a seventeenth-century commonplace: the distinctions—of times, places, objects, persons—we customarily make as we move about in the world are the illusory creations of a limited perspective; if our visions were sufficiently enlarged, we would see that all things visible were not only framed by (Hebrews 11:3) but are informed by (are manifestations of) the word that is God: "Thy word is all."

Herbert's poems characteristically ask us to experience the full force of this admission in all its humiliating implications. If God is all, the claims of other entities to a separate existence, including the claims of the speakers and readers of these poems, must be relinquished. That is, the insight that God's word is all is *self*-destructive, since acquiring it involves abandoning the perceptual and conceptual categories within which the self moves and

From *Self-Consuming Artifacts: The Experience of Seventeenth-Century Literature.* ©1972 by The Regents of the University of California. University of California Press, 1972.

by means of which it separately exists. To stop saying amiss is not only to stop distinguishing "this" from "that," but to stop distinguishing oneself from God, and finally to stop, to cease to be. Learning to "spell" in these terms is a self-diminishing action in the course of which the individual lets go, one by one, of all the ways of thinking, seeing, and saying that sustain the illusion of his independence, until finally he is absorbed into the deity whose omnipresence he has acknowledged (thy word is *all*).

There is nothing easy about the "letting go" this poetry requires of us. We are, after all, being asked to acquiesce in the discarding of those very habits of thought and mind that preserve our dignity by implying our independence. Naturally (the word is double edged) we resist, and our resistance is often mirrored in the obstinate questionings and remonstrations of the first-person voice. The result is a poetics of tension, reflecting a continuing dialectic between an egocentric vision which believes in, and is sustained by, the distinctions it creates, and the relentless pressure of a *re*solving and *dis*solving insight. That dialectic takes many forms, but its basic contours remain recognizable: the surface argument or plot of a poem proceeds in the context of the everyday world of time and space, where objects and persons are discrete and independent; but at the same time and within the same linguistic space, there is felt the pressure of a larger context which lays claim to that world and everything in it, including speaker, reader, and the poem itself:

> *Lord, my first fruits present themselves to thee;*
> *Yet not mine neither: for from thee they came,*
> *And must return.*

("The Dedication")

The return of these fruits and of everything else to the God of whose substance they are is the self-consuming business of these poems, which can be viewed as a graduated series of "undoings" and "letting go's": (1) the undoing of the perceptual framework in which we live and move and have our (separate) beings. This involves the denying of the usual distinctions between "this" and "that"—a *"making of one place everywhere"*—and the affirmation of a universe where God is all. An inevitable consequence of this undoing is the gradual narrowing (to nothing) of the distance between the individual consciousness (of both speaker and reader) and God; that is, (2) the undoing of the self as an independent entity, a *"making of no thine and mine"* by making it all thine, a surrender not only of a way of seeing, but of initiative, will, and finally of being (to say "I am" is to say amiss). To the extent that this surrender is also the poet's, it requires the silencing of his voice and the relinquishing of the claims of authorship, and therefore (3) an undoing of the poem as the product of a mind distinct from the mind of God. This undoing, or letting go, is an instance of what it means, in Herbert's own words, to *"make the action fine"* (by making it not mine). And finally, and inevitably, Herbert's poems are undone in still another sense when (4) the insight they yield ("thy word is all") renders superfluous the mode of discourse and knowing of which they themselves are examples. These poems, as they ask their readers to acknowledge their complete dependence, act out that acknowledgment by calling attention to what they are not doing, and indeed could not do. In their final radical modesty, they perform what they require of us, for as they undermine our reliance on discursive forms of thought, and urge us to rest in the immediate apprehension of God's all-effective omnipresence, they become the vehicles of their own abandonment. "God only is," writes Thomas Browne, "all others . . . are something but by a distinction." To read Herbert's poems is to experience the dissolution of the distinctions by which all other things are.

MAKING ONE PLACE EVERYWHERE

The preceding is a summary statement that raises as many questions as it answers. If the insight of God's omnipresence is violated by the very act of predication ("This or that is"), how does a poet who is committed to that insight practice his craft? How does one avoid saying amiss if language is itself a vehicle for the making of invidious distinctions? How can God's prerogatives be preserved if one produces sentences which automatically arrange persons and objects in hierarchical relationships of cause and effect? Answering these questions will be the burden of this chapter, but we can begin by noting that Herbert baptizes language by making it subversive of its usual functions. In his poetry words tend to lose their referential fixity, and syntactical patterns often obscure the relationships they pretend to establish. In short, Herbert avoids saying amiss in an ultimate context by deliberately saying amiss in the context of a perspective he would have us transcend.

The peculiar force of a Herbert poem, then, often depends on our awareness that the terms in which we are being encouraged to formulate a concept are inadequate to it. In some poems, this awareness is only a momentary thing, the (by) product of a single phrase:

> Subject to ev'ry mounter's bended knee
> ("The Holy Scriptures (I)" 1:14)

To read this line is to experience the insufficiency of its mode of discourse. It is a miniature exercise in epistemology. "Mounter's" involves the reader in the most conventional of homiletic practices, the figuring forth of a spiritual distinction by a spatial image; but "bended" undermines the simple formula (up-good, down-evil) on which the analogy depends, forcing the reader to let go of the image and of the way of thinking that has generated it, and calling into question the very possibility of comprehending spiritual matters in spatial forms. It is called into question in a more substantive way in "The Temper (I)":

> How should I praise thee, Lord! how should my rymes
>   Gladly engrave thy love in steel,
>   If what my soul doth feel sometimes,
>   My soul might ever feel!
>
> Although there were some fourtie heav'ns, or more,
>   Sometimes I peere above them all;
>   Sometimes I hardly reach a score,
>   Sometimes to hell I fall.

If, as Arnold Stein has argued, the "plain intention" of this poem is "to transform its initial attitude into its concluding one," that transformation is the result of exchanging one way of looking at the world for another. The "initial attitude" is one of complaint: Herbert's inability to praise God as he would like to is a condition, he maintains, of his inability to sustain the occasional moment of perfect joy ("Sometimes I peere above them all"); and that, in turn, is a condition of God's fitful presence. The stated wish to praise God, then, is a thinly disguised accusation of him. Were he more faithful, more constantly in attendance, the poet's lines and rhymes would flow easily and everlastingly. (God here has the role assigned to inspiration in the laments of secular poets.) Of course this (hidden) argument holds only if one limits God to times and places, and that is exactly what Herbert is doing in the extended image of the second stanza. Presumably God resides in that fortieth heaven to which the poet occasionally ascends; lower levels receive proportional shares of his emanations and in hell there is (literally) no trace of him at all.

But while this localization of God's presence is consistent with certain Neoplatonic systems and even with the three-tiered universe of popular tradition, it will hardly do for the deity of whom Augustine speaks when he says, "He came to a place where He was already." This statement (if it is a statement) illustrates the Christian solution to the problem of thinking and talking about God in terms whose frame of reference he transcends. One uses the terms (no others are available), but simultaneously acknowledges their insufficiency, as Herbert does in the concluding and, in view of his earlier complaint, triumphant, stanza of this poem:

> Whether I flie with angels, fall with dust
> Thy hands made both, and I am there:
> Thy power and love, my love and trust
> Make one place ev'ry where.
>
> (25-28)

The speaker's dilemma, both as would-be praiser and God-seeking man, exists only in his formulation of it, and its solution is effected when that formulation is abandoned or let go. The process of letting go is set in motion in the first line: the pointing of the "whether—or" construction (one supplies the "or") suggests that Herbert is still committed to the divided worlds of the opening stanzas, but at the same time the alliteration of "flie" and "fall" is pulling us in a different direction, toward the dissolving of the distinctions—between angels and dust, heaven and hell—the syntax is supporting. By the end of the following line, "ev'ry where" has been made one place through the agency of the precisely ambiguous "there," which refers neither to the earth ("dust") nor to the ("fourtie") heavens, but to God's hands, the framers, supporters, and therefore, in a real sense, the location, of both. The point of doctrine is, as always, a commonplace—since all things were made by God (John 1:3) and by him all things consist (Colossians 1:17), everywhere is his "there"—but the peculiar value of its appearance here resides in the process through which Herbert makes his readers approach it. The reader who negotiates the distance between "Whether" and "there" passes from a (syntactical) world where everything is in its time and place to a world where specification of either is impossible, to a *uni*verse. This same movement is compressed into an even smaller space in the final line, where "one place" actually does become "ev'ry where" in the twinkling of a reading eye. And, of course, the ease with which we take in the paradox is a direct result of the experience of the preceding lines.

As is often the case in a Herbert poem, the resolution of the spiritual or psychological problem also effects the resolution of the poetic problem. For when the speaker is able to say "Yet take thy way; for sure thy way is best" (21) he removes the obstacle to his singing of God's praises; that obstacle is not his uneven spiritual experience, but his too easy interpretation of that experience as a sign of God's desertion. Once he gives up that reading of his situation, he is free to see in it a more beneficent purpose:

> This is but tuning of my breast,
> To make the musick better.
>   (23-24)

Thus the very condition the speaker laments finally yields the praise he thought himself debarred from making, and itself becomes the occasion for, because it has been the stimulus to, praise. That is, the sense of heaven's desertion leads to the mental exertions which produce the poem which generates the intuition that God's way is best. What begins as a complaint against God ends with the realization that the supposed basis of the complaint, when properly seen, is something to be thankful for. The poem's movement in effect anticipates the counsel of Sir Thomas Browne, who advises us "so to dispute and argue the proceedings of God as to distinguish even His judgments into mercies" (*Religio Medici*, I).

Just how great a mercy God affords Herbert here can be seen in the poem's penultimate line:

> Thy power and love, my love and trust.
>   (27)

What this does is give the poet a part in the action of the concluding line—making one place everywhere ("make" has a multiple subject). God's power and love, his continuing presence in the world, are of course the final cause of this effect, but the poet's love and trust in that other love are necessary for its perception since the perceiving consciousness he was born with suggests something else altogether (that "this" or "that" is).

Making one place everywhere, in contradiction to the appearance (or illusion) of a multiplicity of places, is also the action and the experience of "Even-Song." As in "The Temper (I)," the opening lines suggest a distinction, in some part spatial, which does not survive the reading experience:

> Blest be the God of love,
> Who gave my eyes, and light, and power this day,
>   Both to be busie, and to play.
> But much more blest be God above,
>   Who gave me sight alone.
>   (1-5)

Apparently the poet prays to two Gods, the "God of love," and that more powerful and more to be thanked "God above," the God presumably, of the higher regions. This halving of the world's empire is immediately suspect and is already being challenged by the unifying force of the rhyme "love-above." By the time the reader takes in the pun in line 8—"But I have got his sonne, and he hath none"—the two deities have become one, or, what is in effect the same thing, two coequal and coidentical members of a trinity, and for the remainder of the poem the speaker addresses his remarks unambiguously to a second person singular.

The dividing and distinguishing tendencies of the human consciousness, however, are irrepressible, and they reassert themselves toward the end of the poem:

> I muse, which shows more love,
>   The day or night.
>
>   (25-26)

The answer is implicit in what has gone before; since they are both God's they show equally his love; and moreover as manifestations of that love they lose their separate identities, which is exactly what happens to them in this stanza:

> I muse, which shows more love,
>   The day or night: that is the gale, this th' harbour;
>   That is the walk, and this the arbour;
>   Or that the garden, this the grove.
>
>   (25-28)

The speaker muses in the (submerged) context of a familiar proverb: "as different as day and night." At first this sense of difference is reinforced; the "gale and harbour" image is made up of easily separable components, distinct in time and place; the gale *brings* one to the harbour. The distinctness of "walk" and "arbour" however is less immediately striking; either they are adjacent or one encloses the other. The third pair of substitute coordinates actually works against the argument it is supposedly supporting; for while "garden" and "grove" are distinguishable, distinguishing between them requires more of an effort than the heavily alliterative verse ("gale," "garden," "grove"; "harbour," "arbour," "garden") encourages. In the very process of (supposedly) expanding an opposition, Herbert has led us surreptitiously and by degrees to a sense of

sameness, and it is this experience that gives force to the triumphant
assertion of the following line:

> My God, thou art all love.
>
>   (29)

Here the poet admits that the question he has posed three lines earlier
was based on assumptions (that "this" day, or "that" night, is) that are found
to be invalid when our perspective on "things" is sufficiently enlarged, as
it has been in the course of the poem. Of course, that invalidated perspective
is the one we must live with (or in), even after its insufficiency has been
demonstrated or experienced, and the speaker returns to it, and to the logical
language which is an extension of it, in the final lines:

> My God, thou art all love.
> Not one poore minute scapes thy breast
> But brings a favour from above;
> And in this love, more then in bed, I rest.
>
>   (29-32)

Once again God is "above" (the rhyme of the opening stanza reappears)
and man "below," but this formulation is now less dangerously distorting
than it might have been at the beginning of the poem because we know
now (what we always knew, but less self-consciously) that this way of
thinking and verbalizing is an accommodation. That is, we know, even as
we read line 32, that resting in bed or anywhere else, we are always resting
in God's love which makes one (any) place everywhere.

Examples of this kind could be multiplied indefinitely, but the point,
I think, has been made: to read many of Herbert's poems is to experience
the dissolution of the lines of demarcation we are accustomed to think of
as real. Perhaps the most spectacular of the poems in this mode is "Church
Monuments," which has been brilliantly analyzed by Joseph Summers:

> The dissolution of the body and the monuments is paralleled
> by the dissolution of the sentences and stanzas.
>   The movement and sound of the poem suggest the "falls"
> of the flesh and the monuments and the dust in the glass. The
> fall is not precipitous; it is as slow as the gradual fall of the
> monuments, as the crumbling of the glass, as the descent of the
> flesh from Adam to dust. . . . With the cluster of consonants,
> it is impossible to read the poem rapidly. The related rhymes,
> with their internal echoes and repetitions, both give phonetic

continuity to the poem and suggest the process of dissolution.
. . . The sentences sift down through the rhyme scheme skeleton
of the stanzas like the sand through the glass and the glass itself
has already begun to crumble.

To this obviously authoritative description of what is happening in the
poem I would add a description of what is happening in (and to) the reader;
for the dissolution of sentences and stanzas and of the objects within them
produces a corresponding dissolution, or falling away of, the perceptual
framework a reader brings with him to the poem and indeed to life. Thus,
in the opening lines the firm sense of time and place, which at first allows
us to distance ourselves from objects and processes, is progressively eroded:

> While that my soul repairs to her devotion,
> Here I intombe my flesh that it betimes
> May take acquaintance of this heap of dust;
> To which the blast of deaths incessant motion,
> Fed with the exhalation of our crimes,
> Drives all at last. Therefore I gladly trust.
>
> (1-6)

The first three lines are replete with distinctions, distinctions of times,
persons, objects, spaces, and actions. The body is distinguished from the
soul and both from the heaps of dust with which they are bid take
acquaintance. The words on which the syntax pivots are "While" and
"Here," time and place markers respectively. Even less essential words, like
"repairs" and "betimes," contribute to the strong impression of local
identities, separable objects, discrete and specifiable moments. Yet no sooner
have these demarcations been established and assumed a kind of reality in
the reader's mind, than the process of undermining them begins. If it is
"impossible to read the poem rapidly" it is also impossible to read the poem
in stages because it affords us no natural resting places. Units of meaning
that seem complete in themselves are unexpectedly revealed to be only the
introductory clauses in a larger utterance, an utterance whose scope finally
expands to include the whole poem. It is, in Herbert's own words an
"incessant motion," and it proceeds by blurring the distinctions it
momentarily establishes. This process begins with "To which" (4), a
transition that forces the reader to keep one eye on the three preceding lines
at the same time he is a witness to, and to some extent the agent of, the
melting into one another of the objects that fill those lines. Initially, the
referent of "which" is assumed to be "dust," but as the "blast" of the verse's

"incessant motion" drives us toward the full stop in line 6, the possibilities widen to include, first, "this heap of dust" and then, when we reach the climactic "all," that other "heap of dust," "my flesh." That is to say, the word" "all" operates retroactively to make earlier words and phrases mean differently. As the poem opens, "intombe my flesh" seems merely a fancifully witty way of referring to the speaker's immobility while at prayer. Now we see that the witticism is a tautology: his flesh *is* its own tombe, one more heap of dust, exactly like those that are the objects of its contemplation. To take acquaintance of *this* heap of dust is to follow (with a vengeance) the Socratean injunction, "know thyself." It is an injunction to which we too must respond for the simple "our" of line 5 does not allow us, as readers, to exempt ourselves from the statement the poem is making. In the first two lines we are insulated from this shock of recognition by the objects that literally stand between us and "this heap of dust"—the church, its monuments, and the speaker—but by the end of line 6 (which, of course, ends nothing), these have all become one ("at last") and that oneness has been extended outward to embrace us too.

Thus when Herbert declares "Therefore I gladly trust," we await the identification of the object of his trust with more than a syntactical interest, and for a moment we are surprised by what we find:

> My bodie to this school, that it may learn
> To spell his elements, and finde his birth
> Written in dustie heraldrie and lines;
> Which dissolution sure doth best discern,
> Comparing dust with dust, and earth with earth.
> These laugh at Jeat and Marble put for signes.
>
> (7–12)

The body would seem to be a questionable repository of trust given the prediction in the first stanza of its imminent dissolution; and, of course, as the line continues the sense changes, forcing us to replace "my bodie" with "this school" as the object of "trust," a grammatical adjustment which mirrors perfectly the life adjustment the poem is urging us to make. In the school to which both the reader and the body are sent the lessons are strangely self-defeating. One *spells* correctly when one *discerns* the indecipherability of the text; discerning is "*sure*" only when the object of discernment dissolves; "*signes*" signify properly only when they become indistinguishable from their surroundings (a word that itself has little meaning at this point); "*comparing*" becomes an excerise in tautology, "comparing dust with dust." The words I have emphasized all receive both a metrical and a sense stress and together, that is, in isolation, they strongly suggest a process by which some measure of phenomenal clarity can be achieved; but between them and surrounding them are the other words, which finally mock the pretensions of this clarifying vocabulary. Consider, for example, lines 9 and 10: The stressed words taken by themselves piece out a strong declarative statement, "Written . . . lines / Which . . . sure . . . discern." But for a reader, the firmness of the past participle "written" is severely qualified by the adjective "dustie" which in its forward movement makes it impossible to take the word "lines" literally; in addition, the noun itself has so many possible referents—the lines of body, the genealogical lines of the body's heraldry, the lines of the epitaph (no longer there), the lines of the poem (which are themselves becoming progressively more "dustie")— that "which" is more a question than a pronoun. The question becomes academic with the next word "dissolution." Whatever "which" was, it is no more, having dissolved; only that dissolution is "sure" and, as the line ends, the verb "discern" completes an irony of which itself is a victim.

The syntactical structures of this poem are no more successful at discerning or distinguishing than are the monuments they so unclearly present. Indeed, the forms of both (syntax and monuments) collapse simultaneously before the reader's eye, and with them collapses the illusion they together perpetuate, the illusion that the world of time and space— where "this or that is"—to which they have reference is permanent or even real. That is to say, discursive linguistic forms, no less then jeat and marble, are extensions of an earthbound consciousness, and, like jeat and marble, they become true (accurate) hieroglyphs only when their pretensions are exposed. Thus in lines 14-16 the imminent failure of the monuments to point out (isolate, individuate) the heaps they have in "trust" (what an irony in *that* word) is imitated in the failure of the syntax to keep separate (point out) its own components:

> What shall point out them,
> When they shall bow, and kneel, and fall down flat
> To kisse those heaps, which now they have in trust?

The fact that Hutchinson feels compelled to provide a full gloss of these lines—"What shall distinguish tomb and bodies, when all are, sooner or later, commingled in one heap of dust?" (499)—is a nice comment on the success of Herbert's strategy. Where his editor obligingly provides the distinguishing specificity of "tombs" and "bodies," the poet gives us only an obfuscating series of pronouns and demonstratives—"what," "them," "they," "those," "they"—with the result that the larger structure of the utterance is progressively undermined. "Them," "they," and "those" become one, not in the future of Herbert's "shall," but in the present of his question. And that question is as much the object of irony as are the markers whose dissolution it predicts; for the very basis for asking a question—for rational predication in general—is taken away when the phenomena to which the question would direct our attention will not stay put and are, in fact, in the process of disintegrating. In other words, this self-consuming question convinces us not only of the insubstantiality of monuments, but of the final irrelevance and insufficiency of the way of thinking (spatially and temporally) the act of questioning assumes.

The same use of language—not to specify, but to make specification impossible—is on display in the final lines, where to monuments and bodies and sentences and questions is joined time, as one more earthly mold whose form dissolves in the context of a more inclusive vision:

> That flesh is but the glasse, which holds the dust
> That measures all our time; which also shall
> Be crumbled into dust. Mark here below.
>
> (20-22)

As before, the referents of the relatives expand so that for the second "which" the reader understands not only "time," but "glasse," "flesh" (one hears an echo of the Biblical "all flesh is grass") and even "measures," all of which have been crumbled into dust. With this in mind, the final gesture of the first-person voice is more than a little suspect:

> Mark here below.

Mark where? and with what? and in what? "Mark" follows immediately upon "dust" (the heavy stresses of the Lydgatian, or "humpbacked," line pushes them up against each other) and the juxtaposition of the two words undermines the pointing motion of the imperative, leaving the reader to look at one more example of "dustie heraldrie." In this context, the final distich—"How tame these ashes are, how free from lust, / That thou mayst fit thy self against thy fall"—can hardly be taken as seriously as its alliterative neatness would suggest. There is finally something facile about the stance of the speaker, who lectures his body as if he were not implicated in either its pride or its fall. The poem laughs not only at the pretensions of jeat and marble, but at its own pretensions, and also at the facility of those readers who thought to escape from it with an easy and pious conclusion. Summers tells us that the hieroglyphic form of "Church Monuments" serves "to reinforce the message," but that message itself crumbles just as we are about to carry it away.

Isabel MacCaffrey has written of Milton that his "worlds all fit exactly inside each other," an observation that also fits Herbert. In fact it might be a description of the action of "Church Monuments," where a succession of worlds or containers, at first separate and discrete, are discovered finally to be perfectly congruent, not only fitting inside each other, but filled with the same substance, dust. Yet in some important respects, this is not a representative poem. More typically the vessels and boxes (a favorite word) of Herbert's poetic landscape, when opened, are found to contain not dust, but Christ. This is uniquely true of the poem "Sepulchure," whose ostensible plot is the search for a lodging suitable to hold Christ's body:

> O Blessed bodie! Whither art thou thrown?
> No lodging for thee, but a cold hard stone?
> So many hearts on earth, and yet not one
> Receive thee?
>
> (1–4)

The speaker's questions depend on two assumptions that do not survive the experience of the poem: (1) that stone and heart are separate and opposed entities, and (2) that the initiative in this situation rests with the heart. The first assumption is challenged even as it is taking form; for while the argument of the stanza distinguishes between heart and stone, their juxtaposition cannot help but bring to mind the Biblical characterization of the heart as hard and stony. The second assumption will be overturned when we realize that Christ's entry into the heart is not conditional on its disposition to receive him, and that, in fact, he is already in residence. That realization, however, is still several stanzas away, and for a time we continue to move within the context of the speaker's complaint:

> Sure there is room within our hearts good store;
> For they can lodge transgressions by the score:
> Thousands of toyes dwell there, yet out of doore
> They leave thee.
>
> But that which shews them large, shews them unfit.
> What ever sinne did this pure rock commit,
> Which holds thee now? Who hath indited it
> Of murder?
>
> (5–12)

These lines apparently confirm and extend the opposition of heart and stone: not only is the latter more hospitable than the former ("out of doore / They leave thee"), but it is the more fitting receptacle. Again, however, the two objects are brought closer together, even as they are distinguished: both are now regarded as sepulchers, one for the body of Christ, the other for the body of sin, and, more significantly, both are drawn into the complex of associations evoked by the charged phrase, "this pure rock":

> for they drank of that spiritual Rock
> that followed them: and that Rock was
> Christ.
> (I Corinthians 10:4)

> Behold I lay in Sion a chief corner
> stone, elect, precious: and he that
> believeth on him shall not be confounded.
> (I Peter 2:6)

In the context of these allusions (and they are hardly recondite), the stanza receives a double reading. The rock of line 10 is simultaneously the stone that holds Christ's body and Christ himself, the sinless rock on which his church (another rock) and all its members ultimately rest. As in "Church Monuments," the components of the poem's scene are beginning to collapse into one another and, as they do, the sense made by the syntax becomes problematical. Literally, "Which holds thee now" is a relative clause, but in the multiple perspectives now available to the reader, it becomes a question. Which sepulcher holds thee now, now that supporter and supported, container and contained, have become one? "Oh blessed body! Whither art thou thrown?"

The answer to these questions is given in the penultimate stanza:

> And as of old the Law by heav'nly art
> Was writ in stone; so thou, which also art
> The letter of the word, find'st no fit heart
> To hold thee.
> (17–20)

Every reader will recognize this as a near paraphrase of II Corinthians 3:2-3: "Ye are our epistle written in our hearts . . . not with ink, but with the Spirit of the living God; not in tables of stone, but in fleshly tables of the heart." Once more, however, the allusion works against the literal sense of the argument, undermining its urgency; for while in the surface rhetoric the problem remains the finding of a fit heart, II Corinthians tells us that the heart has been made fit by the very person who occupies it. That is to say, "this pure rock" has already made pure the rock which holds it *now*, not the actual stone sepulcher, which, after all, is empty—"And they entered in, and found not the body"—but the sepulcher of our once stony hearts, soften so by the Word inscribed upon them that they are able to produce laments and self-accusing poems.

Reading "Sepulchure," then, is like the experience of reading the Scriptures— "This verse marks that, and both do make a motion / Unto a third, that ten leaves off doth lie"—and with each expansive motion, the lines of demarcation with which we began seem less and less real. The answer to the question "O Blessed bodie! Whither art thou thrown?" is finally discovered to be "everywhere" (now made one place), but especially in the inhospitable heart which by virtue of its occupation has become what it is so often termed in another galaxy of Biblical allusions—the temple of God. The solution of the problem that was the poem's occasion ("No lodging for thee?") coincides with the *dis*solution of its phenomenal distinctions, and both solution and dissolution are confirmed in the final stanza:

> Yet do we still persist as we began,
> And so should perish, but that nothing can,
> Though it be cold, hard, foul, from loving man
> Withhold thee.
>
> (21-24)

In these lines the poem's two arguments finally converge, one asserting plainly what the other has all the while been suggesting: the active force in this situation, as in every other, is not the heart but Christ. Paradoxically, this plain point is underlined by the ambiguity of the concluding line and one-half. Is it that nothing (either stone or heart or stony heart) cold, hard, and foul can keep Christ from loving (adjective) man? or that nothing cold, hard, and foul can keep Christ from loving (participle) man? The pressure to resolve the ambiguity is minimal, because the distinctions that would make one reading better than the other—between loved and loving man, between the heart as agent and Christ as agent, between letting in and forcing entry—are no longer operative. In a world where Christ occupies every position and initiates every action, ambiguity—of place, of person, of agency—is the true literalism. His word is all.

HELEN   VENDLER

Alternatives: The Reinvented Poem

One of the particular virtues of Herbert's poetry is its provisional quality. His poems are ready at any moment to change direction or to modify attitudes. Even between the title and the first line, Herbert may rethink his position. There are lines in which the nominal experiences or subjects have suffered a sea-change, so that the poem we think we are reading turns into something quite other. The more extreme cases occur in Herbert's "surprise endings," in what Valentina Poggi calls his "final twist," in which Herbert "dismisses the structure, issues, and method" of the entire poem, "rejecting the established terms" on which the poem has been constructed. A case in point is "Clasping of Hands," which ends, after playing for nineteen lines on the notions of "thine" and "mine," with the exclamation, "Or rather make no Thine and Mine!" In cases less abrupt, Herbert's fluid music lulls our questions: we scarcely see his oddities, or if we see them, they cease to seem odd, robed in the seamless garment of his cadence. When in "Vertue" he breathes, "Sweet rose," we echo, "Sweet rose," and never stop to think that nothing in the description he gives us of the rose—angry in hue, pricking the eye of the rash beholder, with its root ever in the grave—bears out the epithet "sweet." Is the stanza about a sweet rose, as the epithet would have us believe, or about a bitter rose? This is a minor example of Herbert's immediate critique of his own clichés ("The Collar" could serve as a major example) and poses, in little, the problem of this chapter: how to give an accurate description of Herbert's constantly self-critical poems, which so often reject premises as soon as they are established.

Herbert's willingness to abolish his primary terms of reference or his primary emotion at the last possible moment speaks for his continually

From *The Poetry of George Herbert*. ©1970, 1975 by The President and Fellows of Harvard College. Harvard University Press, 1975.

provisional conduct of the poem. In "Grace," after begging, for twenty lines,
for God's grace to drop from above, Herbert suddenly reflects that there is,
after all, another solution, equally good: if God will not descend to him,
he may be brought to ascend to God:

> O come! for thou dost know the way:
> Or if to me thou wilt not move,
> Remove me, where I need not say,
>   *Drop from above.*

In part, this change of terms is simply the cleverness of finding a way out
of a dilemma; but more truly, in Herbert's case, the ever-present alternative
springs from his conviction that God's ways are not his ways— "I cannot
skill of these thy wayes." If man insists on one way—that his God, for
instance, drop grace on him—it is almost self-evident that God may have
a different way in store to grant the request, and Herbert bends his mind
to imagining what it might be—in this case, that God, instead of moving
himself, should remove Herbert. The pun in the "solution" shows verbally
the pairing of alternatives to accomplish the same object.

Precision is all, and when Herbert catches himself in careless speech,
he turns on himself with a vengeance. In "Giddinesse," human beings are
reproved for fickleness, and God is asked, first, to "mend" us; but no we
are beyond mending, and so Herbert must ask God to "make" us anew;
but no, one creation will not suffice—God will have to "remake" us daily,
since we sin daily:

> Lord,   *mend*
>   or rather   *make* us; one creation / Will not suffice our turn;
> Except thou   *make us dayly,* we shall spurn
>   Our own salvation.

Equally, when Herbert finds himself lapsing into conventional pulpit
oratory in the poem "Miserie," he pulls himself up sharply from his clichés
about "man" and in the last breath turns inward: "My God, I mean myself."
These second thoughts are everywhere in Herbert. The wanton lover, he
says, can expend himself ceaselessly in praising his beloved; why does not
the poet do the same for God? "Lord, cleare thy gift," he asks in "Dulnesse,"
"that with a constant wit / I may—" May what? we ask, and if we continue
the analogy, we would say, "That I may love and praise thee as lovers their
mistresses." Something like this must have passed through Herbert's mind,

and have been rejected as presumptuous, so that instead he writes:

> Lord, cleare thy gift, that with a constant wit
> I may but look towards thee:
> *Look* onely; for to *love* thee, who can be,
> What angel fit?

The italicized "look" and "love" show Herbert doing, as it were, the revision on his poem in public, substituting the tentative alternative for the complacent one. He takes into account our expectation, prompted by his analogy with lovers, of the word "love," and rebukes himself and us for daring to preempt such a divine gift. The proper reading of the poem must realize both the silent expectation and the tacit rebuke, as Herbert changes his mind at the last moment.

Some of Herbert's most marked and beautiful effects come from this constant reinvention of his way. One of the most spectacular occurs in "A True Hymn," where Herbert has been praising the faithful heart over the instructed wit, and says:

> The fineness which a hymne or psalme affords,
> Is, when the soul unto the lines accords.
>
> . . . If th'heart be moved,
> Although the verse be somewhat scant,
> God doth supply the want.

He then gives an example of God's supplying the want:

> As, when th'heart sayes (sighing to be approved)
> *O, could I love!* and stops: God writeth—

Logically, what God should write to reassure the soul is, *"Thou dost love."* To wish to love is to love; but to love God, Herbert bethinks himself, is first to have been loved by God (as he tells us in "Affliction [I]"), and so God, instead of ratifying the soul's wish, *"O could I love!"* by changing it from the optative to the declarative, changes the soul from subject to object and writes *"Loved."* If we do not intuit, as in "Dulnesse," the "logical" ending (*"Thou dost love"*), we cannot see how Herbert has refused a banal logic in favor of a truer metaphysical illogic, conceived of at the last possible utterance of the poem. He stops in his course, veers round, writes *"Loved,"* and ends the poem in what is at once a better pride and a better humility.

What this means about Herbert's mind, this rethinking of the poem

at every moment, is that he allows his moods free play and knows that logic
is fallible: one may want one thing today and quite another on the Last
Day, for instance. When, in "The Quip," Herbert is tormented in turn by
the jeering of worldly Beauty, Money, Glory, and Wit, he remains silent,
but says in his heart that on the Last Day he will be revenged, when his
God will answer his tormentors for him: *But thou shalt answer, Lord, for
me.* And yet, as soon as he truly thinks of that scene on the Last Day, he
reinvents it. The last stanza of "The Quip" shows Herbert's God, not
vindicating at large the now-triumphant soul, not administering an
anathema to the defeated worldly glories, but engaging in an almost silent
colloquy alone with the faithful soul:

> Yet when the houre of thy designe
> To answer these fine things shall come;
> Speak not at large; say, I am thine:
> And then they have their answer home.

When we hear, in "Love Unknown," of God's wishes for Herbert (which
amount to Herbert's best wishes for himself), we learn that "Each day, each
houre, each moment of the week, / [He] fain would have [him] be new,
tender, quick." Nothing is to be taken for granted, nothing should be
habitual, nothing should be predictable: every day, every hour, every
moment things have to be thought through again, and the surface of the
heart must be renewed, quickened, mended, suppled.

An accurate description of Herbert's work implies the locating of his
true originality. A few years ago this was the subject of some debate between
William Empson and Rosemond Tuve, when Empson claimed as "original"
images that Tuve proved traditional in iconographic usage. Empson
retorted that traditional images could nevertheless bear a significant
unconscious meaning, and that choice of image in itself was indicative.
Certainly "tradition" is used differently by different poets, and each poet
decides what décor he will choose from the Christian storehouse in order
to create his stanzas. Though every single image in a poem may be
"traditional," the choice of emphasis and exclusion is individual and
revealing. Herbert often begins poems with, or bases poems upon, a
traditional image or scene or prayer or liturgical act or Biblical quotation;
but a question crying out for answer is what he makes of the traditional
base. A similar question would ask what he does with the experiential
donnée, personal rather than "traditional," of an autobiographical poem.
In short, what are some of Herbert's characteristic ways of "conducting"
a poem? My answer, in general, appears in the title of this chapter, and in

the examples I have so far offered: Herbert "reinvents" the poem afresh as he goes along. He is constantly criticizing what he has already written, and he often finds the original conception inadequate, whether the original conception be the Church's, the Bible's, or his own. Nothing is exempt from his critical eye, when he is at his best, and there is no cliché of religious expression or personal experience that he does not reject after being tempted into expressing it. A poem by Herbert is often "written" three times over, with several different, successive, and self-contradictory versions coexisting in the finished poem. A different sort of poet would have written one version, felt dissatisfied with the truth or accuracy of that account, written a second, more satisfactory version, then rethought that stage, and at last produced a "truthful" poem. Herbert prefers to let his successive "rethinkings" and reinventions follow one another, but without warning us of the discrepancies among his several accounts, just as he followed his original qualification of the rose as sweet with a description of the rose as bitter, without any of the usual "buts" or "yets" of semantic contradiction. I should add that the evidence of the Williams manuscript, which gives Herbert's revisions of some poems, supports these conjectures on Herbert's rethinking of his lines, but what I wish to emphasize is not his revisions before he reached a final version but rather the reinvention of the the poem as it unfolds toward its final form. . . .

In addition to correcting himself, whether in the impersonal terms of "Prayer (I)" or in the terms of repeated experience in "The Temper (I)," Herbert corrects his autobiography too, but as usual without flaunting his reinventions. They are for us often the discoveries of a second reading, since at first we take them wholly for granted. The blandness of most critical paraphrase of Herbert indicates that readers have been misled by the perfect grace of the finished poems and have concluded that an uninterrupted cadence means an uninterrupted ripple of thought. Herbert knew better: he said his thoughts were all a case of knives. The wounds of those knives are clearest in the three greatest autobiographical poems, "Affliction (I)," "The Flower," and "The Forerunners."

In "The Forerunners," the simplest of the three, Herbert complains that in age he is losing his poetic powers, and in explaining the loss he offers several alternative explanations which a more anxious poet would be at pains to reconcile with each other. Herbert simply lets them stand: truth, not coherence, is his object. First, the harbingers of age come and evict his "sparkling notions," who are of course guiltless since they are forcibly "disparked." They and Herbert suffer together. Next, the "sweet phrases, lovely metaphors" are apparently not being evicted but are leaving of their own free will. Echoing Wyatt, Herbert asks reproachfully, "But will ye leave me thus?" accusing them of ingratitude after all his care of them. Next, they are no longer ungrateful children leaving home but are fully of age, seduced virgins: "Has some fond lover tic'd thee to thy bane?" Finally, they are debased, willingly prostituting themselves in the service of the lover who loves dung. In Herbert's last bitterness, even their essence and power are denied them: they are no longer creative "enchanting" forces but only "embellishments" of meaning. There is no resolution to these successive metaphors of loss—no comprehensive view is taken at the end, and we suffer with Herbert the final defensive repudiation of those servants who have in fact deserted him. His powerful love of his "beauteous words" has its own independent force within the poem, but so does his gloomy denial of value to those words at the end. The only true critical description of poems such as this must be a successive one; a global description is bound to be misleading.

"Affliction (I)," like "The Forerunners," depends on a series of inconsistent metaphors for a single phenomenon, God's treatment of his creature. Herbert's ingenuity is matched only by his frankness: his God is at first a seducer, "enticing" Herbert's heart; next he is a sovereign, distributing "gracious benefits"; then an enchanter, "bewitching" Herbert into his family. He is an honest wage-paying master, a king dispensing hope of high pleasure, and a mother, indulgent:

> At fist thou gav'st me milk and sweetnesses;
> I had my wish and way.

But then God becomes one who inflicts sickness, and the poet groans with the psalmist, "Sicknesses cleave my bones." Worse, God becomes a murderer—"Thou took'st away my life"—and an unfair murderer at that, leaving his creature with no means of suitably vengeful retaliation— "A blunted knife / Was of more use than I." God sends famine, and Herbert becomes one of Pharaoh's lean kine: "Thus thinne and lean without a fence or friend, / I was blown through with ev'ry storm and winde." In two lines of sinister genius, God is said to "betray" Herbert to paralysis (a "lingring" book) and death (he "wraps" Herbert in a gown made unmistakably shroudlike by the sequence of verbs). Next, God becomes a physician, deluding Herbert with his "sweetned pill," but then cruelly undoes his own healing when he "throws" Herbert into more sicknesses. God's last action seems his wickedest, surpassing all his previous enticements and tortures: he "clean forgets" his poet, and the abandonment is worse than the attention. These indictments of God are only one strain in this complaint, with its personal hesitations, accusations, self-justifications, and remorse, but they show Herbert's care and accuracy in describing his own notions of God as they changed from episode to episode. There is a remarkable lack of censorship; even with the Psalms as precedent, Herbert shows his absolute willingness to say how things are, to choose the accurate verb, to follow the truth of feeling. We can only guess at Herbert's inconsistencies of self-esteem underlying the inconsistencies in this portrait of God. This God, changeable as the skies—first lightening, then love, and then lightening again—is reflected from a self first proud and then craven and then proud again, a self that does not know whether it is a child or a victim or a dupe, a self for whom all self-assertion provoked a backwash of guilt.

The inconsistent God addressed in "Affliction" may at first cause us some dismay. Yet I believe that Herbert had a reason for choosing each of his metaphors, and though his "underthought" may not emerge as explicit accusation, the metaphors he chooses to employ (in respect to God and God's actions) are on the whole accusatory. While the tradition of religious poetry does not forbid the reproaching of God, it scarcely ever refuses, as Herbert does here, to allow God a response, and the confounding of Job shows the usual course of such divine responses, imitated by Herbert in "Dialogue."

In "Affliction" the metaphors respresenting God's inflictions and Herbert's afflictions are the vehicles of the narrative, but the length of the narrative and the cumulative addition of metaphors are themselves metaphors for the cruellest infliction of all—duration, repetition, inventively varied torture in which respites only intensify recurrences. Yet all the retrospective narration, though painful, memorializes only the suffering possible to receptivity: Herbert is passive in both torment and delight. There are tempests raining all night here, as in "The Flower," but "The Flower" postulates a personal sin of presumption, which justifies God's wrath, and by so doing assumes an intelligible universe in which anyone can read his proper state:

> These are thy wonders, Lord of love,
> To make us see we are but flowers that glide . . .
>   Who would be more,
>   Swelling through store,
> Forfeit their Paradise by their pride.

In "Affliction," however, there is no such assumption of personal guilt, and God seems capricious and arbitary. Only his first "enticing" actions are explicable, used as they are for seductive purposes; after that, there is no predicting what cordials or corrosives are to follow, nor in what sequence, nor for what cause. "Now I am here," says Herbert, "What thou wilt do with me / None of my books will show." This is the central affliction of the poem, the utter unintelligibility of the universe, a universe which, seeming patternless, was an especial torment to a poet whose nature bent everything to form, neatness, order, and music, to whom randomness was the ultimate temperamental antithesis.

Herbert asks for nothing less than a law to encompass God, a law by which God's actions can be brought into the range of a reasonable hypothesis like that in "The Flower," where God's chastisements always mean that one has sinned. In "Affliction," as in many of Herbert's strongest lines, simplicity encompasses former meanings in its resonance. "Now I am here" means, at this point in the poem, "Now I am here enticed, bewitched, wrapped in a gown, betrayed to a book, thrown into sicknesses, bereft of friends, without fruit or profit"; and "What thou wilt do with me" reads, "What—after enticing me, making me ill, murdering me, killing my friends, giving me false medicine, cross-biassing me—thou wilt do with me / None of my books will show." It is as though Herbert had drawn an elaborate map of a journey as well as the history of his life, so that he can say "Now" and "Here" and "What" to an audience who can fill in the data of "Before" and "Then" and other "Whats."

We might expect, in his Job-like case, a reply from a voice out of the whirlwind. But Herbert's situation is worse than Job's: he is answered only by silence. God has forgotten him, and Herbert's cries are, as Hopkins was to say later, "Cries like dead letters sent / To dearest him that lives alas! away." But Herbert's response is neither to curse God and die nor to announce that he is gall and heartburn; with less vital force to spare, he withdraws dangerously into abstraction, apathy, and loss of ego: "I reade, and sigh, and wish I were a tree." God visits no afflictions on trees: they flourish in due season, they bear fruit, and they house birds. Their "justice" inheres in mere being, not doing. In what lies man's justice?

> I say more: the just man justices;
> Keep grace; that keeps all his goings graces.

So said Hopkins, confronting the same problem of being and doing: all natural things—and a just man is a natural thing—radiate themselves in their actions. But for Herbert, choice is meant to reign over instinct or physical laws, and in the case of man the problem of will intersects obliquely with the effortlessness of being. Herbert does not see any possible parallel between himself and the tree: he lacked Hopkins's confidence in the fundamentally just nature of mere being.

God, says Herbert, arrogates to himself all the right to change, but expects Herbert to be steadfast—stout in weakness, meek in trouble, ever the faithful servant. "Well, I will change the service," Herbert retorts, "and go seek / Some other master out." The defiance sounds plausible until we remember that Herbert had earlier told us that he had come to a place where he could neither go away nor persevere. If he could do neither of these, it is hardly more likely that he could swerve sharply away from his lifelong path. It is also true that the mere summoning of the notion of another master would make Herbert recall that there are only two: God and Mammon, in one formulation; God and the Devil, in another. The alternative of another master is terrifying even in the naming of it and accounts for Herbert's frightened "Ah my deare God!"

Although the Christian pilgrimage, in its usual appearance, is beset with dangers and difficulties, these are normally attributed either to the pilgrim's weakness or to the intervention of wicked tempters, not to the agency of God himself. Even in *Job*, it is not God who *causes* evil to befall his servant. Herbert's boldness in attributing direct agency to God in respect not only to joy but also to trouble is imitated by Hopkins:

> How wouldst thou worse, I wonder, than thou dost
> Defeat, thwart me?

The morass into which "Affliction" has led us is not easily quitted, and perhaps Herbert has not so much resolved as ended his poem. A satisfactory ending would in some way exculpate God, reconcile Herbert to remaining in God's service, and offer him the renewal of energy he needs to persevere or to advance, extinguishing his helpless exhaustion. Terrified by his own threat to abandon his master, Herbert recoils with his first epithet of affection, "Ah my deare God!" In the beginning of the poem Herbert's heart was brought into God's service (by whatever seductive means) and he must deal, as he has not yet done, with that primal fact. His own emotions are, in short, the missing factor in the poem up to this point. His life investment—his only life investment—has been in God, and should he leave God, his heart would be entirely empty. Love that has been placed in one hope alone is not so soon transferred. Whether or not we consider the object of that love a chimera makes no difference: the absence of love, Herbert realizes, is worse, as a suffering, than the loss of health, life, or friends; it would be the worst of afflictions to be prevented from loving. And so his final paradox hastily reaffirms his love and swears that if he fails to love, God may punish him by preventing him from loving. In this way, God is reestablished as the source of value—value being love—and Herbert's love, his motive for perseverance, is renewed.

It is impossible to know to what extent Herbert was conscious of the many uneasy phrasings in "Affliction." Paralleling the irreconcilable metaphors for divinity are the equally unsettling versions of the self. One way to look at the poem is to say the poet is engaged in constructing an ideal self and is experiencing the psychological stages of that construction. The ideal self is modeled on expectations putatively coming from God, but from a psychological point of view one may equally well see the expectations as issuing from the self. The construction of a "better self" seems at first inspection a task bringing only the delights of self-approbation. The self identifies itself wholly with God and becomes quasi-divine in sharing God's benefits, God's furniture, God's stars, God's pleasures. The natural self, in this phase of construction, seems only a happy base to the celestial self: besides his "natural delights" Herbert will have God's "gracious benefits." This harmonious supposition seems mostly of Herbert's own making, as the phrases I have italicized reveal:

> *I thought* the service brave:
> So many joyes *I writ down* for my part . . .
>
> I looked on thy furniture so fine
>   And *made it fine to me* . . .
> Such starres *I counted mine* . . .
>
> What pleasures could I want, whose King I served?

None of these appropriations and conjectures is of God's doing. The leap into identity with God makes the self intensely happy with its new superimposed construct, and in a burst of confidence the soul entirely forgets its moral nature:

> Thus argu'd into hopes, my thoughts reserved
>   No place for grief or fear.

There is a childlike pleasure in the apparent reconcilliation of the natural and supernatural selves; and the integral harmony of childhood, the loss of which drove the soul to the construction of a second self, is regained in "milk and sweetnesses," "flow'res and happinesse."

Sorrow and sickness, woe and pain are so closely intertwined in the forth and fifth stanzas that psyche and soma become one. The terrible influx of this sorrow (which seems to have caused Herbert's physical sickness, rather than the reverse) is unexplained: "With my yeares sorrow did twist and grow." Later, some causes of Herbert's sorrow are suggested—his loss of health, the death of friends, his dissatisfaction with academic life. But it is truer to the poem to believe that after Herbert's complacent construction of an easy spritual life, the inevitable war broke out between instinct and conscience. Herbert's demands on himself were never other than extreme, so much so that even he himself was conscious of the eventual severity of his conscience, scratching at him tooth and nail, as he says in "Conscience," carping and catching at all his actions. This cruelty of the self to the self continues throughout the rest of "Affliction," and though the attacks of the self against itself are projected onto God, they are, to speak psychologically, Herbert's own doing. Moved by aspiration, conscience, and the ideal, he chose academic life over the worldly inclinations of both birth and spirit, as he tells us, thinking thereby to approve more of himself. Instead, he found himself in a rage. The rage, an advance in psychological truth over his earlier sorrow, plunges him into more sicknesses. In wishing to forgo his mortal nature by becoming a tree, Herbert is retreating from the siege of one self by the other, just as by reading and sighing he retreats from his former rage. His boast that he will seek out "some other master" is, in this interpretation, meaningless: he has no other internalized self to serve. The principle of annihilation lurking in the final paradox (since not to love is not to be) reflects this quandary. To seek another master is equivalent to extinguishing a self long-constructed, and this recognition, though not explicit, acts as a temporary resolution to the problem of the two selves. Rage solves nothing; only the love of one self for the other can restore inner harmony. But a constant guilt resurfaces and causes the many phases of Herbert's autobiography.

With guilt comes a sense of God's absence, and that experience, habitual with Herbert, is the central topic of the third of these autobiographical poems, "The Flower." Just as the sonnet "Prayer" redefines over and over, with increasing approximation to the truth, what prayer is, so "The Flower" redefines over and over, with increasing approximation to the truth, what has in fact been happening to Herbert. We are told that he has suffered a period of God's disfavor, during which he drooped, but that God has now returned to him, making him flourish once again. This simple two-stage event could have been told, presumably, in a plain chronological account; but instead, we are given several versions of the experience undergone. It is this repetitiveness, incidentally, here and elsewhere in Herbert, which causes Palmer to class this poem with others as redundant, lacking that fineness of structure he saw in Herbert's simpler two-part and three-part poems. The redundancy is apparent, but not real; each time the experience is redescribed, it is altered, and each retelling is a critique of the one before.

The first version of Herbert's experience is a syntactically impersonal one, told without the "I." Herbert could be meditating on some universally known phenomenon:

> How fresh, O Lord, how sweet and clean
> Are thy returns! ev'n as the flowers in spring;
>   To which, besides their own demean,
> The late-past frosts tributes of pleasure bring.
>   Grief melts away
>   Like snow in May
>   As if there were no such cold thing.

Now these last three lines say something not strictly true. We do keep a memory of grief. But in the first flush of reconciliation, Herbert generously says that God has obliterated all past grief in the soul. This version of the incident also says that God has been absent and has now returned, just as spring absents itself and then returns, in a natural cyclical process. We, and Herbert, shall discover in the course of the poem how untrue these statements—about the cyclical absence of God and the obliteration of grief—are.

The second stanza gives us yet another, and almost equally rosy, view of Herbert's experience, this time in the first person:

> Who would have thought my shrivel'd heart
> Could have recover'd greennesse? It was gone
>   Quite under ground; as flowers depart
> To see their mother-root, when they have blown;
>   Where they together,
>   All the hard weather
>   Dead to the world, keep house unknown.

Here the period of grief is represented as, after all, not so difficult: it was not really God who went away, but rather Herbert; and his absence was on the whole cosy, like the winter hibernation of bulbs, where the flowers, in comfortable company, visiting their mother the root, keep house together with her, while the weather is harsh aboveground. This certainly does not sound like a description of grief, but like a situation of sociable comfort. The only ominous word, keeping us in touch with the truth, is "shrivel'd," which sorts very ill with the familial underground housekeeping.

So far, a cloak of palliation lies over the truth. But when Herbert has to summerize what his experience of grief followed by joy has taught him, he admits that he finds the God who lies behind such alternations of emotion an arbitrary and incomprehensible one, who one day kills (a far cry from absenting himself) and another day quickens, all by a word, an absolute fiat. We are helpless to predict God's actions or to describe his intent; we await, defenseless, his unintelligible decisions, his arbitrary power:

> These are thy wonders, Lord of power,
> Killing and quickning, bringing down to hell
>   And up to heaven in an houre;
> Making a chiming of a passing-bell.
>   We say amisse,
>   This or that is:
> Thy word is all, if we could spell.

An early anthologist of Herbert cut off the poem here; for him, and probably for Palmer, too, the poem might just as well have ended with this summarizing stanza. For Herbert, however, it cannot: he has presented us with too many contradictions. Does God absent himself cyclically, like the spring, or arbitrarily and unpredictably? Is God benevolent only, or in a fact a malevolent killer as well? Was it he who was absent, or Herbert? Was the absence a period of hellish grief or of sociable retirement? The poem had begun in earthly joy, but now, with the admission that we cannot spell and that God's word is arbitrary and incomprehensible, Herbert's resentment of his earthly condition has gained the ascendancy, and he repudiates wholly the endless emotional cycles of mortal life:

> O that I once past changing were,
> Fast in thy Paradise, where no flower can wither!

Not God's changeableness, but his own, is now the issue; the "withering" and "shriveling" are now uppermost in his mind, as once again his past grief, tenacious in memory and not at all melted away, comes to his mind.

Yet once more, for the forth time, he recapitulates his experience. This time he does it in the habitual mode, the present tense of habit, emphasizing its deadly repetitiveness:

> Many a spring I shoot up fair,
> Offring at heav'n, growing and groning thither . . .
>
> But while I grow in a straight line,
> Still upwards bent, as if heav'n were mine own,
>   Thy anger comes, and I decline.

This habitual recapitulation leads Herbert to realize that his God's actions
are in fact not arbitrary, as he had earlier proposed, but that punishments
come for a reason: Herbert has been presumptuous in growing upwards as
if heaven were his own, and therefore he has drawn God's terrible cold wrath
upon himself.

We must stop to ask whether this confession of guilt on Herbert's part
is a realization or an invention. The intolerable notion of an arbitrary and
occasionally malevolent God almost necessitates the invention of a human
fault to explain such punishments. That is Herbert's dilemma: either he
is guilty, and therefore deservedly punished, or he is innocent, and his God
is arbitrary. Faced with such a choice, he decides for his own guilt. We cannot
miss the tentative sexuality of his "budding" and "shooting up" and later
"swelling"—one question the poem puts is whether such self-assertion can
ever be guiltless, or whether every swelling is followed by a punitive
shriveling. The answer of the poem is equivocal: his present "budding"
seems innocent enough, but the inevitable alternation of spring and winter
in the poem, of spring showers and icy frowns, tells us that we may always
expect God's wrath. When that wrath directs itself upon the sinner,

> What frost to that? What pole is not the zone
>   Where all things burn,
>   When thou dost turn,
> And the least frown of thine is shown?

There is no more talk about keeping house snugly underground through
all the hard weather. Herbert, on the contrary, has been nakedly exposed
to the hard weather, has felt the freezing cold—the tempests of God. The
truth is out; he *has* suffered, and he still remembers his grief. Oddly, once
the truth is out, Herbert has no more wish to reproach his God; he feels
happier considering himself as guilty than indicting God. It is not God,
he says, who is arbitrary and capricious, but we; God's actions only follow
ours; he is changeless, and we are the changeable ones. Herbert, having put
off the old man, scarely recognizes the new man he has become:

> And now in age I bud again;
> After so many deaths I live and write;
> I once more smell the dew and rain,
> And relish versing: O my only light,
>   It cannot be
>   That I am he
> On whom thy tempests fell all night.

In the unearthly relief of this stanza, Herbert returns to the human norm. His two constant temptations are to be an angel or a plant, but, the second half of "The Flower," like the second half of "Prayer," discovers human truth after the self-deception of the first half. With the unforced expression of relief, Herbert can acknowledge that in truth he was not comfortably visiting underground, but was being beaten by tempests. The paradisal experience of "budding again," like any paradisal experience in life, is forfeit if the reality of past grief is denied: the sharpened senses that once more smell the dew and rain are those of a Lazarus newly emerged from the sepulcher; to deny the cerements is to deny the resurrection. At this point, Herbert can engage in genuine "wonder." The previous "These are thy wonders, Lord of power" may be translated "These are thy tyrannies"; but now that Herbert has assuaged his anxiety by deciding that power is not arbitrary and perverse but rather solicitous and redemptive, he can say, "These are thy wonders, Lord of love." The poem is one of perfect symmetry, marked by the two poles of "wonder." It is redundant, if one wishes to call it that, in circling back again and again to the same experience, but each time it puts that experience differently.

The end of the poem embodies yet another self-reproof on Herbert's part, put this time as a warning to all who, like himself, may have been presumtuous in thinking heaven their own:

> These are thy wonders, Lord of love,
> To make us see we are but flowers that glide:
> Which, when we once can finde and prove,
> Thou hast a garden for us, where to bide.
> Who would be more,
> Swelling through store,
> Forfeit their Paradise by their pride.

This homiletic neatness is probably a flaw in the poem, and the harsh judgment that Herbert passes, in so impersonal and universal a way, on his earlier presumption makes this one of his comparatively rare poems with an "unhappy" ending. Since the fundamental experience of the poem is one of resurrection, and since the best lines of the poem express that sense of renewal, we may reasonably ask why the last lines are so grim. They are, I think, because of the two truths of experience at war in the poem. One is the immediate truth of renewal and rebirth; the other is the remoter, but larger, truth of repeated self-assertion, repeated guilt, repeated punishment. Until we are "fast in Paradise," the poem tells us, we are caught in the variability of mortal life, in which, however intense renewal may be when it comes, it comes uncertainly and not for long. Intellectually, the prospect is depressing, with innocence and relish spoiled by guilt and punishment. The hell of life may continue into a hell after life. But this, since it is an intellectual conclusion, cannot fundamentally damage the wonderful sense of restored life that has made the poem famous. It speaks, however, for Herbert's pained fidelity to fact that he will not forget the gloomy truth in the springlike experience.

The inveterate human tendency to misrepresent what has happened is nowhere more strongly criticized than in Herbert. Under his repetitive and unsparing review, the whole truth finally becomes clear. Herbert knows that to appear pious is not to be pious; to pay formal tribute is not to love; servilely to acknowledge power is not to wonder; to utter grievances is not to pray. His readers, often mistaking the language of piety for the thing itself, are hampered by dealing with an unfamiliar discourse. We have a rich sense of social deception in human society and can detect a note of social falseness in a novel almost before it appears; but it sometimes does not occur to us that the same equivocations, falseness, self-justifications, evasions, and defensive reactions can occur in a poet's colloquies with his God. We recognize defiance when it is overt, as in "The Collar" or "Affliction (1)," but other poems where the presentation is more subtle elicit assenting readings and token nods to Herbert's sweetness or humility. Herbert spoke of himself in "Affliction (IV)" as "a wonder tortur'd," and his own estimate of himself can be a guide in reading his poems.

Even in that last-placed and most quietly worded poem, "Love (III)," which is spoken in retrospect by the regenerate soul from the vantage point of something understood, the old false modesty lingers. There is, as Herbert says in "Artillerie," no articling with God, but in this poem the soul is still refusing to give up the assertion of the private self. When Herbert catches glimpses of God's order, which may be termed the best order he can imagine for himself, he finds it almost unnatural, odd, even comic. His impulse is to deny that he has any connection with such a disturbing reordering of the universe, to feel a sense of strain in attempting to accommodate himself to it. Often, he prays that his God will remake him to fit in with a divine scheme: "Lord, mend or rather make us." But sometimes Herbert rejects this claim on God's indulgence. At his best, and at our best, says Herbert, God refuses to accept the view we like to take of ourselves as hopelessly and irremediably marred and ignorant creatures. Herbert's protests that he is not capable of glory are not catered to; expecting a gentle solicitude from God, he is confronted by an equally gentle but irreducible immobility. Each of his claims to imperfection is firmly, lovingly, and even wittily put aside, and he is forced to accept God's immage of him as a guest worthy of his table. What Herbert wants is to linger in the antechambers, to serve, to adopt any guise except the demanding glory of the wedding garment, but Love is inflexible, and the initial "humility" of the guest is revealed as a delusive fond clinging to his mortal dust and sin.

Herbert's God asks that he be more than what he conceives himself to be. Herbert may have invented this sort of God to embody the demands that his own conscience put upon him, a conscience formed by that "severa parens," his mother. But even in such a brief poem as "Love (III)," Herbert's originality in transforming his sources, in reinventing his topic, strikes us forcibly. We know that the poem depends on St. Luke's description of Jesus' making his disciples sit while he served them; and on the words of the centurion transferred to the Anglican communion service, "Lord, I am not worthy that thou shouldst enter under my roof"; and on Southwell's "S. Peter's Complaint," in which St. Peter knocks on sorrow's door and announces himself as "one, unworthy to be knowne." We also know, as Summers first made clear, that Herbert's actual topic is the entrance of the redeemed soul into Paradise. Now, so far as I know, this entrance has always been thought of as an unhesitating and joyful passage, from "Come, ye blessed of my father" to "The Saints go marching in." The link between St. Peter knocking at a door and a soul knocking at St. Peter's door is clear, but it is Herbert's brilliance to have the soul give St. Peter's abject response, while standing hesitant and guilty on the threshold, just as it is a mark of his genius to have the soul be, instead of the unworthy host at communion, the unworthy guest in heaven. When we first read "Love," it strikes us as exquisitely natural and humanly plausible; it is only later that the originality of conception takes us aback. As in "Dooms-day," Herbert looks at the event as it really would be, not as tradition has always told us it would be. If the redeemed soul could speak posthumously and tell us what its entrance into heaven was actually like, what would it say? And so the process of reinvention begins.

Herbert's restless criticizing tendency coexists with an extreme readiness to begin with the cliché—roses are sweet, redeemed souls flock willingly to a heavenly banquet, sinners are swinish, Doomsday is awesome, past grief was not so painful. Over the cliché is appliquéd the critique—roses are bitter and smarting, the soul would in reality draw back from Love's table, sinners are, in desire, indistinguishable from saints, Doomsday would in fact be agreeably social, past grief was, if truth to be told, intolerable. It makes little difference to Herbert where he finds his *donnée*—in the images of courtly poetry, in the Bible, in his personal experience. The artless borrowed beginning soon becomes the scrutinized personal statement. The anxiety that must have made Herbert want to begin with the safe, the bland, the familiar, and the taken-for-granted coexists permanently with the aggression that impelled him almost immediately to criticize the received idea. He seems to have existed in a permanent reversible equilibrium between the two extremes of tradition and originality, diffidence and protest, the filial and the egotistic. His poems do not "resolve" these extremes into one attitude; rather, they permit successive and often mutually contradictory expressions of the self as it explores the truth of feeling. At any moment, a poem by Herbert can repudiate itself, correct itself, rephrase itself, rethink its experience, reinvent its topic. In this free play of ideas lies at least part of Herbert's true originality.

A. R. CIRILLO

Crashaw's "Epiphany Hymn": The Dawn of Christian Time

Posterity has not been as kind to Richard Crashaw, the poet, as it has been to Richard Crashaw, the man. Literary history, which is quite willing to regard Crashaw's disrupted life and enforced wanderings with sympathy, would seem to deny him a place among the elect poets, and perhaps this is just. Few could argue convincingly that he belongs on Parnassus. Yet, in our judgment of his religious poetry, we seem to have applied unfair or alien standards and found his wanting. Our condemnation of his "excesses" stems from a religious tradition ironically more common to us than to him, a tradition which he was not really trying to emulate and which he would not have found exclusive. Anglo-Saxon countries are heir to an essentially Puritan attitude toward religious devotion (even when the belief in such devotion itself is on the wane) which holds that when God speaks to man, He speaks in a plain style; any heightening of that style is more suspect as it becomes more elaborate. As a result, we celebrate Herbert and Vaughan, and even Donne (whose virtues need no defense) at the expense of Crashaw's "baroque sensibility."

But Crashaw's best religious poetry belies that usually pejorative and frequently vague description, and a careful reading of this poetry shows that it contains a richness of detail and evocation, a pattern of careful, orderly development that is not only especially significant, but also perfectly welded to the form and temper of its expression. It is not the true manner of the "Donne tradition," and perhaps it is time to lay that ghost to rest when

---

From *Studies in Philology* 67, no. 1 (January 1970). ©1970 by The University of North Carolina Press.

dealing with seventeenth-century religious poetry. Louis Martz, who has taken the most significant step in this direction, has admirably defined the issue in terms of individual response and experience: meditative style expressed not only that which the poet has in common with humanity, but that which is uniquely his, his personal *way* of reacting to his faith and belief.

Whether one wants to call the style "meditative," "devotional," or even "religious," the issue is not about terminology but about a poem's effectiveness as an eloquent expression of religious feeling. One does not need to be a High Anglican to respond to Herbert's deeply felt faith in *The Temple*, nor a Christian Hermetist to sense the divinity Vaughan finds in nature. These are "quieter"poets and their works are seldom, if ever, filled with the turbulent energy, rich color, and unsettling imagery one finds in Crashaw. Perhaps the difference is between the High Mass of the Romans with its color, pageantry, and the appeal to the senses, and the simple service of the rural English church. The modes are different, but the feeling and communion is not necessarily less intense or more effective in either case. Within such terms it is possible to find in Crashaw's devotional poetry a profundity not usually associated with his art; and it is in these terms that I propose to examine,in the following pages, Crashaw's hymn, "In the Glorious Epiphanie of Our Lord God," from the 1652 volume, *Carmen Deo Nostro*.

This hymn and the three which precede it in that volume—"To The Name Above Every Name, The Name of Jesus," "In the Holy Nativity of Our Lord God," and "New Year's Day"— form a sequence with a remarkable structural and progressive unity of themes climaxed in the "Epiphany Hymn." Before I focus on this last hymn, however, I should like to review the entire sequence as it contributes to that poem.

I

As a glance at the *Roman Breviary* will show, there are two principal cycles to the liturgical year: the cycle of Christmas or Incarnation with its preparatory season of Advent, and the cycle of Easter or Redemption with its preparatory season of Lent (*Quadrigesimae*). Within the first cycle fall all four of the feasts celebrated in these hymns, and it is this cycle which will be the main concern here, for it closes with the feast of the Epiphany. In the principle metaphor of these four hymns there is a significant correspondence with the cycle of the day and the cycle of the sun, so that the four poems form, externally, the first cycle of the church year, internally reflected by the development of an enigmatic "day" from poem to poem. An apotheosis of these cycles occurs in the "Epiphany Hymn."

The first and most important poem—one that might be called the precursor of the cycle of Incarnation which it invokes—is the "Hymn To The Name Above Every Name, The Name of Jesus." In the Roman Catholic liturgical year of the seventeenth century the feast of the Holy Name was rapidly assuming its position as a permanent feast in early January between the feasts of the Circumcision and Epiphany. Though nominally an occasional piece, Crashaw's poem represents more than the celebration of a particular church feast; in the course of its 239 lines it extends the meaning of devotion to the Holy Name to include restoration of spiritual harmony in Christian terms, within the context of musical ecstasy and Renaissance moral views of concord.

Concurrent with this harmonic structure in the poem is the enigmatic use of the word "day." In its immediate usage the word refers to the festival which gives the poem its name; but the literal referent is far from final, since in the cumulative thought progression of the poem, the concept of a *series* of days or comings of Christ evolves with crescendo-like effect within the basic harmonic metaphor. In the "Hymn to the Name" this *day* is more than the feast day devoted to the adoration of the name of Christ; its meaning expands to include a series of three advents: past, present, and future, which cover all of time. In his third, fourth, and fifth sermons on Advent St. Bernard explains the three advents in terms common to the Christian theological tradition. The first is the Incarnation as a moment in history, the day of the first coming in the flesh *to men*. This advent is the first step in the restoration of moral and cosmic harmony lost at the Fall, and it comes in time, or rather, at the beginning of time for the Christian. The second is closely connected with and comes in virtue of the first: Christ's coming *into men*, into the soul as its Redeemer and the Restorer of the harmony of light darkened through Adam's Fall. In Catholic ritual, the act of transubstantiation is a daily reiteration of both of these advents simultaneously; that is, a daily coming of the Name on an actual yet mystical level wherein the Name takes flesh in the host and enters the soul of the communicant. Man can avail himself of these advents in the sacrifice and reception of the Eucharist:

> And ten Thousand PARADISES
> The soul that tasts thee takes from thence.
>   (187–8)

This is an advent which is always in process, a perpetual coming to the well-disposed soul.

The third and final advent implicit in the "Hymn to the Name," is that which St. Bernard labels the coming *against men*, the final coming in power and majesty, alluded to in the final section:

> Alas what will they doe
> When stubborn Rocks shall bow
> And Hills hang down their Heaun-saluting Heads
>   To seek for humble Beds
> Of Dust, where in the Bashfull shades of night
> Next to their own low NOTHING they may ly,
> And couch before the dazeling light of thy dread majesty.
> They that by Loue's mild Dictate now
>   Will not adore thee,
> Shall Then with Iust Confusion, bow
>   And break before thee.
>
> (229-39)

Reference to the final coming relates the whole conception of the poem to another cycle which may be expressed in terms of the sun. In the tradition that accrued to Genesis and its account of creation, the seventh day on which God rested was thought of as a perpetual sabbath. After the six days of creation God withdrew to a timeless vantage over all; this constitutes the seventh day, and since all time, for God, is present, the seventh day is the continuing duration of the present—a continuing duration sustained for the Christian by the perpetual advent. With the final judgment, however, at the end of time, the natural sun will again darken, ending the seventh day and human time, as Christ, the sun of the eighth day, rises in light and glory.

The theme of harmony, the cyclic structure, and the threefold conception of advent are central to this poem and the three which follow it. Light is the primary symbol of harmony, of the dawn of Christian time, the new era of redemption which reaches its apex in the Epiphany, the manifestation and illumination of Christ as a true and more brilliant light to the Gentiles. On this focal image of light, which has a natural relationship to the multi-layered conception of "day" I have just discussed, Crashaw builds a series of themes and paradoxes, both historical and moral, that make the final hymn a fitting climax to and illumination of the three advents evoked initially in the "Hymn to the Name."

Opening with the diction and measures of a love song, the "Nativity Hymn," takes the light of the first advent on its primary level of nature. The sun yields in brilliance to Christ the light of incarnate grace. This is the *first* day, the day of Incarnation as historical fact, and Christ becomes The light of the rising sun: "It was THY day, SWEET! & did rise / Not from the EAST, but from thine EYES" (21-2). But the perpetual advent, that moral coming into men in the light brought by Christ to the moral realm, is implied later, in one of Crashaw's favorite metaphors, that of the child in the Virgin's bosom like the sun in the eastern clouds:

> We saw thee in thy baulmy Nest,
> Young dawn of our aeternall DAY!
> (31-2)

The full chorus which concludes the hymn sets up the moral paradox of the Incarnation in natural cyclical terms—the birth of Christ on a winter night heralding the coming of day and summer:

> Wellcome, all WONDERS in one sight!
> Eternity shutt in a span.
> Sommer in Winter. Day in Night.
> Heauen in earth, & GOD in MAN.
> Great little one! whose all-embracing birth
> Lifts earth to heauen, stoopes heau'n to earth.
> (79-84)

The hymn for the Circumcision, or New Year's Day, returns to the equation of Christ with a moral day (lines 1-4), the sun again losing in comparison with the light of Christ:

> When he hath done all he may
> To make himselfe rich in his rise,
> All will be darknes to the Day
> That breakes from one of these bright eyes.
> (25-8)

The final stanzas of this hymn lead to the climactic movement of the cycle seen in the "Epiphany Hymn," which will transmute this contrast of lights into a new order. The prophetic lines refer to the coming of the Magi from the east, abandoning their false gods and false light:

> And soon this sweet truth shall appear
> Dear BABE, ere many dayes be done,

> The morn shall come to meet thee here,
> And leaue her own neglected Sun.

> Here are Beautyes shall bereaue him
> Of all his eastern Paramours.
> His Persian Louers all shall leaue him,
> And swear faith to thy sweeter Powres.
>
> (29-36)

With this theme of adoration of Christ, an echo of the concluding lines of the "Hymn to the Name" ("Shall Then with Iust Confusion, bow / And break before thee"), we move into our major concern, the "Epiphany Hymn," a poem which, working on simultaneous orders of meaning, prunes the more sensuous elements of the earlier poems and joins the themes of light, advent, and harmony inherent in a Christian hymn into the conclusion of one cycle of liturgical and Christian time, the cycle of the Incarnation—or of the first advent and its accompanying moral advent into the soul of man.

II

Light and its tangents—day, dawn, and the sun—now become joined with another unitive light, the star of the Magi, in a spiritual conflict of night and day. Ruth Wallerstein and Austin Warren have recognized that, in relation to the "Nativity Hymn," the central metaphor of the "Epiphany Hymn" is once more the comparison of Christ to the sun, supernature and nature, a comparison Crashaw had been making throughout much of his poetry. For example, in his adaptation of Marino's *Sospetto d'Herode* he had stated the essential paradox of the Incarnation in its relation to time:

> That hee whome the Sun serves, should faintly peepe
> Through clouds of Infant flesh: that hee the old
> Eternall Word should bee a Child, and weepe.
> That hee who made the fire, should feare the cold;
> That Heav'ns high Majesty his Court should keepe
> In a clay-cottage, by each blast control'd.
> That Glories selfe should serve our Griefs, & feares:
> And free Eternity, submit to yeares.
>
> (stanza 23)

In the same poem Crashaw had introduced one of the central concerns of the present hymn: the advent of Christ in light as the dispeller of the darkness associated with sin and the old law. Lucifer, the personification of this darkness, gives the Incarnation perspective in the moral drama:

> Hee has my Heaven (what would he more?) whose bright
> And radiant Scepter this bold hand should beare.
> And for the never-fading fields of Light
> My faire Inheritance, hee confines me here,
> To this darke House of shades, horrour, and Night . . .
>
> (stanza 27, lines 1-5)

> Darke, dusty Man, he needs would single forth,
> To make the partner of his owne pure ray . . .
>
> (stanza 28, lines 1-2)

It is this inner presence that Crashaw alludes in speaking of the mystic or interior coming of Christ to man in the "Hymn to the Name":

> I Sing the Name which None can say
> But touch't with An interior Ray:
> The Name of our New Peace; our Good:
> Our Blisse: & Supernaturall Blood . . .
>
> (1-4)

Keynoted by the symbolism of light, this theme is brought to a climax in the "Epiphany Hymn." Light is the link connecting the main themes of the hymn. Each of the three comings of Christ is related, in some way, to illumination: the first, Incarnation, is associated with the light of the star and the burning Seraphim; the second, or mystic coming, is the illumination of the soul, the alleviation of the darkness of sin, articulated in Cornelius à Lapide's commentary on a text of Isaiah used in the Epiphany mass. On the second verse of Isaiah 60 ("For behold, darkness shall cover the earth and a mist the people: but the Lord shall arise upon thee and his glory shall be seen upon thee" [Douai-Rheims]) he says, "Christ removed this darkness first from the Jews and then from the Gentiles like the sun rising from high." On the third verse from the same chapter, taken as a prophecy of the Epiphany ("And the Gentiles shall walk in thy light, and kings in the brightness of thy rising"), Lapide quotes an interpretation of the Church as the sun of truth and grace. Those who are outside of it are in perpetual night unless they yield to that sun which shines through the Church. In effect, the identification of Christ with light on levels of natural and moral meaning, is evident in texts both exegetical and literary from the Gospel of St. John through the Renaissance. Christ is the day which dispels the night of the old law, the darkness of spiritual blindness and ignorance. He is the light of the soul, and his incarnation as an event in time marks the dawn of the Christian era, the day of redemption:

> Away, then, away with our forgetfulness of the truth! Let us remove the ignorance and darkness that spreads like a mist over our sight; and let us get a vision of the true God, first raising to Him this voice of praise, "Hail, O Light." Upon us who lay buried in darkness and shut up in the shadow of death a light shone forth from heaven, purer than the sun and sweeter than the life of earth. That light is life eternal, and whatsoever things partake of it, live. But night shrinks back from the light, and setting through fear, gives place to the day of the Lord. The universe has become sleepless light and setting has turned into a rising.
>
> [Clement of Alexandria, trans. G.W. Butterworth]

The relationship of truth and light, ignorance and darkness, is a traditional part of the extended metaphor of the cycle of the day. Dawn, as one part of the cycle of the day, the sun, the east—all aspects of the central light—are related to the coming of Christ in terms of light.

Commonly, the Epiphany (often called Twelfth Day in England) is interpreted as the manifestation of Christianity to the Gentiles in the persons of the Magi; but the Greek root of the term gives the more essential meaning of a "shining forth, an illumination," symbolized by the star which guided the Magi to the nativity site. This star was the subject of much commentary among exegetes who associated it with Christ, faith, the state of perfection, and even with martyrdom. Taking its place in the sequence of the *Roman Breviary* for the Epiphany, the star appears as an additional manifestation of light:

> and now the glorious light of his Manifestation is breaking upon us. . . . and now the guiding star leadeth the wise men to worship Him, that from the rising of the sun to the going down thereof, the Birth of the true King may be known abroad.

The art of Crashaw's "Epiphany Hymn" lies in the ease with which it harmonizes these traditional themes in a poem that simultaneously celebrates the feast day of the Epiphany and the true coming of Christ to man's soul in the light of grace.

The poem begins with an implicit statement of the central metaphor—Christ as the sun—in the form of a sung invocation: "Bright Babe!" in which Christ is identified with the sun and its light, an image which will take on a richer context as the poem progresses. Here, on the Epiphany, Christ's first advent is manifested to the Gentiles in a burst of light; but with this advent also comes the illumination of the soul and of nature. Christ has come as the dawn of a new day and becomes, on a moral level, the disinheritor of the physical sun. His supplanting of the day suggests not only the paradox of his birth at night (the day is born at night) but also the birth of a moral day for mankind, a day represented in Roman Catholic devotion by the presence of the host in the Monstrance, a vessel designed to resemble the radiating light of the sun around the centrally placed Eucharist, just as the face of Christ, and Christ himself, is the center of the day of grace, or the second advent into the soul of men.

In "The EAST is come" (line 13) the chorus sets up one of the contributing paradoxes of the poem: Christ as the sun receives the adoration of the east which moves to him in a cycle of light and love. So, St. Bernard describes the Magi as coming from the east, seeking the rising sun of justice ("magi ab Oriente venerunt, ortum Solum justitiae requirentes"). Though the *topos* of Christ as the sun is of long-standing duration, the Crashaw passage is working with it as another aspect of the redemptive context. As the sun, Christ ushers in the new day from the east and through his divine love brings this redemptive day to man, as Crashaw had stated this in the general context of the "Hymn to the Name": "the loue-crowned Doores of / This Illustrious DAY" (42-3). But it is the east, personified in the Magi, which has come to Christ, the sun. The paradox of the Incarnation and Redemption cycles is established in its supertemporal context as the first day of Christian time. The first day of light for the soul has come in one physical manifestation reflected in the cycle of night and day: as the world revolved about the sun, the east comes to Christ who has himself come to men, descending that they might ascend.

This theme is continued in the following lines (15-47) sung by the Kings, where the darkness-light paradox refers to the conception of spiritual darkness that existed before the coming of Christ and also to the Magi's particular moral darkness, representative, as they were, of that ulterior world where pagan rites were the erroneous brightness of worshipping false gods. Thus, they were "Lost in a bright / Meridian night, / A Darkenes made of too much day" (16-8). Through the intercession of another light, the star, they have found the way out of their natural and moral night to the true sun, Christ, the day of night and, consequently, the "east of west" (their journey was towards the west). The whole conception of Christian time is concentrated in the description of Christ as the "All-circling point," "The world's one, round, Eternall year." (26-7), where Crashaw returns to the harmonic theme so brilliantly elaborated in the "Hymn to the Name" and so implicit in the Christian *hymn* as a genre. Associating the east and the rosy morn with both the natural dawn and the supernatural moral dawn brought on by the Incarnation and the consequent act of redemption, Crashaw locates his hymn within the context which Leo Spitzer has identified as a morning song of the God-loving soul to the Creator, a love song of the creature for his redeemer. Thus Christ, receiving adoration in the image of the sun, as the new pattern of nature, corresponds to the incarnate image evoked in the "Hymn to the Name":

>   Powres of my Soul, be Proud!
>   And speake lowd
> To All the dear-bought Nations This Redeeming Name,
> And in the wealth of one Rich WORD proclaim
> New Similes to Nature.
>   May it be no wrong
> Blest Heauns, to you, & your Superiour song,
> That we, dark Sons of Dust & Sorrow,
>   A while Dare borrow
> The Name of Your Delights & our Desires,
> And fitt it to so farr inferior LYRES.
>
>   (92–102)

The "All-circling point," the "round Eternal year" are phrases that reflect the harmonic and temporal concepts implicit in the Fall and the restoration of harmony through love-incarnation and redemption. Christ, as Orpheus who appeased fallen nature, is an embodiment of moral *temperatura* in a physical and temporal universe that has lost its physical *temperatura*, expressed in "Not vext & tost / 'Twixt spring and frost" (32–3). He is a perpetual sun, a perpetual light, *lumen de lumine*, not alternating with darkness, but shining through it. For Him there is no time; His year is an eternity. In this context, the singers (the Magi as the Gentiles) are moved into the timelessness of meditation on Christ's coming into the soul as the soul purges itself of the world and moves to Christ. Time yields to eternity in the sun of this mystical "day."

The passage beginning "To Thee, to Thee" (42) brings the poetic movement to a rejection of the natural sun (a star in its own right) and to an implicit identification of it as the false light of error before the light of grace. That it embodies some figurations of the fallen star, Lucifer, the origin of falsehood, becomes more explicit in the section beginning "Farewell, the world's false light" (48), followed by the related rejection of the false gods and black idolatry associated with Egypt. Because of the illumination from this new light, this other sun, mankind abandons the old law and its rites as "The proud & misplac't gates of hell" (55) which stand in the way of the new day of Christ. These were not only false ways to God but, glowing with that false light that deceives man, they also represented the night of death for the soul. On this note the complexus of light, sun, and guiding star imagery is raised to the moral and spiritual level, as the shining of Christ on the new day becomes "the world's sure Way!/ Heavn's wholsom ray" (60-1), forming an inner union of the soul and Christ: "Wellcome to vs; and we / (SWEET) to our selues, in THEE" (62-3).

The union of the individual with Christ is but an echo of the desire for the Incarnation expressed in the "Hymn to the Name":

> Come, louely NAME! Apeare from forth the Bright
> > Regions of peacefull Light
> Look from thine own Illustrious Home,
> Fair KING of NAMES, & come.
> Leaue All thy natiue Glories in their Gorgeous Nest,
> And giue thy Self a while The gracious Guest
> Of humble Soules, that seek to find
> > The hidden Sweets
> > Which man's heart meets
> When Thou art Master of the Mind.
> > > > > (115-24)

Later, in the same poem, when the Name appears it ushers in the new day of grace that is developed in the "Epiphany Hymn":

> WELCOME to our dark world, Thou
> > Womb of Day!
> Vnfold thy fair Conceptions; And display
> The Birth of our Bright Ioyes.
> > > > (161-4)

In the "Epiphany Hymn" (64) the Magi's song continues with the prevailing day-light-sun metaphor ("The deathles HEIR of all thy FATHER'S day!") which is central to the whole redemptive cycle, but with additional elements. I refer, first of all, to the idea of a morning love-song mentioned earlier in relation to the east and the rosy morn. The pagan dawn, personified in Aurora ("No more that other Aurora" [68-9]) is no longer entitled to her love songs; she is replaced by the Virgin who becomes the

rosy morn encompassing the true sun/son, the heir of his father's day, for
it is God the Father who first separated day from night; it is the Father from
whom this sun/son proceeds; and it is also in virtue of the Father's love
and mercy that his *deathless* heir is to die to restore day to man's soul. So,
in the Christmas Breviary, Christ is addressed, "Tu lumen, tu splendor
Patris."

With this the song moves into another ambiguity implicit in the sun
metaphor of,

> We (Pretious ones!) in you haue won
> A gentler MORN, a iuster sun.
> His superficiall Beames sun-burn't our skin;
> But left within
> The night & winter still of death & sin.
>
> (73-7)

The beams of the natural sun (nature unrestored by grace, the darkness after
the Fall and before the Incarnation) as the light in darkness mentioned in
"More desperately dark, Because more bright" (59), sunburnt the skin only
superficially. Death was still without the promise of resurrection, and sin
was still unrelieved by the baptism of Christ's merits. Opposed to the darts
of materiality and material beauty which pierce our eyes but spare our hearts
"which needeth nurture most," to use a phrase from Spenser's "Hymne in
Honour of Love" (38-9), Christ's darts—the light of his grace—pierce the
heart and spare the eyes (78-9) in a true mystic manifestation of that second
advent which comes in virtue of the first, incarnate one. This is an implicit
rejection of the old law of pagan religion elaborated in succeeding lines:

> The doating nations now no more
> Shall any day but THINE adore.
> Nor (much lesse) shall they leaue these eyes
> For cheap Egyptian Deityes.
>
> (85-8)

Nature uninfused by grace before the coming of Christ is embodied in the
sun as a symbol of man's adoration of the light of false gods.

Following this long section on the rejection of the sun as the false light
of pagan faith (48-117), Crashaw returns to a conception of nature alluded
to in the "Hymn to the Name." The sun itself repents of its former position
as the center of the universe of false adoration (treated as a *deliquium* or
eclipse [116-7]), for when it was most venerated it was a mere eclipse
compared to the light of Christ. (Again, the reference is back to line 59,

"More desperately dark, Because more bright.") But the sun went into true eclipse on the day of the crucifixion (118-21), the day when the cycle of redemption was completed. On the day of nature before grace, before the coming of Christ, nature wept in the form of dew, thus calling for redemption.

The context here, of course, is supplied by the Renaissance theory, expressed in Milton's second Prolusion, that with the fall came moral and natural discord as well as man's loss of the faculty of hearing the harmony of the spheres. In

> This dayly wrong
> Silenc't the morning-sons, & damp't their song
> Nor was't our deafnes, but our sins, that thus
> Long made th'Harmonious orbes all mute to vs,
>
> (130-3)

Crashaw relates the theory of discord after the Fall to the highly versatile symbol of the sun as a concretization of man's darkness in light before the coming of the true light once again restored him to the way of harmony.

A theme that has been insinuated throughout the poem is one inherent in the nature of the hymn itself, one integral to the cycle of rising and setting, and implicit in the liturgical cycle: namely, the movement out of darkness into light. Nature, in the figure of the sun, represents the false light in darkness of the consequences of the Fall. Just as Christ died that man might live, descended that man might ascend, the sun is darkened at the crucifixion that man might see. With the Incarnation, as with the rising of the sun, comes the beginning of Christian time and the new day which transcends time, a day in which Christ is the sun, the true light dispelling darkness.

Christ's is the new day to which the sun at last yields—unlike the fallen star Lucifer—going into eclipse at the crucifixion as a reflection in nature of the *apparent* eclipse of the true sun/son. Liturgically, time begins in the church year with the preparation for the reception of Christ incarnate when the inner harmony of the Christian soul will be restored with the coming of grace. The hymn, then, contains what Spitzer has called a harmonic tetrachord: grace-nature-music-harmony, as nature illuminated by the light of grace leads to the harmony of a hymn *sung* by the Magi.

The most explicit but necessarily paradoxical expression of this interest in time and its relation to the new light of Christ is found in the long section beginning, "Time has a day in store" (134-89), where the darkening of the sun at the crucifixion is transformed into the very light which will show men the new law of grace. All of this is continued in the terms of light and

dark. Thus, the sun, a spark adored by the "love-sick" world which has so
far found false redemption in nature, lights the way by taking shelter in
the shadow of the cross. Another darkening of the sun, at the end of time,
corresponds to the one at the crucifixion:

> That dark Day's clear doom shall define
> Whose is the Master FIRE, which sun should shine.
> That sable Iudgment-seat shall by new lawes
> Decide & settle the Great cause
>   Of controuerted light,
> And natur's wrongs rejoyce to doe thee Right.
> That forfeiture of noon to night shall pay
> All the idolatrous thefts done by this night of day;
> And the Great Penitent presse his own pale lipps
> With an elaborate loue-eclipse
>   To which the low world's lawes
>   Shall lend no cause.
>
>   (144-55)

This final coming of Christ in glory and majesty will be to reject those who
have rejected the light of his grace.

The meaning of lines 164-8,

> As by a fair-ey'd fallacy of day
> Miss-ledde before they lost their way,
> So shall they, by the seasonable fright
> Of an vnseasonable night,
> Losing it once again, stumble'on true Light,

lies in the context of the crucifixion when the darkening of the natural sun
created a wholesome fear lighting misled men to the true sun/son of grace.
The Magi, who are singing this hymn as surrogates for those outside the
original pale of grace, had lost their way in the night of nature only to be
led by the light of the star—a natural manifestation of the supernatural—
to the true light where they knelt in adoration. On the other hand, the
darkening of the natural sun on the last day will be a sign for all those who
have rejected this light to "bow and break" before Christ.

The paradox of light in darkness (opposed to the former darkness in
light of the earlier sections of the hymn) is thus related to the order of nature
and to the order of grace. The Magi allude to the two darkenings of the

sun, in lines which are controlled by this enriching ambiguity:

> So his officious blindness now shall be
> Their black, but faithfull perspectiue of thee;
> His new prodigious night,
> Their new & admirable light;
> The supernaturall DAWN of Thy pure day.
>
> (171–5)

The cycle of nature as comprehended in a day is a reflection of the cycle of grace in the first two advents of Christ. Christ's is the supernatural dawn of a pure ray because He is the light who expels the darkness of sin, and the darkness of the old law and the Fall; for we are, according to St. Paul, "children of the light" (I Thess. 5:5).

While continuing to develop the symbol of the darkened sun as the revelation of the true way of God, the Magi's song begins to move to the comtemplative mode which is the true object of the poem. The darkening of the sun becomes the darkening of the world, a renunciation of the flesh in order to meditate on Christ and join in the mystical advent. As St. Bernard suggested in his third sermon on the Epiphany, "Our sermon has two purposes, contempt of the world and mortification of the flesh." Night, or the darkening of the world, becomes the light, like a miraculous star, leading to Christ.

Thus the Dionysian system of the *via negativa* alluded to in lines 192 ff. ("The eight-ey'd Areopagite / Shall with a vigorous guesse inuade / And catche thy quick reflex; and sharply see / On this dark Ground / To descant THEE") is not a new element imposed on the light-darkness motifs of the poem, as Wallerstein states, but serves as a cumulative reflection and transmutation of what has preceded. With this as his vehicle Crashaw moves the whole Incarnation-Redemption cycle initiated in the "Hymn to the Name" to the contemplative process implicit in the darkness-light contrast. Contemplation on the restoration of harmony through the Incarnation was begun as a mystic prophecy and invocation in the "Hymn to the Name"; now, through the liturgical celebration and actual coming of the Name in the flesh, and its spiritual coming into the soul, the "Epiphany Hymn" reaches its climatic point and becomes a mystic rapture through the music of the Christian's interior harmony consonant with the light of Christ's interior advent. It is through the darkness that one can "sharply see . . . To descant THEE."

No longer need Crashaw talk of sweets, rubies, and nests, those sensuous images so characteristic of him, for these accidents of color and materiality are no longer necessary. Now, all is a cosmic harmony of light through darkness, paralleling and heightening the physical light which had led the Gentiles to Christ. With the ecstatic exclamation, "O prize of the rich SPIRIT!" (197), Crashaw has reached the crucial section of the hymn. In terms of the Dionysian way, the sun of Christ is chosen over the sun of the earth, the true star over the false, the spirit over the flesh. What L.C. Martin takes as a mere reference to Christ's eyes, "o ye two / Twinne SVNNES" (204-5), is clearly part of this reiterated duality of the light of nature and the light of grace in Christ, the deliberate darkening of the material order to reach the true light. In a give-and-take of "controverted light," what follows (up to line 219, "Borrowing day & lending night") is a celebration of this paradox which has been central to the poem. The lesson of the negative way is to be taken from Dionysius, "that reverent child of light" (206), taught to *negotiate* Christ (205) (*negotiate*, in the same bargain metaphor by which Christ *redeemed* man) by learning of that new night— the night of the soul in the darkening of materiality before illumination.

This is the way to make Christ the mystic day in the cycle by which day follows night, that day being His illumination of the soul, a day begun by the Incarnation. Mankind can learn the meaning of Christ's coming through the negative light of internal purgation. Internal darkness hence leads to and serves the day of grace just as the sun of nature darkens itself and yields to the sun of grace. This is the "commerce of contrary powres," the "trade / Twixt sun & Shade," the "Borrowing day & lending night" (215-9), the new law for the old, grace relieving sin, the illumination of the Epiphany—a commerce of trade consummated in the mercantile act of redemption when the sun was darkened that men might see.

With magnificent economy, in the following lines (220-33) Crashaw takes a traditional image and uses it in a movement that asserts the potential divinity of man and, in retrospect, opens the meaning of the whole hymn as a mystical manifestation of still another order. The lines, "all the noble powres / That (at thy cost) are call'd, not vainly ours" (220-1), indicate man's primacy over nature while he is yet dependent on the redemption of Christ's merits. They also assert the use of these powers to soar upwards towards His light. The illustrative image of the eagle in flight ("Now by abased liddes shall learn to be / Eagles" [232-3]) compresses considerable meaning. As John Steadman has indicated, the eagle was an image of contemplation particularly because of the belief that it could approach the sun without blinking. For Hugh of St. Victor it referred to those who forsake the earthly and seek the celestial through contemplation, and Stephan Batman recounts the theory that the eagle is always willing to share its prey with others, a characteristic which Crashaw uses purposefully:

> In stead of bringing in the blissfull PRIZE
> And fastening on Thine eyes,
> Forfeit our own
> And nothing gain
> but more Ambitious losse, at lest of brain.
>
> (227–31)

In Crashaw's terms, this is the soul in the hymnal music of ecstatic harmony soaring like the eagle up to the divine light of the new sun incarnate. In this key the total meaning of the poem and of the cycle which had begun with the "Hymn to the Name" reaches fulfillment. Instead of confining themselves to the order of nature and the first coming of the Name in the flesh, the Magi, as representatives of all Christians, so irradiated by Christ's interior light, become contemplative eagles, winged souls, using "Heavn's wholsom ray"—the ray of this supernatural sun—as a way of internal purification and elevation. From the darkness of ancient error they ascend on the ray of truth to the sun of truth.

The phrase "and shutt our eyes that we may see" (233) brings the hymn back to the sun-darkness contrast and still another characteristic of the eagle. As the eagle ages, his eyes become covered with a mist whereupon he goes in search of a fountain. Having found it, he flies up to the sun singeing his wings and evaporating the mist over his eyes with the sun's rays. Following this, he dips himself three times in the fountain and is instantly renewed in the splendor of his vision. Now, in addition to the manifestation to the Gentiles, the Epiphany celebrated two other manifestations, the baptism of Christ and his changing of the water into wine at Cana. Thus, in this Epiphany poem, the eagle's eyes are cleared of darkness as it approaches the sun; as the eagles of contemplation, the Magi or the Christian soul, close their eyes to the natural sun, to the world, so that in this self-imposed mist their eyes may be cleared by the true sun, as their souls are cleared in the fountain of his baptism. It is easy to see the various connotations that the story implicit in the hymn has taken. On the purely natural level, Christ comes at night, and in terms of the *darkness visible* of "More desperately dark, because more bright" (59), the false religions, the things of the world from which the Magi came, have been a false day in a true night. Now the approach to the spiritual sun is one through voluntary darkness and self-imposed night.

Adoration is the keynote of *The Close* (234 ff.) where, in a final resolution of the main themes, the sun itself joins the Magi in their symbolic act of kneeling before Christ in an acceptance of "Love's mild Dictate" as they "couch before the dazeling light" of Christ's dread majesty. In one aspect of this resolution, the sun which through worldly blindness has been called "the eye" (45) is now rather "delegated" (237) the eye of day, surrendering its precedence, its splendor, and its gifts to Christ. The identification of the sun's gold, myrrh, and frankincense with the gifts of the Magi extends the application of these to the putting aside of the splendor of the world for the spendor of Christ. In effect, the sun becomes a mere star compared to Christ: a shadow reflection on the natural level of Christ on the supernatural. Like the miraculous star of the Magi which guided them through the night, the sun becomes a guidepost to the true sun above all, "The world's & his HYPERION" (254), returning the whole hymn, in the cycle of rising and setting and the cycle of the day, back to the center of the new day, the sun/son image with which the poem has opened, "Bright Babe!"

Crashaw's "Epiphany Hymn," then, develops its own cycle of movement from darkness in light through light in darkness, while it continues the cycle of Incarnation instituted in the "Hymn to the Name." The "Epiphany Hymn" is the liturgical climax of the incarnation cycle— the celebration of the inner manifestation of the second advent. With it the first phase of Christian time is completed, as the three kings and the sun yield to the new light of Christ, synthesizing and transcending time and nature.

LOUIS MARTZ

Henry Vaughan

MODES OF COMMUNION

In the year 1649 Richard Crashaw died in exile at Loreto, a little more than six months after his master King Charles died on the scaffold at Whitehall. An era had ended for English political and religious institutions, and also for English religious poetry. With Crashaw's death the power of liturgical and eucharistic symbols died away in English poetry of the seventeenth century: the symbols earlier celebrated by Southwell, Alabaster, Donne, and Herbert. These poets had their doctrinal differences, and I do not wish to minimize those differences; but they had something more in common: a devotion to the mysteries of the Passion and to a liturgy that served to celebrate those mysteries. All five of these poets entered into holy orders; all five would have agreed with George Herbert's vision of "The Agonie":

> Who knows not love, let him assay
> And taste that juice, which on the crosse a pike
> Did set again abroach; then let him say
>   If ever he did taste the like.
> Love is that liquour sweet and most divine,
> Which my God feels as bloud; but I as wine.

In 1650 Andrew Marvell wrote his famous "Horatian Ode" in honor of the man who

> Could by industrious Valour climbe
> To ruine the great Work of Time,

From *The Paradise Within: Studies in Vaughan, Traherne, and Milton.* ©1964 by Yale University. Yale University Press, 1964.

And cast the Kingdome old
Into another Mold.

And in the same year appeared the first edition of Henry Vaughan's *Silex Scintillans*, a volume that, along with Milton's miscellaneous *Poems* of 1645, marks the emergence of the layman as a central force in religious poetry of the period. Vaughan's volume, though written by a staunch Royalist and Anglican, nevertheless stands as a sign of a profound mutation in human affairs. Without neglecting the highly individual qualities of Vaughan's vision, I should like here to consider his volume of 1650 as the symbol of a vital transformation in the religious outlook of the age.

It is important to look closely at *Silex Scintillans*, 1650. For Vaughan's enlarged volume of 1655, with its second part and its greatly expanded opening matter, presents a modified outlook, a less consistent fabric, and a weaker body of poetry, despite the fact that seven or eight of Vaughan's finest poems did not appear until the 1655 edition. The common charges against Vaughan's poetry—that his poems often begin with a flash of power, but then dwindle off into tedious rumination, that he works by fits and starts, that he cannot sustain a whole poem—these charges find their chief support in Book II of *Silex*, which reveals many signs of a failing inspiration. There is a greater reliance on the ordinary topics of piety, especially in the many labored poems based on Biblical texts; there is a marked decline in the frequency of Herbertian echoes, and a corresponding rise in the use of conventional couplet-rhetoric, after the manner of the Sons of Ben Jonson: a school to which Vaughan showed his allegiance in his undistinguished volume of secular poems in 1646. At the same time the crabbed and contentious Preface of 1655 strikes a tone quite out of line with the dominant mode of the poems in the 1650 volume, here bound up as the first "book" of what has now become a religious miscellany. But the volume of 1650 is a whole, like Herbert's *Temple*; and indeed there are many signs that the volume was deliberately designed as a sequel, a counterpart, and a tribute to Herbert's book.

Vaughan's subtitle is exactly the same as Herbert's: "Sacred Poems and Private Ejaculations"; but the main title represents a vast difference, enforced, in the 1650 volume alone, by the engraved title page presenting the emblem of the Flashing Flint—the stony heart weeping, bleeding, and flaming from the hand of God that strikes direct from the clouds, steel against flint. Furthermore, a careful look at this flinty heart will reveal something that I never noticed until my friend Evelyn Hutchinson, examining this title page with his scientific eye, asked, "Do you see a human face peering forth from within the heart?" It is certainly so: a man within can be clearly seen through an opening in the heart's wall. And facing this we have, again in the 1650 volume only, an intimate confession in the form of a Latin poem, explaining the emblem. Perhaps a literal version of this cryptic Latin will show how essential this poem and this emblem are for an understanding of the 1650 volume as a whole.

The Author's Emblem (concerning himself)

You have often touched me, I confess, without a wound, and your *Voice*, without a voice, has often sought to counsel me; your diviner breath has encompassed me with its calm motion, and in vain has cautioned me with its sacred murmur. I was deaf and dumb: a *Flint*: You (how great care you take of your own!) try to revive another way, you change the Remedy; and now angered you say that *Love* has no power, and you prepare to conquer force with *Force*, you come closer, you break through the *Rocky* barrier of my heart, and it is made *Flesh* that was before a *Stone*. Behold me torn asunder! and at last the *Fragments* burning towards your skies, and the cheeks streaming with tears out of the *Adamant*. Thus once upon a time you made the *Rocks* flow and the *Crags* gush, oh ever provident of your people! How marvellous toward me is your hand! In *Dying*, I have been born again; and in the midst of my *shattered means* I am now *richer*.

Authoris (de se) Emblema.

Tentâsti, fateor, sine vulnere saepius, & me
  Consultum voluit Vox, *sine voce, frequens;*
Ambivit placido divinior aura meatu,
  Et frustrà sancto murmure praemonuit.
Surdus eram, mutusq; Silex: *Tu, (quanta tuorum*
  Cura tibi est!) aliâ das renovare viâ,
Permutas Curam: Jamq; irritatus Amorem
  Posse negas, & vim, Vi, *superare paras,*
Accedis propior, molemq;, & Saxea *rumpis*
  Pectora, fitq; Caro, *quod fuit ante* Lapis.
En lacerum! Coelosq; tuos ardentia tandem
  Fragmenta, *& liquidas ex* Adamante *genas.*
Sic olim undantes Petras, Scopulosq; *vomentes*
  Curâsti, O populi providus usq; tui!

Quam miranda tibi manus est! Moriendo, *revixi;*
Et fractas *jam sum* ditior *inter* opes.

At once, after this story of a sudden, violent illumination, comes the
short and simple poem headed, like the opening poem of Herbert's *Temple,*
"The Dedication"; it contains a number of verbal echoes of Herbert, and
the whole manner of the poem represents a perfect distillation of Herbert's
intimate mode of colloquy.

> Some drops of thy all-quickning bloud
> Fell on my heart, these made it bud
> And put forth thus, though, Lord, before
> The ground was curs'd, and void of store.

These three elements, then: engraved title page, Latin confession, and
Herbertian dedication form the utterly adequate preface to *Silex Scintillans,*
1650. They introduce a volume that will have two dominating themes: first,
the record and results of the experience of sudden illumination; and second,
a tribute to the poetry of George Herbert, which, it seems, played an
important part in cultivating Vaughan's peculiar experience. Thus, toward
the middle of Vaughan's volume, after hundreds of unmistakable echoes of
Herbert in title, phrasing, theme, and stanza-form, Vaughan at last openly
acknowledges his debt by accepting the invitation of Herbert's poem
"Obedience," where Herbert offers his poetry as a written deed conveying
himself to God, with this conclusion:

> He that will passe his land
> As I have mine, may set his hand
> And heart unto this Deed, when he hath read;
> And make the purchase spread
> To both our goods, if he to it will stand.
>
> How happie were my part,
> If some kinde man would thrust his heart
> Into these lines; till in heav'ns Court of Rolls
> They were by winged souls
> Entred for both, farre above their desert!

Vaughan, in "The Match," answers in Herbert's own mode of familiar
address:

> Dear friend! whose holy, ever-living lines
> Have done much good
> To many, and have checkt my blood,

My fierce, wild blood that still heaves, and inclines,
But is still tam'd
By those bright fires which thee inflam'd;
Here I joyn hands, and thrust my stubborn heart
into thy *Deed*

As we look back, this joining of hands and hearts between Vaughan and
Herbert is almost equally evident in the opening poem of the volume proper:
"Regeneration." Here the allegorical mode of the painful quest, the imagery
of struggling upward toward a "pinacle" where disappointment lies, the
sudden cry mysteriously heard upon this hill, and even some aspects of the
stanza-form—all these things show a poem that begins by playing variations
on Herbert's poem "The Pilgrimage," which leads the speaker through "the
wilde of Passion" toward the hill suggesting Calvary:

When I had gain'd the brow and top,
A lake of brackish waters on the ground
Was all I found.

With that abash'd and struck with many a sting
Of swarming fears,
I fell, and cry'd, Alas my King!
Can both the way and end be tears?
Yet taking heart I rose, and then perceiv'd
I was deceiv'd:

My hill was further: so I flung away,
Yet heard a crie
Just as I went, *None goes that way*
And lives: If that be all, said I,
After so foul a journey death is fair,
And but a chair.

But Vaughan's pilgrimage has quite a different theme: in the fourth
stanza the Herbertian echoes fade out, as Vaughan's pilgrimage is called
away into an interior region of the soul, here imaged with the combination
of natural and Biblical landscape that often marks Vaughan at his best:

With that, some cryed, *Away*; straight I
Obey'd, and led
Full East, a faire, fresh field could spy
Some call'd it, *Jacobs Bed*;
A Virgin-soile, which no
Rude feet ere trod,

> Where (since he stept there,) only go
> Prophets, and friends of God.

The allusion to Jacob's vision and journey toward the East (Genesis 28: 10-22; 29:1) is only the first of many such allusions by Vaughan to the "early days" of the Old Testament; here the scene begins an allegorical account of the mysterious workings of grace; the pilgrim enters into a state of interior illumination, where he is prepared to apprehend the presence of God and to hear the voice of the Lord. In the remaining six stanzas the setting mysteriously changes to another landscape, a springtime scene, where a grove contains a garden with a fountain; the state of grace is imaged by combining the natural imagery of spring with subtle echoes of the most famous of all spring-songs: the Song of Solomon. The key to these stanzas is given by Vaughan himself in a verse from the Canticle appended to the poem: "Arise O North, and come thou South-wind, and blow upon my garden, that the spices thereof may flow out." It is the Garden of the Soul: one of the great central symbols in the Christian literature of meditation and contemplation. For Vaughan's poem here we need to recall especially the four verses of the Canticle (4:12-15) that immediately precede Vaughan's citation:

> A garden inclosed is my sister, my spouse; a spring shut up,
> a fountain sealed.
> Thy plants are an orchard of pomegranates, with pleasant
> fruits; camphire, with spikenard,
> Spikenard and saffron; calamus and cinnamon, with all
> trees
> of frankincense; myrrh and aloes, with all the chief spices:
> A fountain of gardens, a well of living waters, and streams
> from Lebanon.

So in Vaughan's spiritual landscape "The aire was all in spice," while

> Only a little Fountain lent
> Some use for Eares,
> And on the dumbe shades language spent
> The Musick of her teares;
> I drew her neere, and found
> The Cisterne full
> Of divers stones, some bright, and round
> Others ill-shap'd, and dull.

>   The first (pray marke,) as quick as light
>   Danc'd through the floud.
>   But, th'last more heavy then the night
>   Nail'd to the Center stood.

Vaughan is developing his favorite image-cluster of light and darkness through symbols that suggest one of his favorite Biblical passages: the third chapter of St. John's gospel, where Nicodemus hears the words of Jesus by night:

>   Except a man be born of water and of the Spirit, he cannot
>   enter into the kingdom of God.
>   That which is born of the flesh is flesh; and that which is
>   born of the Spirit is spirit.

So in Vaughan's allegory, the spiritual part of man is here reborn, made bright and "quick" as light; while the fleshly part remains dull and heavy, nailed to the earth. Much the same significance is found in the following scene, where in a bank of flowers, representing his own interior state, the speaker finds

>   Some fast asleepe, others broad-eyed
>   And taking in the Ray

And finally, all the images and themes of this poem coalesce with a threefold allusion to the "winds" of grace: the "rushing mighty wind" of Pentecost (Acts 2:2), the winds that are prayed for in Vaughan's quotation from the Canticle, and the wind described in the words of Jesus to Nicodemus: "The wind bloweth where it listeth, and thou hearest the sound thereof, but canst not tell whence it cometh, and whither it goeth: so is every one that is born of the Spirit." And so the poem concludes:

>   Here musing long, I heard
>   A rushing wind
>   Which still increas'd, but whence it stirr'd
>   No where I could not find;

>   I turn'd me round, and to each shade
>   Dispatch'd an Eye,
>   To see, if any leafe had made
>   Least motion, or Reply,
>   But while I listning sought
>   My mind to ease

By knowing, where 'twas, or where not,
It whisper'd; *Where I please.*
Lord, then said I, *On me one breath,*
And let me dye before my death!

So the poem, like dozens of others by Vaughan, begins with echoes of
George Herbert, whose simplicity of language and intimacy of tone pervade
the whole poem and the whole volume of 1650; but, like all of Vaughan's
better poems, "Regeneration" moves away from Herbert to convey its own
unique experience through its own rich combination of materials, in which
we may discern three dominant fields of reference: the Bible, external Nature,
and the interior motions of the Self. There is in "Regeneration" not a single
reference that could be called eucharistic. Yet Herbert opens the central body
of his poems with an emblematic Altar, typographically displayed upon the
page, and he follows this with the long eucharistic meditation entitled "The
Sacrifice," where he develops the meaning of the Passion through a variation
on the ancient Reproaches of Christ, spoken from the Cross as part of the
Good Friday service. Nothing could speak more eloquently of the vast
difference between these two poets.

In accordance with his central symbols at the outset of his *Temple*
Herbert gives seventy-seven stanzas of epigrammatic advice on how to lead
a good life, under the title, "The Church-porch"; these stanzas form a
preparation for the mental communion that constitutes the heart of
Herbert's central body of poetry, "The Church," as he makes plain by these
lines on the threshold:

Thou, whom the former precepts have
Sprinkled and taught, how to behave
Thy self in church; approach and taste
The churches mysticall repast.

Now Henry Vaughan also has a group of stanzas in this epigrammatic form,
under the title "Rules and Lessons"; they come exactly in the center of the
1650 volume, as though the advice there given formed the center of the
volume's devotional life. But Vaughan's advice bears no relation to any
ecclesiastical symbolism: it is as though the earthly church had vanished,
and man were left to work alone with God. Vaughan's rules and lessons
for the devout life lay down, in twenty-four stanzas, certain ways of
individual communion with God in every hour of the day, from early

morning, through the worldly work of midday, and on through night, until
the next day's awakening: one couplet gives the essence of the rules:

> A sweet *self-privacy* in a right soul
> Out-runs the Earth, and lines the utmost pole.

Man's duty is to cultivate the inner self, using as aids the two "books" that
we have seen in "Regeneration": the Book of Nature, and the Book of
Scripture, as Vaughan suggests in his advice for morning devotions:

> Walk with thy fellow-creatures: note the *hush*
> And *whispers* amongst them. There's not a *Spring*,
> Or *Leafe* but hath his *Morning-hymn*; Each *Bush*
> And *Oak* doth know *I AM*; canst thou not sing?
> > O leave thy Cares, and follies! go this way
> > And thou art sure to prosper all the day.
>
> Serve God before the world; let him not go
> Until thou hast a blessing, then resigne
> The whole unto him; and remember who
> Prevail'd by *wrestling* ere the *Sun* did *shine*.
> > Poure *Oyle* upon the *stones*, weep for thy sin,
> > Then journey on, and have an eie to heav'n.

Note the rich and curious complex of the Biblical and the natural: the
allusion to the bush from which Moses heard the voice of God; the extended
reference to the time when Jacob wrestled with the mysterious stranger
"until the breaking of the day," when he won the stranger's blessing, and
knew at last that he had "seen God face to face" (Genesis 32:24–30); and
the shorter allusion to the familiar scene of Jacob's vision, after which
"Jacob rose up early in the morning, and took the stone that he had put
for his pillows, and set it up for a pillar, and poured oil upon the top of
it" (Genesis 28:18).

The Bible, Nature, and the Self thus come together in a living harmony,
as in Vaughan's "Religion" (a poem that, typically, seems to take its rise
from Herbert's poem "Decay"):

> My God, when I walke in those groves,
> And leaves thy spirit doth still fan,
> I see in each shade that there growes
> An Angell talking with a man.

Under a *Juniper*, some house,
Or the coole *Mirtles* canopie,
Others beneath an *Oakes* greene boughs,
Or at some *fountaines* bubling Eye;
Here *Jacob* dreames, and wrestles; there
Elias by a Raven is fed,
Another time by th' Angell, where
He brings him water with his bread;
In *Abr'hams* Tent the winged guests
(O how familiar then was heaven!)
Eate, drinke, discourse, sit downe, and rest
Untill the Coole, and shady *Even*.

One must read several stanzas before it becomes clear that the "leaves" here are essentially the leaves of the Bible, where the self can learn to live intimately with God; but at the same time the vivid apprehension of natural life here may suggest that nature itself is still inspired by the divine presence.

The fact that Vaughan so often, in his best poems, seeks out these individual ways of communion with God does not mean that he chooses to neglect or ignore traditional devotions to the Eucharist. On the contrary, he is acutely aware of the importance of the eucharistic allusions in Herbert's *Temple* for he makes frequent efforts to follow Herbert's central mode of mental communion. But he does not often succeed, as we may see in four sizable poems in the 1650 volume that are devoted to eucharistic celebration. His poem "The Passion" is an extended effort to meditate upon the traditional themes, but the poem is wooden, labored, and forced in its effect. One may perhaps trace a cause of this failure to the fact that Vaughan does not visualize the Passion "as if he were present," in the ancient tradition of such meditations; instead he puts the whole occasion in the past. He does not memorialize the Passion as a present reality. In another poem, "Dressing," he performs a preparation for "Thy mysticall *Communion*," but the poem is so worried by contemporary doctrinal quarrels that it ends with a bitter attack on Puritan views, and not with any devotional presence. Another poem, entitled "The Holy Communion," begins by echoing the first two lines of George Herbert's eucharistic poem, "The Banquet": "Welcome sweet, and sacred feast; welcome life!" but Vaughan's poem immediately veers away from the feast to ponder the action of grace within the self, and the operation of God's creative power over the entire universe.

Vaughan's one and only success in this kind of poetic celebration comes significantly in his poem "The Sap," where he approaches the Eucharist indirectly, through a tale told to himself by his inmost self:

> Come sapless Blossom, creep not stil on Earth
>   Forgetting thy first birth;
> 'Tis not from dust, or if so, why dost thou
>   Thus cal and thirst for dew?
> It tends not thither, if it doth, why then
>   This growth and stretch for heav'n? . . .
> Who plac'd thee here, did something then Infuse
>   Which now can tel thee news.
> There is beyond the Stars an hil of myrrh
>   From which some drops fal here,
> On it the Prince of *Salem* sits, who deals
>   To thee thy secret meals . . .
> Yet liv'd he here sometimes, and bore for thee
>   A world of miserie . . .
> But going hence, and knowing wel what woes
>   Might his friends discompose,
> To shew what strange love he had to our good
>   He gave his sacred bloud
> By wil our sap, and Cordial; now in this
>   Lies such a heav'n of bliss,
> That, who but truly tasts it, no decay
>   Can touch him any way . . .

The whole poem, as several readers have pointed out, bears some resemblance to Herbert's poem "Peace," but the contrasts are more significant. In Herbert's poem the seeker after peace comes upon a "rev'rend good old man" who tells him the story of "a Prince of old" who "At Salem dwelt"—alluding to Christ under the figure of Melchizedek, who "brought forth bread and wine" (Genesis 14:18; Hebrews 7). Herbert's poem presents an allegory of the apostolic succession: the "good old man" offers the bread of life derived from the "twelve stalks of wheat" that sprang out of Christ's grave:

> Take of this grain, which in my garden grows,
>   And grows for you;
> Make bread of it: and that repose
>   And peace, which ev'ry where

With so much earnestnesse you do pursue,
Is onely there.

But Vaughan does not end his poem with such an echo of the ecclesiastical ritual; instead he closes with what appears to be yet another tribute to the poems of George Herbert, as he seems to echo here at least four of Herbert's eucharistic poems.

Then humbly take
This balm for souls that ake,
And one who drank it thus, assures that you
Shal find a Joy so true,
Such perfect Ease, and such a lively sense
Of grace against all sins,
That you'l Confess the Comfort such, as even
Brings to, and comes from Heaven.

But this comfort remains, in Vaughan's poetry a promise and a hope: his central channels of communion lie elsewhere, channels with a long and venerable history.

THE AUGUSTINIAN QUEST

Perhaps the discussion of Vaughan's characteristic triad, the Bible, Nature, and the Self, has already suggested the three "books" cultivated by the medieval Augustinians, and especially by St. Bonaventure: the Book of Scripture, the Book of Nature, and the Book of the Soul. The three books are, essentially, one: the revelation given in the Bible shows man how to read, first nature, and then his own soul. That is to say, in Augustinian terms: man, enlightened by Biblical revelation, can grasp the Vestiges, the "traces," of God in external nature; and from this knowledge he can then turn inward to find the Image of God within himself. It is an Image defaced by sin, but with its essential powers restored by the sacrifice of Christ. Man is not simply fallen: he is fallen and redeemed. It is man's responsibility, with the omnipresent help of grace, to clear and renew this Image, until it may become a true Similitude. But the renewal can never be wholly accomplished in this life: thus, as in "Regeneration," the poems that relate Vaughan's journey of the mind toward God end with a cry for help, a prayer for some momentary glimpse of perfection, as in his "Vanity of Spirit,"

where he performs a journey like that in Bonaventure's *Itinerarium*, first
searching through all Nature, and then finding at last within himself

> A peece of much antiquity
> With Hyerogliphicks quite dismembred,
> And broken letters scarce remembred.
> I tooke them up, and (much Joy'd,) went about
> T' unite those peeces, hoping to find out
> The mystery; but this neer done,
> That little light I had was gone:
> It griev'd me much. At last, said I,
> *Since in these veyls my Ecclips'd Eye*
> *May not approach thee, (for at night*
> *Who can have commerce with the light?)*
> *I'le disapparell, and to buy*
> *But one half glaunce, most gladly dye.*

In this effort to piece together broken letters scarce remembered, by the
aid of an interior light, Vaughan displays the essential action of that kind
of meditation which may be termed Augustinian. Its finest explanation is
still the one most easily available: it lies in the great climactic section of
Augustine's *Confessions*, the chapters of the tenth book (6-27) where he
marvels at and meditates upon the power of Memory. If we read and reread
these chapters, we may come to feel them acting more and more as a
commentary upon the poems of *Silex Scintillans*, 1650; and we may come
to understand more clearly the ways in which Vaughan's finest poetry draws
its strength from the great central tradition of Platonic Christianity.

The process of Augustinian meditation begins, as Vaughan's volume
of 1650 begins, with an effort to apprehend the meaning of an experience
of sudden illumination: *percussisti cor meum verbo tuo, et amavi te*—"Thou
hast strucken my heart with thy word, and therupon I loved thee. . . . What
now do I love, whenas I love thee?"

> not the beauty of any *corporall thing*, not the order of times; not
> the brightnesse of the *light*, which to behold, is so gladsome to
> our eyes: not the pleasant *melodies* of songs of all kinds; not the
> fragrant smell of flowers, and oyntments, and spices: not *Manna*
> and honey, nor any *fayre limbs* that are so acceptable to fleshly
> embracements.
> I love none of these things, whenas I love my God: and yet

> I love a certaine kinde of *light,* and a kind of *voyce,* and a kinde
> of *fragrancy,* and a kinde of *meat,* and a kind of *embracement.*
> Whenas I love my God; who is both the *light,* and the voyce,
> and the sweet *smell,* and the *meate,* and the *embracement* of my
> inner man: where that *light* shineth unto my soule, which no
> place can receive; that *voyce* soundeth, which time deprives me
> not of; and that fragrancy *smelleth,* which no wind scatters . . .
>   This is it which I love, when as I love my God.

Here is the spiritual landscape of the redeemed soul, described by Vaughan
in his "Regeneration," glimpsed throughout his volume in the many fresh
images from nature that he uses to relate the experience, and summed up
once again near the close of the volume, in the poem "Mount of Olives."
This title represents a traditional symbol of the soul's retirement to prayer
and meditation, here to recall, like Augustine, a moment which gave his
life its meaning:

> When first I saw true beauty, and thy Joys
> Active as light, and calm without all noise
> Shin'd on my soul, I felt through all my powr's
> Such a rich air of sweets, as Evening showrs
> Fand by a gentle gale Convey and breath
> On some parch'd bank, crown'd with a flowrie wreath;
> Odors, and Myrrh, and balm in one rich floud
> O'r-ran my heart, and spirited my bloud . . .
> I am so warm'd now by this glance on me,
> That, midst all storms I feel a Ray of thee;
> So have I known some beauteous *Paisage* rise
> In suddain flowres and arbours to my Eies,
> And in the depth and dead of winter bring
> To my Cold thoughts a lively sense of spring.

With the memory of such an experience within him, the Augustinian
seeker turns to question external nature, as in the *Confessions*:

> I askt the *Earth* and that answered me, *I am not it*; and whatsoever
> are in it, made the same confession. I asked the *Sea* and the *deepes,*
> and the *creeping things,* and they answered me, *We are not thy
> God, seeke above us.* . . . I asked the heavens, the Sunne and
> Moone, and Starres, Nor (say they) are wee the *God* whom thou
> seekest.
>
>   (10.6)

All creatures give for Augustine the same answer: "they cryed out with a loud voyce, *He made us*" (10.6). It is the questioning of nature that runs throughout Vaughan's poetry, where "Each *tree, herb, flowre* / Are shadows of his *wisedome*, and his Pow'r." Thus in "The Tempest" Vaughan prays that man "would hear / The world read to him!" and declares:

> all the vast expence
> In the Creation shed, and slav'd to sence
> makes up but lectures for his eie, and ear.

(lectures in the old medieval sense, readings of the book, with commentary and elucidation:)

> Sure, mighty love foreseeing the discent
>   Of this poor Creature, by a gracious art
>   Hid in these low things snares to gain his heart,
> And layd surprizes in each Element.
>
> All things here shew him heaven; *Waters* that fall
>   Chide, and fly up; *Mists* of corruptest fome
>   Quit their first beds & mount; trees, herbs, flowres, all
> Strive upwards stil, and point him the way home.

And the way home lies through an interior ascent, climbing upward and inward through the deepest regions of the human soul:

> I beg'd here long, and gron'd to know
> Who gave the Clouds so brave a bow,
> Who bent the spheres, and circled in
> Corruption with this glorious Ring,
> What is his name, and how I might
> Descry some part of his great light.
> I summon'd nature: peirc'd through all her store,
> Broke up some seales, which none had touch'd before,
> Her wombe, her bosome, and her head
> Where all her secrets lay a bed
> I rifled quite, and having past
> Through all the Creatures, came at last
> To search my selfe, where I did find
> Traces, and sounds of a strange kind.
>
>   ("Vanity of Spirit")

So Augustine turns to search within himself and comes "into these fields and spacious palaces of my *Memory*, where the treasures of innumerable *formes* brought into it from these things that have beene perceived by the *sences*, be hoarded up."

> And yet doe not the things themselves enter the *Memory*; onely the *Images* of the things perceived by the *Sences*, are ready there at hand, when ever the *Thoughts* will recall them. . . .
>
> For there have I in a readinesse, the heaven, the earth, the sea, and what-ever I can thinke upon in them. . . . There also meete I with my *selfe*, I recall my *selfe*, what, where, or when I have done a thing; and how I was affected when I did it. There be all what ever I remember, eyther upon mine owne experience, or others credit. Out of the same store doe I my selfe compare these and these likelyhoods of things; eyther of such as I have made experience of, or of such as I have barely beeleeved upon experience of some things that bee passed: and by these do I compare actions to *come*, their *events* and *hopes*: and upon all these againe doe I meditate, as if they were now present. . . .
>
> Great is this force of *memory*, excessive great, O my *God*: a large and an infinite roomthynes [*penetrale*: inner room], who can plummet the bottome of it? yet is this a *faculty* of mine, and belongs unto my nature: nor can I my self comprehend all that I am.
>
> (10.8)

Yet things even more wonderful lie beyond, as he probes ever and ever more deeply into the recesses of the memory. "Here also bee all these precepts of those *liberall Sciences* as yet unforgotten; coucht as it were further off in a more inward place" (10.9). These things could not have been conveyed within by the senses; how was it then that he came to accept these precepts as true?

> unlesse because they were already in my memory; though so farre off yet, and crowded so farre backeward as it were into certaine secret caves, that had they not beene drawne out by the advice of some other person, I had never perchance beene able so much as to have thought of them?
>
> (10.10)

Here the hint of the presence of something like innate ideas in the deep caves of the soul leads directly to a long account of what might be called the dramatic action of Augustinian meditation. It is an action significantly different from the method of meditation later set forth by Ignatius Loyola and his followers; for that later method shows the effects of medieval scholasticism, with its powerful emphasis upon the analytic understanding, and upon the Thomist principle that human knowledge is derived from sensory experience. Ignatian meditation is thus a precise, tightly articulated method, moving from the images that comprise the composition of place into the threefold sequence of the powers of the soul, memory, understanding, and will, and from there into the affections and resolutions of the aroused will. But in Augustinian meditation there is no such precise method; there is, rather, an intuitive groping back into regions of the soul that lie beyond sensory memories. The three powers of the soul are all used, but with an effect of simultaneous action, for with Augustine the aroused will is using the understanding to explore the memory, with the aim of apprehending more clearly and loving more fervently the ultimate source of the will's arousal.

> Wherfore we find, that to learne these things whose *Images* we
> *sucke* not *in* by our Sences, but perceive *within* by themselves,
> without Images, as they are; is nothing else, but by *meditating*
> to *gather together*, and by diligent *marking*, to take notice of
> those same *notions* which the *memory* did before contayne more
> scatteringly and confusedly.
>
> (10.11)

But these things are evasive and elusive; unless we engage in a continual act of re-collection, "they become so drowned againe, and so give us the slip, as it were, backe into such remote and privy lodgings, that I must be put againe unto new paines of meditation, for recovery of them to their former perfection . . . they must be *rallied* and drawne together againe, that they may bee knowne; that is to say, they must as it were be *collected* and *gathered together* from their dispersions: whence the word *cogitation* is derived" (10.11).

The seventeenth-century translator has been frequently rendering the word *cogitare* by the word *meditate*, thus providing his own account of Augustinian meditation: to draw together these things scattered in the memory. It would seem that poetry composed under the impulse of this kind of meditation would differ considerably in its structure from any poetry written under the impulse of the Ignatian mode of meditation—such as Donne's Holy Sonnets. The poetry of Augustinian meditation would perhaps tend to display an order akin to that which Pascal saw in the writings of Augustine: "Cet ordre consiste principalement à la digression sur chaque point qu 'on rapporte à la fin, pour la montrer toujours." That

Pensée may at least suggest the poetry of Vaughan, where the order often consists chiefly in what appear to be digressions, but are really exploratory sallies or *excursus* in the manner indicated by the following passage of the *Confessions*:

> Great is this power of Memory; a thing, O my God, to bee amazed at, a very profound and infinite multiplicity: and this thing is the minde, and this thing am I. . . . Behold, in those innumerable fields, and dennes, and caves of my memory, innumerably full of innumerable kinds of things, brought in, first, eyther by the *Images*, as all *bodies* are: secondly, or by the *presence* of the *things* themselves, as the *Arts* are: thirdly, or by certaine *notions* or *impressions*, as the *Affections* of the mind are . . . Thorow all these doe I runne and tumble [*discurro et volito*]; *myning* into them on this side, and on that side, so farre as ever I am able, but can finde no bottome. So great is the force of memory, so great is the force of this life of man, even whilest hee is mortall.
>
> (10.17)

Thus in many of Vaughan's best poems, as in "Regeneration," the characteristic movement is a "mining" of associations, a roving search over a certain field of imagery, a sinking inward upon the mind's resources, until all the evocative ramifications of the memory have been explored; and then the poem ends rather abruptly, with a cry for divine help, or some generalizing moral conclusion. The movement is seen at its best in "Corruption," where the mind lingers over the memories of the "early days" of Genesis:

> Sure, It was so. Man in those early days
>   Was not all stone, and Earth,
> He shin'd a little, and by those weak Rays
>   Had some glimpse of his birth.
> He saw Heaven o'r his head, and knew from whence
>   He came (condemned,) hither,
> And, as first Love draws strongest, so from hence
>   His mind sure progress'd thither.

Under the impulse of this love, Vaughan's mind progresses backward to recover the memory of Paradise:

> He sigh'd for *Eden*, and would often say
>   *Ah! what bright days were those?*
> Nor was Heav'n cold unto him; for each day

> The vally, or the Mountain
> Afforded visits, and still *Paradise* lay
>   In some green shade, or fountain.
> Angels lay *Leiger* here; Each Bush, and Cel,
>   Each Oke, and high-way knew them,
> Walk but the fields, or sit down at some *wel*,
>   And he was sure to view them.

Deep within all such associations lies that essential memory toward which Augustine's digressive and "tumbling" meditations have been subtly and inevitably leading: the memory of a "happy life," a "blessed life," *beata vita.*

> Is not an happy life the thing which all desire; and is there any man that some way or other desires it not? But where gate they the knowledge of it, that they are so desirous of it? where did they ever see it, that they are now so enamored of it? Truely we have it, but which way, I know not . . .
>
> How they come to know it, I cannot tell: and therefore have they it by, I know not, what secret notice; concerning which, in much doubt I am, whether it bee in the memory or no: which if it bee, then should wee sometimes have beene blessed heretofore. [*quia, si ibi est, iam beati fuimus aliquando; utrum singillatim omnes, an in illo homine, qui primus peccavit . . . non quaero nunc; sed quaero, utrum in memoria sit beata vita.*]
>
> But whether every man should have beene so happy as severally considered in himself, or as in the loynes of that man who first sinned . . . I now inquire not: but this I demaund, whether this blessed life bee in the memory, or no?
>
> (10.20)

It must be so, he concludes, for it is known to people in different languages, under different names: "And this could not bee, unlesse the thing it selfe expressed by this name, were still reserved in their memory." But what, precisely, is this thing?

> there is a ioy which is not granted unto the ungodly; but unto those onely which love thee for thine owne sake; whose ioy thy selfe art. And this is the blessed life, *to reioyce unto thee, concerning thee,* and *for thy sake*: this is the happy life, and there is no other.
>
> (10.22)

a happy life is a ioying in the truth: For this is a ioying in thee, who art the truth, O God my light, the health of my countenance, and my God. This is the blessed life that all desire . . . Where therefore gaynd they the knowledge of this happy life, but even there, where they learned the truth also? . . . which yet they would not love, were there not some notice of it remayning in their memory . . . For there is a dimme glimmering of light yet un-put-out, in men: let them walke, let them walke, that the darknesse overtake them not.

(10.23)

It is the central image of *Silex Scintillans*: the flash, the spark, the glance, the beam, the ray, the glimmering of light that comes from the memory of an ancient birthright of blessedness—*utrum singillatim omnes, an in illo homine, qui primus peccavit*: whether it be a memory of each man's individual life, or whether it be a memory of Adam's original happy life— that memory remains, yet un-put-out in men. The image is notable in the poem "Silence, and stealth of dayes," where this Augustinian motif is used in recalling the memory of a loved one who has died (evidently Vaughan's brother):

> As he that in some Caves thick damp
>   Lockt from the light,
> Fixeth a solitary lamp,
>   To brave the night
> And walking from his Sun, when past
>   That glim'ring Ray
> Cuts through the heavy mists in haste
>   back to his day,
> So o'r fled minutes I retreat
>   Unto that hour
> Which shew'd thee last, but did defeat
>   Thy light, and pow'r,
> I search, and rack my soul to see
>   Those beams again.

The "Sun" here is the "solitary lamp" within the cave of the speaker's soul: the memory of his loved one is the light within that serves as an interior sun. Sometimes, carried toward the things of the outer world, the speaker tends to walk away from that "glim'ring Ray," but, remembering that he has forgotten, he walks, he walks, in Augustine's way, back toward the memory of light. The beams of this loved one's soul, he comes to realize, now shine in heaven, and he cannot track them there; yet something bright remains within, as he concludes:

> Yet I have one *Pearle* by whose light
> All things I see,
> And in the heart of Earth, and night
> Find Heaven, and thee.

It is the indestructible Image of God, apprehending the presence of God in the memory: "Sure I am, that in it thou dwellest: even for this reason, that I have preserved the memory of thee, since the time that I first learnt thee: and for that I finde thee in my memory, whensoever I call thee to remembrance" (*Confessions*, 10.25).

So the memory of that inner presence runs throughout Vaughan's volume of 1650, as Vaughan struggles backward on his ancient journey of return toward the memory of blessedness. Sometimes the journey backward takes the form of "The Retreate" toward the days of the individual's childhood:

> Happy those early dayes! when I
> Shin'd in my Angell-infancy.
> Before I understood this place
> Appointed for my second race,
> Or taught my soul to fancy ought
> But a white, Celestiall thought,
> When yet I had not walkt above
> A mile, or two, from my first love,
> And looking back (at that short space,)
> Could see a glimpse of his bright-face;
> When on some *gilded Cloud*, or *flowre*
> My gazing soul would dwell an houre,
> And in those weaker glories spy
> Some shadows of eternity . . .
>   O how I long to travell back
> And tread again that ancient track!
> That I might once more reach that plaine,
> Where first I left my glorious traine,
> From whence th'Inlightned spirit sees
> That shady City of Palme trees;
> But (ah!) my soul with too much stay

> Is drunk, and staggers in the way.
> Some men a forward motion love,
> But I by backward steps would move,
> And when this dust falls to the urn
> In that state I came return.

The poem presents the essence of the *Phaedo*, as qualified and developed by Christian Platonism. Indeed, the *Phaedo* gives the closing image of the drunken man, in an important passage that suggests the kernel of this poem:

> And were we not saying long ago [asks Socrates] that the soul when using the body as an instrument of perception, that is to say, when using the sense of sight or hearing or some other sense . . . were we not saying that the soul too is then dragged by the body into the region of the changeable, and wanders and is confused; the world spins round her, and she is like a drunkard, when she touches change? . . .
>
> But when returning into herself she reflects, then she passes into the other world, the region of purity, and eternity, and immortality, and unchangeableness, which are her kindred.

In Vaughan, as in Augustine's *Confessions*, there is of course only the most guarded and glancing use of the Platonic doctrine of reminiscence: any hint of the soul's preexistence is used by Vaughan as a metaphor of innocence; and the whole poem is toward the close clearly transmuted into orthodox Christianity. The poet superimposes upon the Platonic suggestions the concept of the "Inlightned spirit" which catches a vision of the promised land, as did Moses when he "went up from the plains of Moab unto the mountain of Nebo . . . And the Lord shewed him all the land of Gilead . . . and all the land of Judah, unto the utmost sea, And the south, and the plain of the valley of Jericho, the city of palm trees" (Deuteronomy 34:1-3).

So the "early days" of the individual's childhood become one with the "early days" of the human race, as related in the Old Testament; and both together form powerful symbols of the memory of a happy life that lives, however glimmeringly, within the soul that has, through regeneration, come into yet a third state of childhood: the state of the "children of God" set forth in the eighth chapter of Romans.

Such is the paradise within, compounded of the Bible, of Nature, and of the Self, which lies at the heart of Vaughan's *Silex Scintillans*, 1650: a vision that results from the constant effort to remember the beauty of the sudden illumination described in his opening Latin confession. That Latin poem and its emblem of the Flashing Flint, with its image of the man within, are once more brought to mind by the well-known passage that concludes Augustine's sequence of meditations on the force of memory:

> Too late beganne I to love thee, O thou beauty both so ancient and so fresh, yea too too late came I to love thee. For behold, thou wert *within* mee, and I *out* of my selfe, where I made search for thee; deformed I, wooing these beautifull pieces of thy workmanship. . . . Thou *calledst*, and criedst unto mee, yea thou even brakest open my *deafenesse*. Thou discoveredst thy beames, and *shynedst* out unto mee, and didst chase away my blindnesse. Thou didst most *fragrantly blow* upon me, and I drew in my *breath* and panted after thee. I *tasted* thee, and now doe *hunger* and *thirst after thee*. Thou didst *touch* mee, and I even *burne* againe to enioy thy peace.
>
> (10.27)

RUTH NEVO

Marvell's "Songs of
Innocence and Experience"

There is a distinct strain of Epicureanism in Marvell's sensibility which would, on the face of it, seem to sort ill with either his Platonism or his Puritanism. But in fact, as his Puritanism is intimately related to his Platonism, so are both conditioned by the claims upon the resolved soul of a high Renaissance culture. The "Drop of Dew," emblematic companion piece to the "Dialogue between the Resolved Soul and Created Pleasure," illustrates the pattern of these relationships.

The equation dewdrop = soul, rose petal = earthly habitation, is never of course made explicit. There is thus scope for wit in the logical manipulation of the emblematic conceit to reveal layer upon layer of implication, all confirmatory of the original premise. The core of the poem's wit, however, lies in the description of the soul's attitude to its material mansion. The dewdrop is "careless" of its mansion new; it "slights" the purple flower; it "shuns" the sweet leaves; "every way it turns away," wound in that "coyest" of figures, the circle. The suggestion is, or would be, of a reluctant mistress in a conventional, mundane amorous affair, save that the real reason for the soul's cool reserve is implicit all the time: not, clearly, coquetry, but its recollection of the clear region where it was born. Both spheres of love are brought together and set off against each other in the concluding antithesis: "Here disdaining, there in Love"; while the true source and final goal of the soul's desire are brought out in the climax of the poem:

From *Studies in English Literature 1500–1900* 5, no. 1 (Winter 1965). ©1965 by William Marsh Rice University.

> But does, dissolving, run
> Into the glories of th' Almighty Sun.

The poem derives its symbolism from the familiar Platonic opposition between fountain of light and shadow of matter, but in the figure of the dewdrop resting upon the rose petal these opposites are brought aesthetically as close together as possible. And this is what is of particular interest in "On a Drop of Dew" and the "Dialogue between the Resolved Soul and Created Pleasure": the exact point of balance between the moral and aesthetic attitudes. Such a tension, and such accommodations as are implied by a free and full recognition of the delights of the senses point to a relationship with those schools of Renaissance Platonism which were anything but blind to the beauties of created nature. Indeed the whole doctrine of the Florentines, of the school of Ficino, at all events, may be regarded as an intricate and elaborate *Apologia pro voluptate sua*. The Epicurean element, issuing in the contention that joy is the true *summum bonum* and not in the least necessarily antithetical to virtue, is everywhere apparent. And in Ficino's *De Amore*, the Neoplatonic circle of love becomes an impassioned statement of the continuity between the glow and glory of God's countenance and the sensuous beauty of the world—an affirmation, in despite of the shadow in the cave, that "this whole earthly beauty . . . is the third face of God." There were, moreover, among Marvell's contemporaries, voluptuaries of nature who needed no apology. But if Marvell was well aware of, and interested in, the *libertin* view of sensuous innocence of a Saint-Amant, he was equally aware of that other great Renaissance tradition which presents the metamorphosis, East of Eden, of a paradise of peace, plenty, liberty, and creatural harmony, into a fool's paradise of sloth, gluttony, license, and animality. Frank Kermode has convincingly argued the case of "The Garden" as what he calls an anti-genre to the libertine celebration of sensuous pleasure. But an anti-genre is by definition a refutation of a case in its own terms. And so, in the solitary and passionless garden itself, the nectarine, the curious peach, and the vine crush their wine upon his mouth. If Marvell was profoundly a Puritan it was not disdain for the batteries of alluring sense that made him so. Yet on the other hand, if the soul is resolved because its love of the Form of the Good subsumes all loves of lower degrees, that Form is not always easy to determine let alone embrace. If the high priests of Neoplatonism could fall out upon the issue of *intellectus* versus *voluptas* as the ultimate felicity, how much more might a remote votary, who was, moreover and above all, an English Puritan. Therefore, when he encamps his mind in the safety and sensuous ease of the forest at Nun Appleton, it is not for a vision of the splendor of the divine light shining through bodies that he begs the courteous briars, but for an imitation of the passion of Christ (stanzas 75–77).

"The Dialogue between the Soul and the Body" culminates in an image which indicates the form in which these contraries impressed themselves most deeply upon his consciousness:

> Who but a Soul could have the wit
> To build me up for Sin so fit?
> So Architects do square and hew,
> Green Trees that in the Forest grew.
>
> (41–44)

Here, it seems, Marvell recognizes his own ambivalence; his stance, historical and personal, at a point where values deriving from a rich humanistic literary inheritance clash with values deriving from a puritan insistence on moral hierarchy and moral directedness, green Trees with purposeful Architects: in Arnold's formulation, spontaneity of consciousness with strictness of conscience. A parallel awareness, Jamesian almost in its duality, of elaborate civilisation as the matrix at once of the mind's highest refinements and basest sophistications provides the ground for a further series of ironic counterstatements, and the immediate motive for his inquiries into the nature of innocence and experience. It is this theme which gives to the body of his lyric verse its particular form and pressure; and it is the object of this paper to show how Marvell's version of pastoral—the genre most adapted to accommodate effects of counterpoint and the recognition of contraries—provide the essential bearings for an account of Marvell's imagination. One of these pastorals can best be understood, I believe, in the light of the treatise which has been called "the bible of the Platonic revival": the *Commentary on the Symposium* which was written, in fifteenth-century Florence, by another Platonising Christian of Epicurean sensibility.

That Marvell was possessed of an imagination at once delicate, profound and capable of the highest moral seriousness is too seldom acknowledged. What he is frequently acknowledged to possess is the accomplishment of a consummate literary stylist; one who himself, as it were, anonymous, makes expression effective by a subtle and flexible rendering of a variety of stylistic idioms, so that he can range from a dry spare wit, or burlesque, to intimations of great strangeness, mystery, or pathos. And this virtue too, is exhibited to perfection in the presentation of the personae which will be discussed here: the Nymph complaining for the death of her fawn, Daphnis and Chloe, and Damon the mower.

"The Nymph Complaining for the Death of Her Faun" has caused difficulty to critics struggling to reconcile the "trivial" story of a girl weeping for the death of a pet with their sense of a deeper, possibly allegorical, possibly religious significance. It is perhaps not surprising that the allegorists themselves are at cross-purposes, one submitting the "stricken Anglican Church," another the brooding love of the Church for the crucified Lamb. Professor LeComte has amusingly disposed of the latter view, suggested by Bradbrook and Thompson, and set the reader on the right zoological and iconographical track with a battery of cervid analogues, literary and mythological, from Pythagoras on. He settles finally for a Virgilian fawn—the pet stag of Sylvia, who had cared for it and tamed it— mortally wounded by Ascanius; with the stag of Artemis at Aulis, whose murder by Agamemnon was expiated by the sacrifice of Iphigenia, in the background. "The Nymph's name," he concludes, "if she has one, is Sylvia rather than Pietà." However, the choice of a Silvia for a Pietà solves no problems. As Karina Williamson instantly pointed out, there are still, among other difficulties, the insistent Canticles echoes to be accounted for, still a puzzling discrepancy between letter and figure, between slender fable and parabolic elaboration. Don Cameron Allen has recently brought his large learning to bear upon the literary antecedents and analogues to the poem's imagery of fawn and garden. He catalogues bejewelled deer of Ovidian story metamorphosed in the course of time into the *candida cerva* of Petrarch and the quarry, or the wounded lover himself, in French and English Renaissance poetry of the *chasse d' amour*; and apocalyptic deer of medieval bestiary and saint's legend which lead up to the romance emblem of the white deer as Christ. In the venerable ancestry of gardens he notes the classical gardens of the mind, and the medieval gardens of love; and the fine metaphorical economy achieved when the Nymph abandoned refers to her "garden" as a "wilderness."

What this controversy, and Allen's *summum*, in fact do is to bring right into the open, and amplify, a total rich context of allusion, classical and Christian, from which the poem derives its associations, variously for various readers. One can never know which or how many of these strings vibrate for a given reader; on the other hand, it is imperative to assume the possibility of some common ground among readers, some selection from the tentacular mass of association—or the meaning disintegrates under centrifugal force and we are left in a wilderness of echoes. But selection tends to follow one direction at the expense of another, and evokes immediate partisan refutation. Neither Renaissance prefiguration nor modern archetypology provides a solution without remainder. The literal actuality of the girl and her fawn are a stumbling block to typology. As a result, critics have tended to fall into two camps: they have looked askance at the poem as an example of baroque exuberance of decoration, or the "fatal facility of octosyllabics"; or they have embraced it as an example of Eliot's definition of metaphysical wit: the recognition, implicit in the expression of every experience, of other kinds of experience which are possible. But neither of these views offers any solution to the main problem of elucidation, and both leave Silvia and Pietà in a state of uneasy truce; while Professor Spitzer's recent attempt to have it both ways, with Niobe substituting for Silvia and a medieval substantiation miracle for Pieta leaves us with neither a comprehensible Nymph nor a coherent narrative.

Certainly solutions are not easy to come by. A packed punning phrase of Marvell himself may provide a hint for a direction. We have to do neither with decorative virtuosity nor with formal allegory, but with the "light Mosaick" of an arcane meaning. Read as "light mosaic" (with the "light" adjectival), the phrase points to that discipline of attentive submission to the internal relations set up within the poem itself which can protect against partisan selection. Read as "Light Mosaic" (with "Mosaic" adjectival) it points to the revelation of unity which occurs when letter and figure, background echoes and foreground emblems converge in a single illumination. The Neoplatonic version of an Aristotelian dictum throws light both on the pun and the poem:

> since the cognition of our minds has its origin in the senses, we
> would never know the goodness hidden away in the inner nature
> of things, nor desire it, unless we were led to it by its manifestation
> in external appearance.

D.C. Allen's statement of the poem's first-level, literal meaning—its external appearance—could hardly be bettered: "it is a sensitive treatment," he says, "of the loss of first love, a loss augmented by a virginal sense of deprivation and unfulfillment." But the poem comes fully into focus only when it can be seen as Marvell's most profound rendering of the theme of Innocence, as "Daphnis and Chloe" is his most sophisticated rendering of the theme of Experience, and Damon the Mower his most complete rendering of the theme of the destruction of Innocence by Experience, though this destruction is implicit in the "Nymph" as well. For Allen's gloss fails to take into account the division of the poem, and of the experience the poem relates, into three phases. The shooting of the fawn and its death constitute the frame of the poem and the occasion of the girl's complaint. But within the frame is set her recollection of the faithless lover whose gift the fawn was, and her memories of the solitary time when she drew comfort in her forlornness from the nimble, beautiful, and affectionate creature. It is worth noticing, further, that the specifically Christian overtones of the imagery occur with greatest density as the two themes of love and death reach a climax in emotional reflection—not when the fawn actually dies, but when the girl first grasps the fact that its life has been taken, and when she recreates the quality of her brief contentment.

The stereoscopic structure of the poem puts it in the tradition of complaint by dream-vision or memory-vision, of which Chaucer's *Booke of the Duchesse* is a complex paradigm, and Wordsworth's "Ode on the Intimations" a later variant. Such a form exists to give expression and definition to the poignant contingency of present grief and past happiness, rapt vision and return to the cold everyday. Hence the moment chosen for the beginning of the poem:

> The wanton Troopers riding by
> Have shot my Faun and it will dye.
> (1-2)

The poem, like others of the kind, develops its theme of present grief and past joy, doubly enacted through the faithless lover and the dying fawn, under the universal categories of spring and fall. It is from this pattern that Marvell's vision of innocence and experience emerges.

One might well begin by asking what precisely is involved in the "classical-landscape-with-figures" evocation of the title, more particularly since that evocation is sharply contradicted by the topicality of the "wanton Troopers" with *their* evocation of civil war and the Scottish covenanting army of 1640. Consonant with the latter evocation is the dramatic figure of the girl herself. For whatever affinities she may have with a Silvia or a Pietà or a Margaret of Goldengrove, her speech in *propria persona* is touched throughout with the deprecatory or diffident accents of a rustic simplicity. So that it is a seventeenth-century Country Maid who is appearing in the guise of a Nymph complaining for the death of her fawn and there is a *discordia concors* in this naming which is Marvell's deliberate exploitation of Renaissance philology. For from the Renaissance landscape the nymphs have not yet departed; nor have the nymphettes yet arrived. Nymphs are maidens *tout court*, young and beautiful and pastorally innocent; but they are also still the semi-divine nature spirits, half-tree half-woman, which inhabited the ancient woodlands; and their "fauns" are indeed fawns, seen pursued by tigers in the most humdrum natural way by Milton in 1667, but for Middleton in 1631, still the lustful offspring of satyrs, half-man half-beast. The poem's opening therefore, sets contrary images to work in the mind: in the background throng forms from that twilit region of the pagan imagination where the continuity deathless and fertile, between the human and the natural, is figured forth in the dual shapes of the creatures and in their ceaseless transformations and metamorphoses; while in the foreground spurred soldiers ride roughshod over a country at war. The two sets of images converge in an intuition of that which unites them: a state of innocence, defined and delimited by the juxtaposed terms of reference. The pagan world of the metamorphoses is innocent because it is without the knowledge of sin; there is as yet no breach between the soul of man and the erotic nature he shares with the rest of the creatures of generation and corruption. The love of the girl for the fawn is innocent because it is sealed off from the experience of sex, the beguiling and false love of the inconstant Silvio, the moral ambiguity and sophistication of whose frivolous *chasse d'amour* is parodied, or stylised, by the puns on Dear and Heart. By way of contrast the sensuous and affectionate nature of the girl meets that of the fawn in reciprocal delight and blessedness.

Now the moral of this little tale is certainly not that one should love fawns rather than swains. The Nymph, it is clear, is constantly aware that the creature is only a creature. It may even, if it lives long, prove as false as Silvio. Nor is it cherished as a reminder of a falsely idealised or sentimentalised love affair, but for its own sake, for its beauty and for its intrinsic spontaneous capacity for response:

> For it was full of sport; and light
> Of foot, and heart; and did invite,
> Me to its game: it seem'd to bless
> Itself in me. How could I less
> Than love it? O I cannot be
> Unkind t'a Beast that loveth me.
>
> (41–46)

The growth of her tenderness and affection for it is outlined with a delicate naturalism which is what has led Allen, no doubt, to remark that it represents for her the child she might have had if Silvio had not proved counterfeit. But it is much more than this. For the "pretty skipping grace" of the fawn changes from naturalistic in effect to visionary, and even apocalyptic, when we are told that

> it was nimbler much than Hindes;
> And trod, as on the four Winds.
> (69-70)

And this flicker of the transcendental is the prelude to the central and crucial garden passage.

What is stressed throughout is the beauty of the fawn as such, as living creature, not as either mere pet or as symbol for some complex abstraction. And this beauty has a genealogy. Whereas for Pico beauty consisted in the harmonizing of discords, Ficino finds the "beauty of bodies" in "activity, vivacity, and a certain grace shining in the body because of the infusion of its own idea." Marvell's description accords remarkably well with Ficino's analysis, and can be put another way: the fawn realises its own gentle and affectionate nature in its "pretty skipping grace" and this is what is seen and cherished by the girl, in that almost reflex impulse of the love which is, in the Platonic conception, desire awakened by beauty. The significance of this view of beauty is explained in the *Commentary*:

> Beauty is a kind of force or light shining from Him through everything . . . first through the Angelic Mind, second through the World-Soul and the rest of the souls, third through Nature, and fourth through Corporeal Matter. It fits the Mind with a system of Ideas; it fills the Soul with a series of concepts; it sows Nature with Seeds; and it provides Matter with Forms. In much the same way in fact, that the single light of the sun lights up four bodies, fire, air, water, earth, so the single light of God illuminates the Mind, Soul, Nature and Matter. Anyone seeing the light in these four elements sees a beam of the sun, and through this beam is directed to the perception of the supreme light of the sun itself. In the same way, whoever sees and loves the beauty in these four, . . . through this kind of glow sees and loves God Himself.

Thus, it is the glow of God in the beauty of the creature that the Nymph sees and loves in the fawn. The account of the nature and origin of love given by Carlo Marsuppini in the role of Agathon is, save in one point, exactly applicable:

> the holy Angelic Mind, because it is unimpeded by any attendance upon the body, reflects upon itself where it sees the face of God engraved within its own breast, and seeing it there, is struck with awe, and clings most avidly to it forever. The charm of that divine countenance we call beauty; the passion of the Angelic Mind seeking inwardly the face of God, we call love. O, that it might touch us also: but our soul, born into a condition in which it is encased by an earthly body, is inclined to the function of generation. Weighed down by this preoccupation, it neglects the treasure-house concealed within itself, and so, involved in an earthly body, it is servant to the needs of the body for a very long time. To this labor it accommodates sense indeed continuously, and reason also more often than it should. Hence it happens that though it does not notice the glow of that divine countenance shining forever within it until the body has at length become mature and the soul purged, it may with reflection contemplate the countenance of God revealed to our eyes in the handiwork of God. Through just this kind of contemplation we advance to beholding him who shines forth from within His handiwork.

It is a spark of his charm and of this love which has touched the Nymph so that what the fawn comes to be the object of is not surrogate passion but contemplative imagination; and what the fawn mediates is the transition from the power of generation yearning to procreate beauty in bodies to the power of intelligence yearning to recreate within itself, and know, the beauty of God.

But this transition comes precisely not to a "mature body and a purged soul." It is, in Marvell's vision, the gift of an innocent soul, awakened to passion but denied its carnal fulfillment, and in retreat in the garden of love, the garden enclosed. Now the garden enclosed is a traditional emblem of the soul, as roses and lilies are emblems of love and innocence, but the emblematic meanings are antecedent, preconditions, as it were, of the girl's present experience. The garden passage is an elaborate trope, the purpose of which is to give concrete representation to the acts of the soul in contemplation, when the mind withdraws into its happiness, and enjoys the pure images of its own conception.

> Among the beds of Lillyes, I
> Have sought it oft, where it should lye;
> Yet could not, till it self would rise,
> Find it, although before mine Eyes.
> For, in the flaxen Lillies shade,
> It like a bank of Lillies laid.
> Upon the Roses it would feed,
> Until its Lips ev'n seem'd to bleed:
>   (77–84)

As in the Song of Songs so here the poem enacts a meaning. What the emblems enact is given in the accumulating imagery of unity: the garden so overgrown with roses and lilies that dividing contours and paths characteristic of gardens are lost in the sameness of wilderness; the white fawn disappearing from view in the whiteness of the lily bed; the feeding upon roses; its lips bleeding roses; the transference of the roses to her lips by the imprinted kiss; and the culmination:

> had it liv'd long, it would have been
> Lillies without, Roses within.
>   (91–92)

This unity is of the loved object with its surroundings, in the girl's mind and through the girl's mind, since the garden is her mind. So that the garden becomes the state of blessedness that the soul enjoys when it shares with the object of its love a perfect unity of being. Contemplation of intelligible form is not set in division against satisfaction of sensual appetite, but knowing and enjoying are one, and thus ultimately, mind and nature are one. Ficino on the mind is again instructive:

> What, then does the intellect seek if not to transform all things into itself by depicting all things in the intellect according to the nature of the intellect? And what does the will strive to do if not to transform itself into all things by enjoying all things according to the nature of each? The former strives to bring it about that the universe, in a certain manner, should become intellect; the latter, that the will should become the universe. In both respects therefore . . . the effort of the soul is directed . . . toward this end: that the soul in its own way will become the whole universe.

Marvell's trope conveys with marvellous felicity this perfection of the soul in temporal terms. The springtime of the year when the fawn loves to disport itself in the garden is both the springtime of the girl's youth, and the perennial spring the contemplative mind creates by the transforming acts of its disinterested and joyous love. The matter of the fall, of experience, of knowledge, and especially of the knowledge of death, is reserved for the frame of the story. Hence the brute fact with which the poem opens:

> The wanton Troopers riding by
> have shot my Faun and it will dye.
>
> (1-2)

It is to be noted, and the girl's outburst draws attention to this, that there is no particular malice or purpose in the act which leads to the fawn's death. It is, precisely, a *wanton* act. A sheer unmotivated overflow of carnal energy, such as soldiers, poised for warfare, or youths (like Silvio) poised for lovemaking, may most generally be supposed to exhibit in the two most common contexts of the word. The nymph's reflections upon this wantonness, this unordained and arbitrary act, move in a rhetorical *gradatio* to draw out its furthest possible moral bearing. Marvell's mastery of decorum is important: the thought moves musingly, reflectively, giving the impression of spontaneous discovery, and is cast in the middle style, not heroic, yet not base, but capable of ranging from a colloquial realism in the girl's account of her feelings, to a measured generality in the moral apothegms. It is this stylistic rendering of simple speech which gives just the right pace and pitch to the movement of ideas: from the girl's prayer to heaven to forget the murder, to the idea of Heaven's register, of unjust "use" of the creatures, of creatural responsibility ("Else Men are made their Deodands"), of guilty hands which cannot be washed clean, of stain in the very grain of humanity, and so finally, to the idea of ultimate sin, Adam's in origin, Cain's in fact, for the expiation of which there is not such another in the world to offer. Whether "such another" be taken as an allusion to Iphigenia (in place of whom Artemis could have accepted a deer) or to Christ (whose death has transcended all pagan sacrifices and rendered them inoperative) dramatically in the context the line gives the speaking girl's sense of the inalienable uniqueness of the living creature which cannot be replaced, and whose death therefore cannot be expiated by a merely human ritualistic act.

The passage, then, registers an expansion of consciousness in the girl's mind—her inescapable knowledge of the mortal condition; a final knowledge which has been preceded, as she goes on immediately to relate, by her first experience of wantonness, of what may be meant by the fallen nature of man, in flight from which she took refuge in her solitude. With the shooting of the fawn, innocence dies as it encounters death, and there is reason in the nymph's statement that the loss of the fawn's warm life-blood wounds her to the heart.

The natural history of innocence which the poem relates then, is as follows: the native possession of youthful inexperience, it comes to self-consciousness at the very moment of its first painful contact with its anti-type Eros ("Thenceforth I set myself to play "). Withdrawn in the enclosed garden of the soul, in loving contemplation it conceives its ideal forms. Fragile as life itself, it is doomed, like all else in the world of the impermanent, to extinction. And it can find, as it weeps for its loss, and yearns for its perpetuation, in the forms of art its only immortality.

For the final stanzas of the poem replace the metamorphosis of fawn into roses and lilies, which is Marvell's metaphor for the contemplative imagination of innocence, with the metamorphosis of nymph into statue, which is his metaphor for the contemplative imagination of experience. The sweet joy of the garden has become the cold pain of the world, symbolised by the weeping stone:

> For I so truly thee bemoane,
> That I shall weep though I be Stone:
> Until my Tears, still dropping, wear
> My breast, themselves engraving there.
>
> (115–8)

Indeed tears, which flow so liberally in seventeenth-century poetry, are here given a special value. They are holy frankincense, wounded balsam, amber; perfume, preservative, and crystal offering at Diana's shrine. They are all these and more, for in this mellow myth of the soul's exile the birth of art is one with the loss of Eden.

> For I would have thine Image be
> White as I can, though not as Thee.
>
> (121–2)

Emphasis upon Marvell's "metaphysical manner" has distracted attention from his gift for narrative verse, where brevity and command of nuance provide for a proper pace without loss of implication. The first stanza of "Daphnis and Chloe" states the nature of the situation with the utmost precision and with the utmost cunning. The climactic position of "all his *Art*" gives to that crucial little word a maximum significance, over which plays a flicker of irony: what business have simple shepherds with "art"— in this context, evidently the art of seduction? The flicker is more than confirmed when the reader hears in stanza two that it is Nature, foe to sex, even her own, as opposed to Art, who teaches Chloe to be coy. Natural feminine modesty seems to be what is at issue. But this impression receives a rude jolt when a certain coarseness, a man-of-the-world matter of factness in the second half of the stanza ("But she neither knew t'enjoy Nor to let her Lover go") places the coyness of Chloe in the context of that kind of predatory sexual egoism which is a basic subject matter of the "naturalistic" Restoration dramatists.

Meantime, under the shadow of sudden parting, Chloe is prepared to let her niceness fall, a consummation, it is implied, which might well have been expected by a reflective mind supplied with the wisdom of the adage: "Sudden parting closer glews." Nature too, it seems, concurs; which puts Nature in a highly equivocal light. Only Daphnis, oddly enough, since he is well read in all the ways by which men their siege maintain (is it a slim volume of Ovid that our shepherd carries about in his pocket?), does not know this way of gaining the Fort. He is, it seems, simpler than we thought, and comes indeed, to the parting so full of his grief that he fails to see his advantage. When he does perceive the purport of his Chloe's tender remonstrances, he is plunged into a turmoil of conflicting emotions. Poor Daphnis is faced with a dilemma which might well unman the most phlegmatic of lovers. Chloe is his, now, for the taking; but alas, her kindness comes too late, and can be no more than the last delicious cup permitted to a condemned man. Rather than thus "enrich his fate," rather than, by gaining all, perforce lose all, Daphnis remains resolved upon a chaste farewell. Moreover, it occurs to him, vividly, if not by the soundest of logical transitions that

> Whilst this grief does thee disarm,
> All th'Enjoyment of our Love
> But the ravishment would prove
> Of a Body dead while warm.
> (73–76)

Gentler times, he therefore concludes, for Love are meant:

> Who for parting pleasure strain
> Gather Roses in the rain
> Wet themselves and spoil their Scent.
> (85–87)

Upon this elegiac note, Daphnis, a Leander in rhetorical resource, a Troilus in sensibility, draws himself up in resolute stoic self-possession to meet his Fate:

> Fate I come, as dark, as sad,
> As thy Malice could desire;
> Yet bring with me all the Fire
> That Love in his Torches had.
>
> (93–96)

Up to this point in the poem we have been offered a finely turned mock-pastoral—a miniature comedy of manners, in which the participants are regarded with an ironic tolerance. The last three stanzas, however, give the ironies of the poem so sharp a twist, provide a shift of perspective so sudden as to make "Daphnis and Chloe" no less than a *locus classicus* for Marvell's treatment of Innocence—through its opposite. Stanza 15 heralds the close. Its reference to one who after long prayer at last makes the sign to the Headsman and receives the parting stroke, is, with regard to what has gone before in the poem, no more than a rather ordinary pun. With reference to what comes after, it very effectively underlines the cynical opportunism of Daphnis:

> Last night he with Phlogis slept;
> This night for Dorinda kept;
> And but rid to take the Air.
>
> (102–4)

The suddenness with which the reader perceives the true purport of Daphnis's behavior is of course an essential part of the effect. That Chloe's imminent consent was not a spiritual embarrassment to a highly-emotional, ardent if foolish young posturer, but an obstacle to the carefully laid plans of a blasé young rake, longing to be rid of her, comes as an unmitigated shock. What had seemed the amusing sophistication of a simpleton now appears in its true colours as the glib talk of a cad. And yet—cad? He has his excuse, which is judicially acknowledged:

> For, according to the Lawes,
> Why did Chloe once refuse?
>
> (107–8)

The Lawes—of the game, of the art of love, take us back to the opening references to Nature. Benign Nature, it was there suggested, keeps Women coy, that is chaste. But the "state of nature" which the poem now reveals as rationalized in the Lawes is not merely a matter of catch-as-catch-can competitive sexual egoism, but the ultimate possible sophistication of human relationships. This is the Experience which stands in polar opposition to Innocence, as that is alternately presented and ironically undermined in the pastoral figures. It is an Experience which has its origin in the very fabric of erotic nature:

> Nature so her self does use
> To lay by her wonted state,
> Lest the World should separate;
> (13–15)

and its milieu in the adulterate and ambiguous motivations of sophisticated society. The beauty of the poem as an instance is that the reader is himself carried through an analogue of change from the state of not-knowing to the state of knowing, by the plot of the little fable of Innocence and Experience.

It is interesting to compare "Daphnis and Chloe" with its obverse, "Clorinda and Damon," and with the lovely and subtle "Mourning." Damon is the spokesman of conscious virtue, of deliberate "innocence," and Clorinda, apparently, the seductress. An ironic distance is achieved by the rapier speed of the duel of definitions, parallel to the touch of burlesque in the description of the disordered locks and rolling eyes of Daphnis in his distress.

> Seest thou that unfrequented Cave?
> D. That den? C. Love's shrine. D. But Virtue's
> Grave.
> (9–10)

But the pastoral imagery insists on radical innocence, and the meeting of the lovers in Pan's praises is taken up, in the chorus, into the grand harmonies of nature and the spheres, so that it seems Damon has been taught that there is a love which is peace as well as one which is rage.

In "Mourning" two contrary interpretations of Chlora's tears—one grounded in an innocent view of her truth and sincerity, the other in a cynical view of her selfish sophistication—are held in perfect equilibrium; the point upon which these two views balance is the exotic image of the Indian divers which cuts into the smooth polish of the *vers de société* with its vision of unfathomable mysteries within the depths of human impulse.

"Damon the Mower," unlike either "Daphnis and Chloe" or "Clorinda and Damon," is a pastoral elegy for the quiet mind disturbed radically by desire

unsatisfied. It is the culminating poem in the Mower series. The first stanza
of "The Mower's Song" is its epigraph:

> My mind was once the true survey
> Of all these Medows fresh and gay;
> And in the greenness of the Grass
> Did see its Hopes as in a Glass;

and the couplet which ends "The Mower to the Gloworms" its text:

> For She my Mind hath so displac'd
> That I shall never find my home.

The poem's fable reflects the history of consciousness in the mower Damon
under the disruptive influence of Juliana-Eros. Love in its aspect of burning
desire repulsed by icy disdain is familiar material for sonneteer and
pastoralist alike, and Marvell is basing his poem on both those traditions,
and on the metaphysic which lies behind both and from which they draw
their life:

> There are two kinds of love: one simple, the other reciprocal.
> Simple love occurs when the loved one does not return his lover's
> affections. In this case the lover is completely dead, for he neither
> lives in himself, . . . nor does he live in his loved one, since he
> is rejected by him.

The distinction of the poem lies in its mythopoeic treatment of the theme:
the dislocation of man from his universe by the impact of frustrated sexual
experience.

The poem turns upon its system of contrasts: heat-coolth; sensuous
gratification-sensual unease; unity-disunity; harmony-disharmony. The
most crucial of these is expressed with remarkable stylistic virtuosity in
Stanzas 1 and 6. In Stanza 6 erotic imagery defines the relationship of Damon
to nature before his mind was displaced from its proper home. Morn, noon,
and evening, the natural cycle of the day, follow the rhythm of the Mower's
labor in an amorous interchange:

> On me the Morn her dew distills
> Before her darling Daffadils.
> And, if at Noon my toil me heat,
> The Sun himself licks off my Sweat.
> While, going home, the Ev'ning sweet
> In cowslip-water bathes my feet.
>
> (43–48)

In Stanza 8 the mower "within" his scythe becomes emblematically identified with the sun itself. Against these, Stanza 1, the preamble to the Mower's song of disappointed passion, presents a painted scene "fit for his complaint" in which the relationship between the emotional and sensuous life of man and nature is external, mechanical, and perfunctory. The day was as fair as her fair eyes, as scorching as his care; his scythe as sharp as his sorrow, the grass as withered as his hopes. The prim little similitudes reflect a nature which has gone dead; a nature (consonant perhaps with the preoccupations of the Royal Society), from which the last flicker of animism has vanished. Language enacts the disorientation of the mower, burning with a heat the sun could never raise.

This heat, which maddens the Dog, which burns the life out of nature so that grasshoppers pipe and frogs dance no more but only, significantly, the Snake "glitters in its second skin," has its source not in the sun in its seasons but in "a higher Beauty . . . which burns the Fields and Mower both." This is the higher beauty of the "Definition of Love"—the object strange and high which is not merely seasonal, natural, but partakes of the act of the mind. And herein lies the irony. For here is no Conjunction of Mind, no magnanimous Despair which like Diotima, can teach better than Hope the proper and saving direction for love to take. Here is the sensual sting, chaos and disharmony and the alienation of nature whose caves, fountains, dews and cowslip water are inefficacious to quench the fires of the hot day, or hot desires. This is the hard lot of unrequited love which

> can [never] exist without an accompanying indignation. Who is not outraged by him who has taken his soul from him? For as liberty is the most pleasing of all conditions, so servitude is the most unbearable. And so you love and hate the beautiful at the same time; you hate them as thieves and homicides, you are forced to love and revere them as mirrors reflecting the heavenly light.

In this state labor is no longer rhythm, but pain, and the unfortunate lover experiences the leaden burden of the soul at odds with itself:

> But now I all the day complain,
> Joyning my Labour to my Pain;
> And with my Sythe cut down the Grass,
> Yet still my Grief is where it was:
>
> (67–70)

As an "Amphibium of Life and Death" his distraction culminates, ironically enough, in his accidentally self-inflicted wound, and his final comment: Natural wounds can be healed by nature's herbs; but for the invisible wound inflicted by Juliana's eyes there is no cure in nature save a reestablishment of the great rhythm of nature when the mower will become one with the grass again in death.

The fairy ring of his innocent and apollonian happiness has vanished. "Love's whole world," which, in *The Definition* and in the *Commentary*, is the image of a wholeness and a plenitude transcending the dichotomies of Innocence and Experience, is beyond the reach of the rustic mower. The breach in his nature can be healed only in the circle of death of which his and Death's scythe is the symbol.

Seventeenth-century circles are always instructive. "To His Coy Mistress" is Marvell's single poetic attempt to find the circle of perfect being in sexual experience itself. It is not perhaps by accident that the poem is by way of being a companion piece to Donne's "The Sunne Rising"; nor is it by chance that the former is a poem of courtship, the latter of consummation. For where Donne's poem affirms the sovereign self-sufficiency of the world of love, Marvell's, through the irony of its reservations admits a precarious subjectivity in the lover's dream of defiance. In the final line, Time, the category of Experience, preserves his dominion, and the rough strife is ultimately in vain. And indeed

> This will be the case, until the time comes when he [Prometheus] is carried back to that same place from which he received the fire, so that, just as he is now urged on to seek the whole by that one beam of celestial light, he will then be entirely filled with the whole light.

HARRY BERGER, JR.

Marvell's "Upon Appleton House": An Interpretation

In this great poem the speaker enacts the process of withdrawal and return in a manner which is traditional when seen against the background of pastoral literature, but unique when explored in terms of other contexts. One such context is that of the lyric or first-person poem, especially as we find it in the late Renaissance or trace it through the line of great English poets from Chaucer. Another context is the so-called "baroque" interest in theatricality and role-playing. For in this as in other poems, the experience about which Marvell writes is identical with the experience the speaker is at once uttering and undergoing, i.e., *what happens* in "Appleton House" happens *now* in and to Marvell while he "says" the poem. And the peculiar tone Marvell imparts to this experience, a tone at once engaged and detached, sensuous and wittily disengaged, is closely connected to the fact that Marvell is staging himself, trying on (and trying out) certain conventional "roles"— attitudes, gestures, habits of mind—and delighting in his play both as participant and audience.

But these contexts are too purely aesthetic to allow us to do justice to other aspects of the poem, and I should like to approach my interpretation by way of another and wider corridor, over the entry of which might be inscribed *"Thinking* reed and thinking *Reed."* The necessary interdependence of these contrary emphases is a commonplace. The great seventeenth-century versions of the commonplace are distinguished by their dialectical and disjunctive stresses, and by their concern with the antipathy of inside to outside, or of small to large. Thought is opposed to extension, time to

From *Southern Review* (Australia) 1, no. 4 (1965). ©1965 by Harry Berger, Jr. University of Adelaide, South Australia, 1965.

space, spirit as psyche to matter as nature, interpretation to phenomena, conscience to authority, soul to state, substance as inner force or process to substance as something static, bounded and extended. The traditional axis of hierarchy—*up* / *down*—tends to be replaced by, or defined in terms of, two other axes, *in* / *out* and *before* / *after*. Kant's systematic analysis of inner-temporal and outer-spatial intuitions concludes an epistemological revolution to which Marvell and Rembrandt and Milton contributed as much in their own way as did Descartes and Leibniz and Newton. In defining space as the order of coexistence. Leibniz discloses the new centre of value, the new criterion of reality, for "the order of coexistence" is a *temporal* concept, i.e., simultaneity.

"It is not from space," remarks Pascal's thinking reed, "that I must seek my dignity, but from the government of my thought. I shall have no more if I possess worlds. By space the universe encompasses and swallows me up like an atom; by thought I comprehend the world." Seventeenth-century statements of the Pauline and Augustinian tenet, "No one will be good who was not first of all wicked," differ from their early Christian predecessors in treating *conversio* as a moment or gesture which is externally a *contractio*, inwardly a *complicatio*. The more bounded man's nutshell the vaster his empire. An interesting corollary of this is the fact that during the seventeenth century political thought returns to the Platonic assumption that the state is less real, or on a lower plane of reality, than the soul.

From St. Paul to Dante the notion of mystical community and that of divinely ordered society prevailed to sustain belief in a socio-political environment whose spiritual substance was interinvolved with that of the souls which constituted it. The aggregate or macrocosm is no less real than the individual or microcosm which it "places," envelopes and defines; membership in a group is an intrinsic attribute of the soul. By the seventeenth century historical and intellectual changes across the whole field of European culture had operated in such a way as to produce a new set of assumptions. Basic to the historical consciousness of the time is the premise that civilization develops by moving toward increasingly smaller and more intricate units of order. *Now*, if not *then* (in medieval and classical times), the human condition tends toward structures which are primarily microcosmic or atomistic, so that the criterion of human culture must (now) be the extent to which it encourages or allows a high degree of intensive, rather than extensive, organization. One virtue of this premise, understood as a normative account of cultural history, is that it can explain the large-scale disorders of the century. If the world is not what it once was, if there is darkness and chaos all around us, it may well be the natural consequence of the fact that civilization develops toward an optimal state of inwardness and spirit. In the modern age, the seventeenth century, we should expect civil and religious disorder, since extensive forms of organization weaken as the locus of human order is displaced from outside to inside. Furthermore, since the individual soul is more real than any aggregate of souls, men can no longer be expected to form themselves naturally into hierarchies, classes, churches, etc.; macrocosmic structures must be artificially established. Hence the attention to Leviathan, to the social contract, to utopias, to the problems of international law.

The sense of the individual soul's burden and responsibility of course increases with the sense of its power and importance. Civil and social disorder become explicitly the extended forms of failure in the individual soul. Problems are to be confronted by withdrawal into the self. The dangers, stresses and complications of the great world are to be reproduced within the little world of soul, mind, garden, estate, etc. They are to be activated in play form and contained in experiments, poems, models, and miniatures. But withdrawal into the self is only fulfilled by return to the world; otherwise it becomes escape. A similar rationale governs what appears to be a contrary impulse—not withdrawal into the self but temporary self-expansion which, in like fashion, is fulfilled in new gestures of self-limitation.

Such an act of return and self-limitation is fulfilled in the brilliantly muted here-and-now of the last stanza of "The Garden":

> Of flow'rs and herbes this Dial new;
> Where from above the milder Sun
> Does through a fragrant Zodiack run;
> And, as it works, th'industrious Bee
> Computes its time as well as we.
> How could such sweet and wholsome Hours
> But reckon'd but with herbs and flow'rs!

We are to visualize a real garden surrounding the poet, a garden disentangled from the metaphoric, emblematic or fantastic pleasances which previously inhibited his mind. Now for the first time he frames his meditation in the actual occasion which prompted it; for the first time he conveys the impression of standing or strolling in a distictive garden whose objects he notices and indicates. The first person plural either draws him closer to us or suggests he is not alone. We are suddenly and belatedly made to feel that this scene supplies the full context which had been working on the poet from the beginning of his meditation. Obviously he is not trapped in a fantasy world as he was during the fifth stanza; he can leave *this* garden

any time he so desires, and the mood of the final couplet—"How *could* [they]
... Be reckon'd" not "How *can*"—suggests that he is placing the experience
behind him. This final stanza thus emphasizes the recreative and temporary
character of his poetic withdrawal, from the perspective of a mind which
has effectually disengaged itself, a mind in process of returning to the world,
all witty passion spent. The stanza is remarkable for its quality of
deanouement: the unknotting of thought leaves the poet relaxed yet alert
to his surroundings, in a mood quite different from the manic langour of
stanza five.

By this return, by framing himself *in* an actual garden which the poem
has transformed to a symbol (or a set of symbols), Marvell at once asserts
the true power of the mind and the proper use of gardens. The poetic act
is not an escape to free fantasy but an interpretation of the actual or real
existence which the mind does not create. The gesture of return is enacted
when the poet *re*-creates within his second world the image of the first; when
this occurs, the second world displays its greenness and is voluntarily
dissolved, sealed off, or transcended. This is the road not taken by the
complaining nymph, but taken in the "Drop of Dew," and it is a road which
Marvell concisely maps towards the end of "Fleckno":

> I, finding my self free,
> As one scap't strangely from Captivity,
> Have made the Chance be painted
> (167-9)

The perversion of this occurs when the mind collapses distinctions between
inside and outside: projecting its fantasies as realities, the expanding self
tyrannizes nature, seduces or forces it to a monstrous hybrid which is neither
art nor nature, mind nor world. "The Mower Against Gardens" complains
of "Luxurious Man" that his lustful curiosity led him to tamper directly
with the physical world and reduce it to an extension of his vice. There is
nothing wrong with being a gardener, but there is something wrong with
luxurious man who can only assert himself, like a gardener, by direct action
on external nature, who lacks the discipline to move inward, like a poet,
and act on the second nature.

As Marvell phrases it in "Upon Appleton House," Luxurious Man
"unto Caves the Quarries drew, / And Forrests did to Pastures hew." He
is bad enough as a gardener, worse as an architect who annihilates all that
is made to "Marble Crust,"

> Who of his great Design in pain
> Did for a Model vault his Brain,

> Whose Columnes should so high be rais'd
> To arch the Brows that on them gaz'd
>   (5-8)

As the ellipsis suggests, he no sooner conceives his *disegno interno* than it appears before his eyes, and a moment later the projected pomps of his airy brain become his house and world:

> Why should of all things Man unrul'd
> Such unproportion'd dwellings build?
> The beasts are by their Denns exprest:
> And Birds contrive and equal Nest;
> The low roof'd Tortoises do dwell
> In cases fit of Tortoise-shell:
> No Creature loves an empty space;
> Their Bodies measure out their Place.
>
> But He, superfluously spread,
> Demands more room alive than dead.
> And in his hollow Palace goes
> Where Winds as he themselves may lose.
> What need of all this Marble Crust
> T'impark the wanton Mote of Dust,
> That thinks by Breadth the World t'unite
> Though the first Builders fail'd in Height?
>   (9-24)

The whole problem is contained in that brilliant line, "The beasts are by their Denns exprest." The beast builds only for use—hiding and sleeping—not for beauty; like an Aristotelian envelope of place, his snug home expresses his shape, signifies the rudimentary nature of animal-withdrawal and therefore virtually squeezes him into the open. The tortoise secretes only enough of itself to produce what for man's body would supply a coffin. We must realize that though these stanzas offer man a genuine model of constraint and humility, the tone is subtly contaminated by the voice of the Body. Animals are neither constrained nor humble; "Nature" does their work for them, or impels them to secrete just enough shell, collect enough straw, or scoop out enough dirt for a bare fit. Were man to follow this model he could save himself a good deal of trouble and at the same time lay claim to simple and primitive, stoic and unaspiring virtues. But this bucolic rationalization will scarcely do. If we did not remember what happened to Spenser's contented rustic, Melibee, when the robbers got hold of him (*Faerie Queene* 6 11:18), Marvell reminds us later of the dangers of the "equal nest":

> Unhappy Birds! what does it boot
> To build below the Grasses Root;
> When Lowness is unsafe as Hight,
> And Chance o'retakes what scapeth spight?
> And now your Orphan Parents Call
> Sounds your untimely Funeral.
>
> (409–14)

Clearly if man is not able to be ex-pressed from his den, he will need not only stronger walls but more room, and this room will have to extend farther in as well as farther out. He learns from the animals, for example, not by imitating them literally and physically, but by converting the model to a mental figure, by reflecting on the differences and correcting the model as needed. That was no foxhole Fairfax built, and even if, as Don Cameron Allen remarks, it was relatively modest "by seventeenth-century aristocratic standards," it was elegant enough to impress an early eighteenth-century (perhaps middle-class) antiquarian. The scale of the human house is determined by its relation to its owner's mind and soul, not his body:

> But all things are composed here
> Like Nature, orderly and near:
> In which we the Dimensions find
> Of what more sober Age and Mind
> When larger sized Men did stoop
> To enter at a narrow loop;
> As practicing in doors so strait,
> To strain themselves through *Heavens Gate*.
>
> (25–32)

> Yet thus the laden House does sweat,
> And scarce indures the *Master* great:
> But where he comes the swelling Hall
> Stirs, and the *Square* grows *Spherical*;
> More by his *Magnitude* distrest,
> Then he is by its straitness prest:
> And too officiously it slights
> That in it self which him delights.
>
> (49–56)

It is the inner man who measures out his place or "secretes" his shell, and it is in terms of the inner man that the shell is at once protective, functional and expressive—to use Sir Henry Wotton's more Vitruvian terms, firm, commodious and delightful (*Elements of Architecture*, 1624). But since this is so, cannot a poem also serve these needs, and does poetry not in fact fulfil them more completely? There is a shadow of double reference in lines 49–50 above, and more than a shadow in the sixth stanza:

> *Humility* alone designs
> Those short but admirable Lines,
> By which, ungirt and unconstrain'd
> Things greater are in less contain'd.
> Let others vainly strive t'immure
> The *Circle* in the *Quadrature*!
> These *holy Mathematicks* can
> In ev'ry Figure equal Man.
>
> (41-48)

If house and garden express their owner, it takes a poet to say so and to articulate the inner connections. Only in Marvell's verbal world is the physical ambience created by Fairfax rendered fully transparent as a gesture of the human spirit. The poem is a more inward *and* a more expressive medium than house and garden; the inner man literally *speaks* the poem, while house and garden bespeak their owner in a more metaphoric, less immediate way. Not until Marvell's mind has played over and penetrated the possibilities suggested by the house does every architectural figure equal Man:

> So Honour better Lowness bears,
> Then That unwonted Greatness wears.
> Height with a certain Grace does bend,
> But low Things clownishly ascend.
> And yet what needs there here Excuse,
> Where ev'ry Thing does answer Use?
> Where neatness nothing can condemn,
> Nor Pride invent what to contemn?
>
> A Stately *Frontispiece of Poor*
> Adorns without the open Door:
> Nor less the Rooms within commends

> Daily new *Furniture of Friends*.
> The House was built upon the Place
> Only as for a *Mark of Grace*;
> And for an *Inn* to entertain
> Its *Lord* a while, but not remain.
>   (57–72)

By the final couplet, even *Inn* assumes its original prepositional force and the house is contained in the soul.

"Upon Appleton House" is surely one of the most remarkable poems of the seventeenth or any century, breath-taking in the virtuosity of its detail but much more impressive in the way Marvell sustains and modulates the lyric experience of withdrawal and return. This experience, and not the house, is Marvell's real subject and it is also the real model of all the themes on which he discourses. I think it is useful at this point to introduce a general description of this experience by Ortega y Gasset since his comparison of man to animals is similar to Marvell's and perhaps, from the zoological standpoint, equally out of date. Ortega remarks that the ape

> cannot take a stand within itself. Hence when things cease to threaten it or caress it; when they give it a holiday; . . . the poor animal has virtually to cease to exist, that is: it goes to sleep. Hence the enormous capacity for somnolence which the animal exhibits, the infrahuman torpor which primitive man continues in part. . . . if man enjoys this privilege of temporarily freeing himself from things and the power to enter into himself and there rest, it is because of his effort, his toil, and his ideas he has succeeded in retrieving something from things, in transforming them, and creating around himself a margin of security which is always limited but always or almost always increasing. This specifically human creation is technics. Thanks to it, and in proportion to its progress, man can take his stand within himself. But conversely, man as a technician is able to modify his environment to his own convenience, because, seizing every moment of rest which things allow him, he uses it to enter into himself and form ideas about this world, . . . to form a plan of attack against his circumstances, in short, to create an inner world for himself. From this inner world he emerges and returns to the outer, but he returns as protagonist.

This is of course, a virtual description of what Marvell does during his poem, also a description of what he counsels Fairfax to do, although, as we shall see, the poet's retirement differs considerably from the lord's.

Appleton House provides Marvell with an external margin of security, but it becomes questionable whether the inner world he creates is one which could be shared or appreciated by Fairfax or any other upstanding man of affairs. The general's retirement is conceived merely as a temporary contraction of interest to the more manageable and orderly, the more exemplary, compass of his domestic microcosm. But Marvell's retirement turns into what can only be called imaginary *implosion*. He expands inwardly as he moves farther away from the house—through garden, meadow, and wood. With the ocean and forest of his mind he creates far other worlds, perspectives in perspectives. His imagination does for him what "Multiplying Glasses" were doing at about the same time for Robert Hooke:

> By this means the Heavens are open'd and a vast number of new Stars, and new Motions, and new Productions appear in them, to which all the antient Astronomers were utterly Strangers. By this the Earth it self, which lyes so neer us, under our feet, shews quite a new thing to us, and in every little particle of its matter, we now behold almost as great a variety of Creatures. as we were able before to reckon up in the whole Universe it self.

But Marvell's experiments are less innocent and not marked by the scientific ideal of "objectivity." His *indecus* behaviour in the forest mocks the very order—sober, constrained and neat—which protects him from the world. By the time he has assumed the role of "easie Philosopher" (561) conversing with birds, his retreat is scarcely motivated by concern "for some universal good" (741). He sees himself as a grotesque lord of misrule: "Under this *antick Cope* I move / Like some great *Prelate of the Grove*" (591-2), a primitive and comical celebrant to and through whom Nature unmediated speaks. His special immunity—that of priest, fool, poet or madman—gives him licence to war on the World, and one feels that Marvell evoking this particular mood would not exclude his equestrian lord and beautiful pupil from the World:

> How safe, methinks, and strong, behind
> These Trees have I incamp'd my Mind;
> Where Beauty, aiming at the Heart,
> Bends in some Tree its useless Dart;
> And where the World no certain Shot

> Can make, or me it toucheth not.
> But I on it securely play,
> And gaul its Horseman all the Day.
>   (601-8)

Such recklessness would seem in fact the point of the joke, the climax of
the imaginative orgy in which a moment later the poet offers himself as
a willing prisoner or sacrifice to the woods, a sylvan Christ shading off into
Bacchus and Merlin.

Having thus "privately" let go, he can move back, refreshed, toward
society, and he does this by imagining another person, one who stands for
the very order he has just upset—Miss Maria, the embodiment of rules,
external constraint, domestic and social decorum. In effect his mind
constrains itself by projecting the image of the censor; therefore Maria is
clearly a pattern or Idea, as Allen has acutely observed. The mind's holiday
is over and the orderly pattern, temporily denied and mocked, appears more
sympathetic after the poet's anarchic release. In her character and
appearance, in her relations to Fairfax and to the poet, Maria embodies all
the attachments by which Marvell is bound to his fellow men, and she
embodies them as something fresh and new, something now acceptable and
even attractive. Maria turns the poet's wild nature into an aristocratic
menage and her image is thus anticipated by two stanzas which indicate
how the poetic orgy has refreshed him and prepared him to face the world:

> For now the Waves are fal'n and dry'd,
> And now the Meadows fresher dy'd;
> Whose Grass, with moister colour dasht,
> Seems as green Silks but newly washt.
> No *Serpent* new nor *Crocodile*
> Remains behind our little *Nile*;
> Unless it self you will mistake,
> Among these Meads the only Snake.
>
> See in what wanton harmless folds
> It ev'ry where the Meadow holds;
> And its yet muddy back doth lick,
> Till as a *Chrystal Mirrour* slick;
> Where all things gaze themselves, and doubt
> If they be in it or without.
> And for his shade which therein shines,
> *Narcissus* like, the *Sun* too pines.
>   (625-40)

Like the seventh and eighth stanzas of "The Garden," the last four lines characterize the poet's previous behavior in an epitome and thus remove it to a distance. His exotic world fades, the cosmos shrinks to a familiar local scene, his orgy has not been a new Fall but a playful swim in the mind's ocean, and he can now revest himself with social thoughts. The final stanza of solitude may faintly suggest that he is turning in mystic fashion into the landscape, but it also presents us with the most familiar and local of images:

> Oh what a Pleasure 'tis to hedge
> My temples here with heavy sedge;
> Abandoning my lazy Side,
> Stretcht as a Bank unto the Tide;
> Or to suspend my sliding Foot
> On the Osiers undermined Root,
> And in its Branches tough to hang,
> While at my Lines the Fishes twang!
> (641–8)

Both the pose and the implied "unity with nature" convey the new sense of ease and relaxation. Communion with the depths is at once expressed and attenuated in the amused figure of the final line. Nobody, the tone implies, nobody would suggest what cosmic mayhem has been let loose inside the mind of this lazy angler—unless, unlike Miss Maria, he had just read the previous *Lines*. Nobody, that is, except Sir Isaak Walton, who knew that angling was like poetry, that it was at once comtemplative and active as well as "honest, ingenuous, quiet and harmless," that it was not only an escape from "the press of people and business and the cares of the world" but also a source of revelation:

> the great Naturalist Pliny says, "That nature's great and wonderful power is more demonstrated in the sea than on the land" . . . doubtless this made the Prophet David say, "They that occupy themselves in deep waters, see the wonderful works of God"; indeed such wonders and pleasures too as the land affords not.

But there is a time for all things, especially since the different sides of the mind see the world in different ways, so that the right side might disapprove of what the left side was doing:

> But now away my Hooks, my Quills,
> And Angles, idle Utensils.
> The *young Maria* walks to night:

> Hide trifling Youth thy Pleasures slight.
> 'Twere shame that such judicious Eyes
> Should with such Toyes a Man surprize;
> *She* that already is the *Law*
> Of all her *Sex*, her *Ages Aw.*
>
> See how loose Nature, in respect
> To her, it self doth recollect
>
> (649–58)

The different sides of the mind to which Marvell gives play during the poem are concisely if perplexingly focused in the final three stanzas. After his praise of Maria he turns and apostrophizes the estate, exhorting it to follow her example and be the best in its class:

> For you *Thessalian Tempe's Seat*
> Shall now be scorn'd as obsolete;
> *Aranjuez, as less,* disdain'd;
> The *Bel-Retiro* as constrain'd;
> But name not the *Idalian Grove,*
> For 'twas the Seat of wanton Love;
> Much less the Dead's *Elysian Fields,*
> Yet nor to them your Beauty yields.
>
> 'Tis not, what once it was, the *World;*
> But a rude heap together hurl'd;
> All negligently overthrown,
> Gulfes, Deserts, Precipices, Stone.
> Your lesser *World* contains the same.
> But in more decent Order tame;
> *You Heaven's Center, Nature's Lap.*
> *And Paradice's only Map.*
>
> But now the *Salmon-Fisher's* moist
> Their *Leathern Boats* begin to hoist;
> And, like *Antipodes* in Shoes,
> Have shod their *Heads* in their *Canoos.*
> How *Tortoise like,* but not so slow,
> These rational *Amphibii* go?
> Let's in: for the dark *Hemisphere*
> Does now like one of them appear.
>
> (753–66)

Antipodes has two different meanings which are actualized in the poem: (1) the same form but upside down, as when one sees one's reflection in the surface of the water; here, it may be observed, the surface conceals the depths in functioning as a mirror; (2) opposite in form, as when one diving through that watery mirror with its "orderly and near" images comes on a strange undersea wilderness—"such wonders and pleasures too as the land affords not," or, as William Empson, who might have been paraphrasing Walton, put it, "all land-beasts have their sea-beasts, but the sea also has the kraken; in the depths as well as the transcendence of the mind are things stranger than all the kinds of the world." As a *rational* amphibian, man lives both in the "land" which surrounds him and in "the Mind that Ocean" which he contains; as a *rational* amphibian, he lives a double life within the mind, oscillating between extremes of extravagance and constraint, wilderness and neatness, nature and art, fantasy and science, contemplation and action, poetry and politics, passionate surrender and rational control, delicious solitude and social demand, self-expansion and self-limitation, love of anarchy and love of law.

These extremes are problematically related by the ambiguous syntax connecting lines 761 and 762: (1) "The world is no longer the rude heap it once was." (2) "The world is no longer what it once was; now it is a rude heap and the paradisaic order of a Former Age is all negligently overthrown." The previous stanza, with its suggestion that the latest is the best, would opt for Baconian optimism, while the political chaos of Marvell's time would encourage chiliastic pessimism. Does civilization gradually improve nature and move through myth and history toward an apex in Appleton House, and is Appleton House a microcosm of a developed culture which is the Daughter of Time? Or is Appleton House a small and precious exception to the work of *tempus edax*, an oasis in the Modern Wilderness? The paradox is only apparent, for each is a familiar extreme, a one-sided response of the mind, and the solution lies in the two meanings of *contains*: in its "more decent Order tame" the lesser world possesses and controls the disordered greater world.

As an escape from contemporary chaos, the lesser world of Appleton House chastens down the wilderness, brings time to a stand-still (*"Admiring Nature* does benum" [672]) and revives the disciplined ideal of an older, purer age when Nature mirrored Reason. One thinks of Romans, especially Virgilian, appeals to the ancient Italian *frugalitas*, not only because of the general tone and the specific reference to Romulus and "his Bee-like Cell" (40) but also because of a distinct echo of *Aeneid* VIII, 362 in which Evander describes how Hercules stooped to enter his humble palace:

> 'haec,' inquit, 'limina victor
> Alcides subiit, haec illum regia cepit.
> aude, hospes, contemnere opes et te quoque dignum
> finge deo, rebusque veni non asper egenis.'
> dixit et angusti subter fastigia tecti
> ingentem Aenean duxit

> that more sober Age and Mind,
> When larger sized men did stoop
> To enter at a narrow loop . . .

> Things greater are in less contain'd . . .

> Yet thus the laden House does sweat
> And scarce indures the *Master* great.

Restraint was natural to uncorrupted men who did not therefore require great space or *opes*: recognizing his own gulfs, his stony and desert places, he bound them in. It was through slackening that the lesser world spread superfluously into the greater, drew the quarries to caves and expressed its unruled pride in rude heaps of marble crust. In Marvell's hands this arcadian commonplace, however stoic, fits easily with the Mower's epicurean argument, *e.g.*:

> Nature here hath been so free
> As if she said leave this to me.
> Art would more neatly have defac'd
> What she had laid so sweetly wast;
> In fragrant Gardens. shaddy Woods,
> Deep Meadows, and transparent Floods.
>   (75-80)

It is in this context that *Antipodes* means mirror-image: nature mirrors reason, earth mirrors heaven, the estate gratefully gives back to Maria "that wondrous Beauty" which "first she on them spent" (689-702).

If, then, the estate is viewed as a restoration of the Former Age, the poetic perspective which so views it may be an even more complete withdrawal from contemporary darkness. Appleton House is at most a garden wilderness, like that of the complaining nymph. The poem describing it describes a Reason which has already been externalized as Nature, and this mirroring surface screens out the other kind of antipodes which lies "behind" or "beneath" it. Of the three scenes which Marvell stages in the meadow (385-417, 418-40, 441-64), the first two conclude the "bloody" lessons of history with funeral-images, but the third wipes these out: it "brings / A new and empty Face of things" (441-2), makes a passing reference to the Levellers, and shifts to the more distant perspectives of art and science; the immediate problems are dissolved in microscopic and telescopic vistas; here disorder is flea-like and order cosmic. The green-world attitude is implicit in the fact that history, insofar as it is admitted, is negative.

This reading of lines 761-2 is counterbalanced by the other: "The world is no longer the rude heap it once was." Civilization is ideally a gradual refinement of matter by mind and flesh by spirit; as human organization increases it should, therefore, ideally contract into forms which are less extensive, more complex and intricately structured, capable of giving play to a richer and broader variety of experience within a smaller or finer expressive compass. But this means that a microcosm is more than merely a miniature of whatever macrocosm it reflects. Its very compression and inwardness, the degree to which it transforms what it reflects into the higher order of spirit or mind or pysche, makes it by definition superior to the macrocosm. Here, "Gulfes, Deserts, Precipices, Stone," would seem to suggest primative and barbaric nature rather than moral chaos; the suggestions of physical extension and force are more literal in such a context, and we are clearly in the presence of what will later be called the sublime; the relation of lesser to greater world is not so much that of domestic order to political chaos, or of individual to state, but that of civilized man to unimproved nature. The cataclysmic and irrational energies of raw nature are contained as vestiges in the mind; they are the underwater antipodes of that reason which is reflected by nature's cultivated surfaces, of that restraining art through which domestic and social orders are stabilized. When these titanic energies erupt, when they are solicited or succumbed to, they produce aesthetic and ethical *indecencies*; lust and pride with their various weapons and structures, war and violence, civil and religious cataclysm, division in friendship, family, sect, and state.

The obvious way to contain these energies is to recognize them for what they are and discharge them in play. Rather than allow eccentric, anti-social, anarchic, Dionysiac, etc., impulses to explode in martial or sexual excess, in socio-political or autoerotic irresponsibility, Marvell practises poetic implosion. As we have seen, he does not abandon himself to the wild and primitive antipodes of reason; he conjures them up, not as immediate orgy or fantasy but as phases of a formal poetic meditation. Where else but in a

poem can the mind creatively let go, annihilate all that's made in what
William James has called "the exuberant excess," the "quest for the superfluous," which distinguishes man from brutes? "Prune down his extravagance," James said, "sober him, and you undo him." For Marvell, however,
man must return to sobriety and to the limits imposed by his own reason,
the limits symbolized in "Appleton House" by the patron and his family.
One prunes down extravagance homeopathically, by being extravagant, and
one justifies the restraint and decency of reason by the same technique. In
this the estate and the poem are differently inflected, the former toward order
the latter toward energy, and they thus serve the two sides of the mind in a
dialectical manner. Like Fairfax's flowery fort, the precipices and gulfs of
the estate are scaled down; they are physically contracted to the dimension
of toy models, but not yet expanded by imagination. Using these physical
models as starting-points, Marvell projects his own vaster and less decent
allusions to chaos:

> And now to the Abbyss I pass
> Of that unfathomable Grass,
> Where Men like Grashoppers appear,
> But Grashoppers are Gyants there:
> They, in there squeking Laugh, contemn
> Us as we walk more low then them:
> And, from the Precipices tall
> Of the green spir's, to us do call.
>
> To see men through this Meadow Dive,
> We wonder how they rise alive.
>
> (369-78)

The progress of implosion in the poem is straightforward: it moves
from world to self, from similes based in observation of landscape to metaphors expressing participation, from Apollonian distance to Dionysiac
involvement. The distance, however, is sustained in relation to the greater
world and its warfare, while the involvement is in the unreal world of the
poet's own making. The most sinister echoes occur in the first meadow scene,
as noted above, when Marvell converts the tawny Mowers to Israelites and
then, by implication, to soldiers who massacre the grass and murder defence-
less birds. Because the bird is immediately made an emblem—"Lowness is
unsafe as Hight"—the transition to the second meadow scene suggests an
actual image of the effects of the Civil War:

> Or sooner hatch or higher build:
> The Mower now commands the Field;
> In whose new Traverse seemeth wrough
> A Camp of Battail newly fought:
> Where, as the Meads with Hay, the Plain
> Lyes quilted ore with Bodies slain:
> The Women that with forks it fling,
> Do represent the Pillaging.
>
> (417-24)

For a moment we feel the extraordinary pressures of the time, the naturally peaceful countryside becomes a scene of carnage. But only for a moment: Marvell turns the image to a happy rural conclusion, separates the heroic from the rustic and, even while keeping the reminders of war, removes them to a distance:

> And now the careless Victors play,
> Dancing the Triumphs of the Hay;
> Where every Mowers wholesome Heat
> Smells like *Alexanders sweat.*
> Their Females fragrant as the Mead
> Which they in *Fairy Circles* tread:
> When at their Dances End they kiss,
> Their new-made Hay not sweeter is.
>
> When after this 'tis pil'd in Cocks,
> Like a calm Sea it shews the Rocks:
> We wondring in the River near
> How Boats among them safely steer.
> Or, like the *Desert Memphis Sand,*
> Short *Pyramids* of Hay do stand.
> And such the *Roman Camps* do rise
> In Hills for Soldiers Obsequies.
>
> (425-40)

The playfulness is reasserted because the two sides of the analogies spring apart; the pastoral scene is felt as a contrast to the ancient wonders and horrors of the great world. The powerful and dynamic ellipsis of the final couplet, together with the local tumuli to which it alludes, point toward the cynic's view of history: "Imperious Caesar, dead and turned to clay, / Might

stop a hole to keep the wind away." The contrast suggests how much of the
great world the lesser world of Appleton House excludes. The lessons of
history are scarcely evident in that timeless bucolic retreat until the poet
warily projects them there; the landscape knows only the recurrent rhythms,
the slow and certain English seasons, of an order in which "nature" and
"society" are harmoniously fused. In so secure a retreat, the mind may safely
make chaos come again without excessive risk. The only risk derives from
those "creative obstacles" inherent in the very forms which offer the margin
of security: the patrons and their vitrified nature, the poet's prudence and
his verse.

From this oblique meditation on man as the destroyer of nature and
man, Marvell withdraws in thought to a scene more innocent, creative, and
artificial:

> A levell'd space, as smooth and plain,
> As Clothes for *Lilly* strecht to stain.
> The World when first created sure
> Was such a Table rase and pure.
> Or rather such is the *Toril*
> Ere the Bulls enter at Madril.
>
> (442–8)

Though man's bloodlust is chastened to game and art in the "more decent
Order tame" of the bullring, it is still present, and I think the modulation
through the Levellers (449–50) to the villagers who "in common chase /
Their Cattle, which it closer rase" (451–2) is meant to refer this sophisticated
form of violence to the utopian or communistic aims of the Levellers. This
violence, as Marvell knew, would reduce us all to cattle—a "Universal
Heard"—and the strategy he himself immediately adopts is precisely the
contrary: where utopians would try to realize their dreams by imposing them
on the world around them, Marvell withdraws still further within himself.
He appeals to the common topos of the flood to create an *imaginary*
destruction of the existing order (465–80), after which he creates his own new
world, his own magical and wish-fulfilling utopia:

> But I, retiring from the Flood,
> Take Sanctuary in the Wood;
> And, while it lasts, my self imbark
> In this yet green, yet growing Ark.
>
> (481–4)

He plays not only Noah but Adam and Eve, running away from trouble in
medio ligni paradisi which meant, as St. Augustine pointed out, retiring

ad seipsos, i.e., to a green thought in a green shade within the *hyle* of imagination.

Here life's problems are diminished to the problems of birds and trees, while history is blurred by being viewed in a cosmic perspective, as when the trees momentarily assume genealogical significance:

> On one hand *Fairfax,* th' other *Veres:*
> Of whom though many fell in war,
> Yet more to Heaven shooting are:
> And, as they Natures Cradle deckt,
> Will in green Age her Hearse expect.
>
> (491-5)

Here chaos is easily and effortlessly transformed to architecture, not by drawing quarries to caves but by a mere focus of the magic eyebeam:

> Dark all without it knits; within
> It opens passable and thin:
> And in as loose an order grows,
> As the *Corinthean Porticoes.*
>
> (505-8)

Here too lowness is as safe as height, the nightingale has Orphean influence rather than an "Orphan Parents Call," her prophetic voice is heeded by Elders, as by the plant previously used to symbolize the prickling leaf of Conscience "which shrinks at ev'ry touch" and is too rare on earth (355-8):

> The *Nightingale* does here make choice
> To sing the Tryals of her Voice.
> Low Shrubs she sits in. and adorns
> With Musick high the squatted Thorns.
> But highest Oakes stoop down to hear,
> And listening Elders prick the Ear.
> The Thorn, lest it should hurt her, draws
> Within the Skin its shrunken claws.
>
> (513-20)

Only in a delightfully incredible world where plants replace men is such harmony possible. Here finally the high seriousness of Original Sin is thrown away on some insights into the local ecology of woodpeckers:

> the Tree . . . fed
> A *Traitor-worm,* within it bred.
> As first our *Flesh* corrupt within

> Tempts impotent and bashful *Sin*.
> And yet that *Worm* triumphs not long,
> But serves to feed the *Hewels young*.
> While the Oake seems to fall content,
> Viewing the Treason's Punishment.
>   (553–60)

In this section the symbolic echoes, such as the allusion to the fall of the Royal oak, are brilliantly in evidence, but again in a disjunctive manner characteristic of greenworld withdrawal: by concentrating on the natural vehicle, shifting away from the human tenor, the poet turns his world into an animated cartoon. What is more logical than that he himself, in the next phase of retreat, should become the arm-flapping conductor of his own Silly Symphony?

> Thus I, *easie Philosopher*,
> Among the *Birds* and *Trees* confer:
> And little now to make me, wants
> Or of the *Fowles,* or of the *Plants*.
> Give me but Wings as they, and I
> Streight floting on the Air shall fly:
> Or turn me but, and you shall see
> I was but an inverted Tree.
>
> Already I begin to call
> In their most learned Original:
> And where I language want, my Signs
> The Bird upon the Bough divines;
>   (561–72)

In the next stanza, he attains, predictably enough, to historical omniscience, though the object of his total knowledge is a cabbala of his own devising:

> Out of these scatterer'd *Sibyls* Leaves
> Strange *Prophecies* my Phancy weaves:
> And in one History consumes,
> Like *Mexique Paintings,* all the Plumes.
> What *Rome, Greece, Palestine,* ere said
> I in this light *Mosaik* read.
> Thrice happy he who, not mistook,
> Hath read in *Natures mystick Book*.
>   (576–84)

Total control of this sort means externalizing one's wishes not only as Nature's mystic book but also as "Chance": "see how Chance's better Wit / Could with a Mask my studies hit!" (585-6). Having thus completed the work of creation and supplied his own apocalypse, the poet reclines into a well-deserved sabbath:

> Then, languishing with ease, I toss
> On Pallets swoln of Velvet Moss;
> While the Wind, cooling through the Boughs,
> Flatters with Air my panting Brows.
> Thanks for my Rest ye *Mossy Banks,*
> And unto you *cool Zephyr's* Thanks,
> Who, as my Hair, my Thoughts too shed,
> And winnow from the Chaff my Head.
>
> How safe, methinks, and strong, behind
> These Trees have I incamp'd my Mind;
>   (593-602)

Since the above passages have as their object the poet in his sylvan activities, I think it worth while to repeat that it is not *there* in the woods but *now* in the course of poetic utterance that Marvell lets go. The descriptive references are general rather than singular: "I confer among the *birds* and *trees,*" "I toss on *pallets,*" "I gaul the world's horsemen *all the day.*" The focus of concrete experience is on the poet *as he imagines* these generalized situations; it is therefore his activity of imagining, as manifested in the play of his rhetoric, analogies, and syntax, which constitutes the return to chaos. His own violence discharges itself as wit; his own pleasure principle, with its archaic inheritance, pursues its levelling and utopian, its destructive and creative tendencies in the controlled form of symbolic play. Into the more "private" and subjective mode of the lyric poem Marvell brings a dominantly theatrical institution, the Vice, on whose saturnalian functions C. L. Barber's study of Shakespeare has thrown much light—as in the following statements, which might have been made with Marvell's reveller in mind:

> Clowning could provide both release for impulses which run counter to decency and decorum. and the clarification about limits which comes from going beyond the limit.
>
> The energy normally occupied in maintaining inhibition is freed for celebration.

The clown or Vice . . . was a recognised anarchist who made
aberration obvious by carrying release to absurd extremes.

Barber's comments on the double plot, inspired by Empson, also illuminate
the poem, since Marvell's implosion is largely a parody of what those in
social, political and intellectual authority do—or try to do—in the great
world of affairs. Shakespeare uses clowns in a traditional way

> to present a burlesque version of actions performed seriously by
> their betters . . . In the early plays, the clown is usually represented
> as oblivious of what his burlesque implies. When he becomes the
> court fool, however, he can use his folly as a stalking horse, and
> his wit can express directly the function of his role as a dramatized
> commentary on the rest of the action.

Marvell, of course, is the court fool playing the *naif*. Having clarified
the limits by going beyond them he returns, as I have already suggested,
and willingly accepts the rulemaking and inhibiting impulses of the mind.
These are projected in the pleasant symbol of Mary Fairfax, *"the Law /
Of all her Sex,* her *Ages Aw."* Similarly the Nature surrounding Maria is
made visually to objectify the present poetic state of mind: "See how loose
Nature, in respect / To her, it self doth recollect." The poet recollects himself
and his loose thoughts by an act of symbolic compression embodied in the
streightness of the image: Maria is an epitome of the domestic order around
her which is in turn an epitome of the social and natural order around it,
etc. If nature was previously a fluid imaginative medium, an ocean of mind,
it is now contracted and solidified to the familiar surfaces of Fairfacian
decorum. It is a nature which aspires to the condition of household art so
as both to mirror and to protect its fair paradigm. Thus "the gellying Stream
compacts below, / If it might fix her shadow so;" fishes hang stupidly like
"Flies in *Chrystal* overt'ane" (675-8), by Maria's flames "in *Heaven* try'd,
/ *Nature* is wholly *vitrifi'd"* (687-8). Furthermore,

> 'Tis *She* that to these Gardens gave
> That wondrous Beauty which they have;
> *She* streightness on the Woods bestows;
> To *Her* the Meadow sweetness owes;
> Nothing could make the River be
> So Chrystal-pure but only *She;*
> *She* yet more Pure, Sweet, Streight, and Fair,
> Then Gardens, Woods, Meads, Rivers are.

Therefore what first *She* on them spent,
They gratefully again present.
The Meadow Carpets where to tread:
The Garden Flow'rs to Crown *Her* Head;
And for a Glass the limpid Brook,
Where *She* may all *her* Beautyes look;
But, since *She* would not have them seen,
The Wood about *her* draws a Skreen.

(689–704)

This gradual recollecting and voluntary straitening is only made possible by utilizing the mind's expanding inward spaces. The poem offers itself as a model or exemplum of this essential human activity. Showing how the domestic order may provide a screen when the social order fails, it doubly glorifies the house. It provides both the answer and the explanation to the question asked in the third stanza:

What need of all this Marble Crust
T'impark the wanton Mote of Dust,
That thinks by Breadth the World t'unite
Though the first Builders fail'd in Height?

The answer is inherent in the concluding image of the salmon-fishers shod in their canoes: to say that "the dark *Hemisphere* / Does now like one of them appear" is simultaneously to contract the hemisphere and expand the tortoise-like fishermen. The object is not only a boat sustaining them above the flood while they fish in the depths; it is also a shoe, a hat, a head, a tortoise-like house, a hemisphere, in short, an *antick cope*. Man's house, his *oikos*, can ultimately be nothing smaller than the universe he creates. A world view or world order is the only magnitude sufficient to contain the wanton mote of dust; it is as natural to man to create, clothe himself in and inhabit a cosmos as it is for a turtle to secrete a shell, and in fact the image suggests that this alone can preserve man on the flood or chaos of his historico-natural environment. Such a *cope*, embracing the universe, occupies very little space. But man's first tendency—the primitive response of the child or of archaic civilization—is always a step in the wrong direction, an attempt to express this impulse in sensuous and extended forms, or to misconstrue the interior constitutive functions of mind as the external functions of nature. The proper response is demonstrated in "Appleton House," where the poet's wanton wit spans the poles, makes contact with the antipodes, connects the world of fleas and the world of stars, recovers the primal wilderness and the archaic mind, and recognizes through all this business at once the reality of the world-making process and the fictive absurdity of the products.

One might expect, from this interpretation, to find the poem resolving its problems in clearcut fashion, to find the poet emerging at the end and fulfilling the rhythm of withdrawal and return. This is indeed the dominant shape of the poetic experience, yet the details make it more tenuous, and complicate the movement with hesitations. For example, consider the final couplet: the sense of the great world as a dark hemisphere may well have been attenuated by the work of the poem until that hemisphere is reduced to the more reassuring silhouette of a salmon-fisher. But on the other hand, the lines may be read this way: "The salmon-fishers appear now, and so does the dark hemisphere. Therefore let's in." "Let's in" is a conventional way to conclude eclogues, and it frequently signifies a new withdrawal after the temporary and often limited resolution achieved within the eclogue. Marvell's image is brilliantly vague and menacing, and his gesture of with-drawal seems more urgent because it includes *us*. It is a gesture which acknowledges the limits of control through the inner discipline of poetry, a discipline which may sustain the self but cannot be expected to renovate the world. The gesture signifies the poet's return from delicious solitude because it implies a sense of the common cause and the common danger—an awareness of human frailty, of the consequent need for human solidarity and thus for political as well as poetical action. Marvell is a little like Prospero who, having gradually surrendered his magic power and prepared to leave his magic island, comes forward to find himself "in this bare island"—this bare platform in England, England as a bare stage—and asks to be released; to be "sent to Naples" is to move back to the redeemed image of actuality in the second world where Prospero has had good effect, and this seems preferable to being trapped in the actuality of the first world, no wonder-working Duke of Milan. Here, this side of the second world where fictions vanish, the poet, like the actor and playwright, is no longer a god but a man among men. He relies on their good will, assistance and esteem, his pleasure and security are mutually bound up with theirs. Yet he comes forward guardedly and hesitantly—long enough to register the fact that the darkness, though moral and political, looms and gathers inevitably as evening. With this, he seems on the verge of retiring once again.

The drift of the ambiguous syntax of this couplet is very much like that of lines 761–2. "'Tis not, what once it was, the *World*." In both cases the poet seems to waver between feeling better and feeling worse; to the extent that his thoughts about Appleton House have made the outside world seem darker and ruder by comparison, he invokes the house even more insistently: *"You Heaven's Center, Nature's Lap, / And Paradice's only Map."* More interesting is the fact that this vacillation, or perhaps we should call it vibrational equilibrium, is projected into the structure of the poem. Marvell's own withdrawal, occupying the centre of the poem, is flanked on the one side by the retirements of the nuns and Fairfax, on the other by that of Maria. Each is more satisfactory than the one it precedes, and the example of Maria obviously provides a healthy contrast to that of the nuns. Yet the cases of both Fairfax and Maria are affected by the poet's ambivalent feelings, and Marvell's treatment of each figure reveals the pressure of his feelings.

When General Fairfax, resigning his command, withdraws to his manor, "His warlike Studies could not cease" and therefore he "laid . . . Gardens out in sport / In the just Figure of a Fort." The poet immediately converts this miniature to a model of a different kind—"with five Bastions it did fence, / As aiming one for ev'ry Sense" (284-8)—but then goes on to develop the lord's martial conceit in four stanzas of recreative fancy, and in a delighted tone which suggests that although he takes his cue from his patron he is less interested in playing war than in the poetic play of analogies. The brief glance at the castle of the body connects Fairfax's miniature with that fortress which the nuns had yielded to Created Pleasure, and Marvell susbsequently relates it to the General's principled rejection of power:

> he preferr'd to the *Cinque Ports*
> These five imaginary Forts:
> And, in those half-dry Trenches, spann'd
> Pow'r which the Ocean might command.
>
> For he did, with his utmost Skill,
> *Ambition* weed, but *Conscience* till.
> *Conscience*, that Heaven-nursed Plant,
> Which most our Earthly Gardens want.
> A prickling leaf it bears, and such
> As that which shrinks at ev'ry touch;
> But Flowrs eternal, and divine,
> That in the Crowns of Saints do shine.
>
> (349-60)

The moral is that external political chaos is caused by defective cultivation of the world within; there are too virtuous men in public life and the reformer's first job must be to retire and set his own house in order. In drawing this moral and making Fairfax a model of proper reform activity, Marvell exemplifies his own relation to the General: the poet depends on his patron not only for his margin of security but also for the subject matter which he then develops according to his own inclination; in return, he carries the patron's model-making tendencies much farther, converting house, garden and owner to figures of thought.

But while praise for Fairfax is the dominant note, the stanzas preceding the above lines (349-60) suggest the presence of another feeling. In elaborating on his patron's toy fort, Marvell describes soldierly bees and flowers safe in a world of "known Allies" and discharging the function of a guard of honour—colours, salute, parade (289-312). There is little chance of war in the garden. Secured by the vigilance and power of cosmic ministers, the sentinel bee has an easy time of it:

> But when the vigilant *Patroul*
> Of Stars walks round about the *Pole*,
> Their Leaves, that to the stalks are curl'd,
> Seem to their Staves the *Ensigns* furl'd.
> Then in some Flow'rs beloved Hut
> Each Bee as Sentinel is shut;
> And sleeps so too: but, if once stir'd,
> She runs you through, or askes *the Word*.
> (313-20)

It is only between stars and bees, in the intermediate world of men, that war is real. Marvell's flight of fancy seems to bring on a genuinely rueful moment, a brief surrender to the longing for escape. The miniature paradise is pressed into the service of this wish, and from such a perspective Fairfax's retirement may be felt as premature:

> Oh Thou, that dear and happy Isle
> The Garden of the World ere while,
> Thou *Paradise* of four Seas,
> Which *Heaven* planted us to please,
> But, to exclude the World, did guard
> With watry if not flaming Sword;
> What luckless Apple did we tast,
> To make us Mortal, and The Wast?
>
> Unhappy! shall we never more
> That sweet *Militia* restore,

When Gardens only had their Towrs,
And all the Garrisons were Flowrs,
When Roses only Arm might bear,
And Men did rosie Garlands wear?
Tulips, in several Colours barr'd,
Were then the *Switzers* of our *Guard*.

The *Gardiner* had the *Souldiers* place,
And his more gentle Forts did trace.
The Nursery of all things green
Was then the only *Magazeen*.
The Winter Quarters were the Stoves,
Where he the tender Plants removes.
But War all this doth overgrow:
We Ord'nance Plant and Powder sow.

And yet there walks one on the Sod
Who, had it pleased him and *God,*
Might once have made our Gardens spring
Fresh as his own and flourishing.
But he preferr'd to the *Cinque Ports*
These five imaginary Forts.

                                   (321–50)

One feels a bare hint of censure: perhaps instead of peaceably playing war in his garden Fairfax should have remained in public life and militantly resisted further Parliamentarian aggression; perhaps at that moment the sick commonwealth needed more tilling and weeding than the exemplary private man. The conduct of toy forts and imaginary wars should be left to poets, not to generals. Marvell's earlier words may, from this vantage point, seem admonitory rather than descriptive: "for an *Inn* to entertain / Its *Lord* a while, but not remain." Thus in taking leave of Fairfax and turning to imagine the meadow—the stanza on conscience is the last sustained reference in the poem—he projects scenes of carnage as if to remind his patron that real war is going on elsewhere and that soldiers may perhaps some day replace mowers even here. This questioning of the wisdom of a retirement which is premature or too final leads into Marvell's own escape and ulimately to its climax:

Bind me ye *Woodbines* in your 'twines,
Curle me about ye gadding *Vines,*

> And Oh so close your Circles lace.
> That I may never leave this Place.
>   (609–12)

There is more irony in the implied advice, "Send the General out, let the Poet retire" ("Send the General out *so that* the Poet may safely retire," cf. the *Horation Ode*) than Allen's summary would seem to allow:

> When Marvell leaves the wood to sing the future of his patron's race, he has, I think, solved his own problem to his immediate satisfaction. He will be the nightingale singing among the lowly thorns. This is the place he hopes "he may never leave." He has advised his patron against retirement as best he can, holding up to him his magisterial duties, the excellence of his qualifications, the urgent necessities of the state of England, and the spiritual impotence and danger of withdrawal from the active life. He knew in his heart of hearts that Fairfax would remain aloof; so he makes his last effort . . . the fortunes of the House of Fairfax depends on Mary.

If the advice is also aimed at the latent politician in Marvell, the poet in him is not prepared to accept it. It is the return to action which seems premature to the poet, who may well claim that the imaginative exercise productive of the sylvan stanzas is the poet's way of weeding Ambition and tilling Conscience, which shrinks at every touch. The return from the woods to Maria is like a return from the voice of the body to the voice of the soul, and it is thus a kind of compromise. It may be incumbent of Fairfax to hurry back into action, but his daughter is after all only twelve years old; she may legitimately remain home a few more years at least, during which time she will need tutoring. If she represents the claims of social and rational order, she does so in a domestic rather than a political context and she symbolizes the halcyon calm of Paradise's only map. To move from the image of Fairfax to that of Maria is therefore a retardation in the rhythm of return. The felt disparity between the young Mary Fairfax and the symbolic Maria, noted by Allen and Joseph Summers, contributes to this effect: safe within this friendly and excellent lesser world, the poet may deal with heaven and hell, with war and politics and passion, *in parvo*. He prefers to manipulate symbols rather than directly to confront their referents.

Allowing for the particular differences of tone, the return to Maria is somewhat like the return from Eveless Eden to the flowery dial in "The Garden." The urge to withdraw from time to thyme is still present, but sharply qualified by the poet's self-consciousness, his acknowledgment *that* the urge is still present. We sense, I think, more resolution and control in the shorter poem, and perhaps one reason the longer poem is longer lies in the fact that it dramatizes the mind's vacillation at closer range, that it shows Marvell moving toward a resolution again and again, yet never quite letting himself achieve it. Thus while he reveals a certain coyness in his own nature by picking Mary Fairfax as symbol, he self-consciously projects his reticence onto the symbol: since Maria would not have her beauties seen, "The Wood about her draws a Skreen."

> For *She*, to higher Beauties rais'd,
> Disdains to be for lesser prais'd.
> *She* counts her Beauty to converse
> In all the languages *as hers;*
> Nor yet in those *her self* imployes
> But for the *Wisdome,* not the Noyse;
> Nor yet that *Wisdome* would affect,
> But as 'tis *Heavens Dialect.*
>
> (705-12)

This is not only a contrast to the nuns, but also an echo of the poet as *"easie philospher."* The ideal order of Appleton House is to be viewed by Maria as preparation for her proper functions in the great world, not as an escape from the dangers attendant on true fulfillment. Yet again, while Marvell contrasts this fulfillment to the perverted self-love of the nuns, his exhortation echoes with images from the sylvan retreat—the *antick cope,* the prelate of the grove, the "double Wood of ancient Stocks":

> This 'tis to have been from the first
> In a *Domestick Heaven* nurst.
> Under the *Discipline* severe
> Of *Fairfax,* and the starry *Vere;*
> Where not one object can come nigh
> But pure, and spotless as the Eye;
> And *Goodness* doth it self intail
> On *Females,* if there want a *Male.*
>
> Go now fond Sex that on your Face
> Do all your useless Study place,
> Nor once at Vice your Brows dare knit
> Lest the smooth Forehead wrinkled sit:
> Yet your own Face shall at you grin,
> Thorough the Black-bag of your Skin;

When *knowledge only* could have fill'd
And Virtue all those *Furrows till'd.*

Hence *She* with Graces more divine
Supplies beyond her *Sex* the *Line;*
And, like a *sprig of Misleto,*
On the *Fairfacian Oak* does grow;
Whence, for some universal good,
The *Priest* shall cut the sacred Bud;
While her *glad Parents* most rejoice,
And make their *Destiny* their *Choice.*
                                        (721-44)

This is a curiously strained passage, at once very emblematic and very
physical, both decorous and unpleasantly suggestive. It is as if Marvell feels
the difficulty of what he is urging, since few eyes are without the wanton
mote. As in "The Picture of Little T.C. in a Prospect of Flowers," the green
prospect is shown to idealize love but also to oversimplify its dangers and
obligations. By making his green metaphor seem a little insistent, a little
inappropriate, Marvell suggests on the one hand the frustration and prudery
related to the fear of exposing oneself to one's sexual and social fate, and on
the other hand a love which may be reduced to genealogical husbandry.
Maria's retired life in the harmoniously responsive world of Appleton House
is fulfilled only when she leaves it behind to open herself to the promising
yet uncertain future, the great world, *"some* universal good." After register-
ing the risk as well as the promise, Marvell turns his thought from the image
of Maria, which has served its purpose, and he moves in the next stanza from
future problems to present joys, from the exemplary human flower to the
real plants around him—"ye Fields, Springs, Bushes, Flowers, / Where yet
she leads her studious Hours."

    In this way, as the poet moves from the nuns to Fairfax to Maria, the
representations of the retired life at Appleton House become increasingly
attractive. Though the general drift of the poem is a praise of Appleton
House as a *temporary inn,* the vectors of return are decelerated, if not
neutralized, by the contrary thrust of new urges to withdrawal. And as the
poem reaches its inevitable conclusion, these countermovements seem to be
intensified. From the moment Marvell introduces Maria, they knot together
in more frequent and compact juxtapositions. Of course the poem as a whole
is characterized by a dominant rhythm of alternating systole and diastole
which affects both spatial and temporal prospects: Marvell's attention

sweeps from the house out to the estate and back to the house ("Let's in"); his meditation moves from the physical presence of "this sober Frame" back in time to the nuns, forward to his patron, inward to the more personal and immediate present of his own withdrawal, outward again to Maria— Thwaites *rediviva* as symbol of the future—and finally, after the brief glance at *her* future, back to the present tense and place, the poet surrounded by the estate and retreating into the house from the approach of darkness. But these vibrations are most drastically compressed at the end: in the "rude heap" stanza, where the poet's focus rapidly widens and narrows, while his temporal prospect seems at once to extend backward and forward in search of paradise; in the restlessness of the final stanza, as his imagination darts from meadow and river to the antipodes, then to tortoises and finally to the dark hemisphere which seems both to expand and contract; in the syntactical alternatives of the "rude heap" and "dark Hemisphere" passages; in the way the brief closing figures—salmon-fishers, antipodes, tortoises, and rational amphibii—recollect and epitomize the oppositions generated through the entire poem.

The work of the poem has led Marvell to sharpen the distinction, which also confronted Prospero, between his reformed symbol or image of actuality and the dark actuality itself; between the lesser world and the rude heap, the friendly family as social microcosm and the chaotic society of which it is a microcosm, the poem as experience and the experience beyond the poem. A controlled return to actuality leads inevitably to a disjunction, to a sense of the gap between the inner and outer orders. If the ambience from which the poet retreats is gradually readmitted into the lesser or second world, it is also tempered. He may not want to step out too far and too hastily into the first world where he is helpless and alone. Yet he knows that ultimately he must, that only the ultimate gesture fulfills the imaginative withdrawal and creation by marking off its limits. Like the return of the flowery dial of "The Garden," the last section of "Appleton House" is tempered surrender, a compromise, which makes itself known as such, and it is this added dimension of self-awareness, this frame of ironic self-diminution, which constitutes the *real* return. Man's *oikos* may expand to a universe, a plurality of universes, yet be no bigger than his head. And though it houses heaven and hell it may nevertheless prove inadequate for its humble primary function in the struggle for existence: to protect man against the dark contingencies— or certainties—of Weather.

GEOFFREY HARTMAN

"The Nymph Complaining
for the Death of Her Faun":
A Brief Allegory

The allegories [previously] proposed have crushed the lightness of nymph
and fawn, the high poetic spirits of Marvell's poem. Why allegorize at all?
The only good reason is that the poem itself teases us into thinking that
nymph and fawn are also something else. This teasing should be respected:
either there is some allegory here, or the poem is deceptively suggestive. Is
the nymph the human soul; the fawn a gift of grace, or some aspect of Christ
or Church? Such thoughts are especially encouraged by images reminiscent
of the Song of Songs.

The fawn is not unlike the young hart of the Song of Songs or its fawns
that feed among the lillies, while the nymph's garden is a kind of *hortus
conclusus* with which fawn and Shulammite are linked. Such allusions, it
is true, freely used in the love poetry of the time, do not of themselves
establish the presence of allegory. Yet when imagery from the Song of Songs
is used in comparable contexts—either directly, as in Crashaw, to celebrate
divine love in passionate terms, or allusively, as in Vaughan, to illustrate the
quest for evidences of election—it reposes on well-established allegorical
tradition. Marvell may have chosen this tradition for its very bivalence, but
a reader cannot miss the sacramental and even christological note emerging
first in lines 13-24 ("There is not such another in / The World, to offer for
their Sin"), crowding around the imagery from Song of Songs (lines 71-93),
and sustained to the end of the poem, whose coda is a series of conceits on

From *Beyond Formalism: Literary Essays 1958-1970*. ©1970 by Yale University.
Yale University Press, 1970.

weeping that remind us strongly of Crashaw—a Crashaw scaled down to sharp diminutives.

If a literal interpretation could account for these features, I would prefer it. Only one nonallegorical approach, however, has been at all successful. According to Leo Spitzer the poem describes a young girl's desire for an impossible purity. He thinks the poem is an oblique psychological portrait. "The description of her pet reflects on her own character by indirect characterization, the increasing idealization of the fawn allowing inferences about the maiden who so idealizes it." It is certainly true that there is something childlike, deliciously naive, and deeply human in the nymph, which breaks through the mythological setting as later in Romantic and Victorian poetry. Yet beside the fact that it would be hard to find, at this time, a single prosopopoeia or "complaint" which is primarily psychological portraiture, Spitzer's view is open to a fundamental objection. It substitutes psychological for mythological categories, assuming that the latter are the poet's means of implying the former. His literalism, therefore, does not take the letter of the poem seriously enough: it refuses to explore the possibility that the nymph is a nymph—not simply a young girl, but a mythic being in a privileged relation to the wood-world of the poem, the world of fawns and nature. Yet Marvell insists clearly enough on the presence of this mythical level. While his troopers and their violence come from a contemporary world, almost everything else is set in a world of myth. The impinging, quick but fatal, of one level on the other should not be obscured by a translation into the psychological.

A second approach, which also claims to be literal, is allegorical despite itself. Romance and pastoral may show the beginnings of passion in an innocent mind, the obliquities of a young girl prey to her first love. The theme derives perhaps from Longus's *Daphnis and Chloe* and contains that special admixture of naiveté in the subjects and sophistication in the author which is to be found here as elsewhere in Marvell. A strong suspicion is raised that the fawn's wound is the girl's, that the poem describes a sexual or at least an initiatory wounding. Yet what the reader may interpret in sexual terms, the nymph's consciousness views in terms of creaturely calamity. By some naive and natural balm of vision, of which allegory is the organized form, she keeps within the confines of a pastoral view of things. She is a nymph rather than a girl precisely because her soul is not yet humanized, her love not yet divided into profane and sacred. The fawn mirrors that undifferentiated love which allows her to pass gradually, and without mystery, from man to beast, from Sylvio to the deer. Her extreme grief, moreover, is so gentle ("ungentle men!") that she still seems to live in the last rays of a world where no sharp distinctions between good and evil obtain. She is too whole for the rage of good against evil, or any understanding of the rage of evil itself. She does not, even now, fall into duality, but abandons the whole (this impossible world) for another whole (the world beyond). The threshold of mature consciousness is not reached—and cannot be reached without a dying of the nymph into a girl or woman.

This ontological interpretation of the poem is, I believe, new. To put it in its simplest form, it respects mythology's insistence that states of soul are correlated with states of being. But it implies a disjunction between the points of view of innocence and of experience, of nymph on the one hand and reader or poet on the other. The poem's playful and artificial flavor, however, betrays a degree of conspiracy between nymph and poet. Naiveté of mood expressed in jeweled conceits is, after all, Marvell's most distinctive trait as author. Instead of arguing that the nymph sees one thing and the poet, who looks at the action from the point of view of experience, sees another, we must suppose a greater unity between the poet and his persona. But once we do this, the nymph begins to appear as a Muse in little, a figure created by the poet to mourn a lost power, perhaps that of poetry itself. The supposition gathers strength if we think of Marvell's poem not in the tradition of complaint or prosopopoeia but in the more comprehensive one of pastoral elegy. The use of pastoral to lament the death of poets was one of its strongest Renaissance developments, and although the lament is usually spoken by an author in *propria persona* and for an individual, Spenser makes the Muses mourn "their own mishaps." It is Marvell's special characteristic to reduce everything to a microcosmic or little-world scale and to view the nymph as a Muse in miniature.

Indeed, the nymph's tradedy, caught in amber, would have reminded a contemporary reader of another tradition cognate with pastoral elegy but now almost extinct. I suspect that the meaning of Marvell's poem became problematic as the tradition lost its natural or commonplace vigor. The medallion, gemlike, or miniature effects found in Marvell can be traced to the epigrams of the Greek Anthology, a considerable portion of which are either verses made for pictures or else little pictures themselves. Those acquainted with the poetry of the Pléiade will remember the impact of the Anacreonta and the Greek Anthology (mediated by the neo-Latin poets) on Ronsard, Du Bellay, and Belleau, who began to develop an alternate tradition to the high style of the great ode which had been their main object of imitation. Not odes but odelettes, not epics and large elegies but little descriptive domestic or rural peoms called *Petites inventions, Bocages, Jeux Rustiques, Pierres Precieuses, Idylles,* now became the delectation of their

Muse. A strange riot of diminutives and diminutive forms begins. The word *idyll*, in fact, was commonly etymologized as a diminutive of *eidos*, a little picture. The idyll, says Vauquelin de la Fresnaie in his *Foresteries* (1555), "ne signifie et ne represente que diverses petites images et graveures en la semblance de celles qu'on grave aux lapis, aux gemmes et calcedoines pour servir quelques fois de cachet. Les miennes en la sorte, pleines d'amour enfantines, ne sont qu'imagetes et petites tabletes de fantaisies d'Amour." The fortunes of this mode of the minor are difficult to follow; it is always merging with so much else—with emblem poetry for example, or with sonnets and their "little rooms," or with various kinds of pictorialism. Its range is so great, its value so variable, that we can go from Belleau's *petite invention* "Le Ver Luisant" (1552) to Marvell's "The Mower to the Glow-Worms" (about a century later), or from a whimsical epitaph on some faithful pet to Ben Jonson's great verses on Elizabeth L.H. ("Wouldst thou hear what man can say / In a little? Reader, stay"), and again from these to Henry King's moving trifle "Upon a Braid of Hair in a Heart" ("In this small Character is sent / My Loves eternal Monument"). The very range of the tradition, however, may be a result of the fact that the recurrent and operative topos of much-in-little constitutes a poetics as well as a theme: it is a defense of poetry's *ignobile otium*, the trivial yet mystical or contemplative nature of art.

Now Marvell's poem is not only an idyll in this sense, but an idyll of idylls. It is a little picture of the spirit of the genre—an apotheosis of the diminutive powers of poetry. Not only is the fawn a spritely embodiment of much-in-little, not only does the whole poem end with a metamorphosis into art, a votive image of nymph and fawn, but, as if to sum up the genre in one monument to itself, "The Nymph's Complaint" brings together the major types of the Greek epigram: dedicatory, sepulchral, ecphrastic, and amatory. An inspired syncretism produces something very like a collage (although, as in reading Homer, one must be taught to recognize the individual bits or formulae), a collage with two important and successful aims. The first is to fuse semipagan forms of sentiment into a recognizably contemporary genre, that of Spenserian pastoral allegory. What Spenser has done is here done again, but in a much less liberal and inventive, a much more deliberate and self-conscious, way. It is an openly synthetic reconstruction, a reassembly of Spenser's already diminished freedoms. Marvell's poetry has something of the embalmer's art, and his diminutive form points to an ideal it would preserve from total dissolution. The poet's second and correlative aim is to translate these various forms of the idyll (pictorial, votive, sepulchral, amatory) into a situation which is the living content of his poem, as if nature and artifice were interchangeable—and this interchange is itself a generative topic of some of the Greek Anthology epigrams, as of the Renaissance "speaking pictures" inspired by them. Though art, in other words, accepts itself as a tour de force, becoming deliberately diminished and artifactual in its aims, it will not give up a magical ambition to rival or supplant nature. The diminished form simply purifies art's power and concentrates its resemblance to hieroglyph, icon, or charm.

In Marvell, therefore, as in every authentic artist, technique is ethos: the form he has chosen—a playful shadow of greater forms, an artful rivalry of naiver forms—is at once a lament and an acceptance of his situation as poet. To understand that situation in its historical context, the vast continued design of Spenserian allegory shrinking and becoming a brief allegory, will help to interpret this "furthest and most mysterious development of English pastoral poetry." The following interpretation can be extended from its specific allegory to the general problem of the status of Spenserian allegory in Marvell's age. A consideration, therefore, of that brief epic "Appleton House" must also concern itself with the problematic status of the epic in Marvell's age. To this double task of finding a specific allegory and of clarifying the status of Spenserian allegory I now turn.

Those who have tried to discover a sustained allegory in "The Nymph" have made a curious error. This error explains not only the failure of their attempt but also why this kind of interpretation is discredited. Instead of basing their allegories on the action, they have immediately sought to decipher the individual agents: nymph, fawn, Sylvio. But in Spenserian allegory it is the action which identifies the agents rather than vice versa. This by no means excludes more static devices: Spenser's figures can have suggestive names, like Sylvio in Marvell, even if the meaning of a figure is disclosed mainly by an intricate pattern of relationships extended (and even scattered like clues) through canto or book. This type of structure was called by Spenser and others continued allegory, and the mistake of applying to Marvell's poem methods of decoding more appropriate to noncontinued allegories comes from the fact that we have so very few lyrical pieces in this mode: Marvell is almost *sui generis* in his short-form use of the dark conceit. The short allegories of Herbert and Vaughan are not really dark, but rather vivified emblems.

Let us begin, therefore, with a description of the action: of what happens in "The Nymph." The nymph traces in retrospect her subtly changing relationship to the fawn. The fawn is first a love gift, then a consolation, and finally a creature loved for its own sake and even gathering to itself the nymph's love for all creatures. The fawn, indeed, becomes so important that, when it is killed, no creaturely consolation seems possible, and the nymph hastens to die.

So highly stylized an action evokes a specific idea of the progress of the soul. The direct object of love is replaced by an indirect one, a live token, which is in turn replaced by a still more indirect one, an icon (lines 111 ff.). And while the token comforts, the icon comforts only, if at all, as a symbol of the impossibility of being comforted: "I shall weep though I be stone." A love that has turned from temporal fulfillment to temporal consolation becomes a disconsolateness which is love still, but removed from this world.

The pattern is general and human enough not to require a special historical locus. It has such a locus, however, in the Christian idea of the soul's progress and the part consolation plays in this. The Christian soul is weaned from worldliness by privations that contain a comfort. That comfort is usually thought of in other-worldly terms, but Marvell's position is rather complex. Though there is an apotheosis of the fawn, analogous to the Assumption of Astrea or other stellar figures (as Crashaw says, "heav'n must go home"), the fawn might have substituted for Sylvio. As Sylvio's surrogate it entices the nymph with a love that remains this-worldly, though chaste or wider than sexual. The fawn's mode of being is, in fact, so peculiarly mixed with nature's that the possibility of a nature-involved consolation seems to die with its ascent out of this world.

The theme of consolation, which points our poem in the direction of allegory, can be traced back to a specific and authoritative analogue. This is the scriptual story of the Comforter in John 14:16, 26, and 16:7 ff. Christ promises the Comforter (Paraclete) to his disciples when they do not suspect or do not understand that he must leave them. For them Christ is part of the approaching and expected apocalypse. But Christ, in preparing them for his absence, for temporality, tells them of the Comforter, who is to be his surrogate and a spirit dwelling with them in his absence, more intimately even than He. (The Paraclete, Donne comments in a sermon, as well as a mediator and advocate, is "in a more intire, and a more internall, and a more viscerall sense, A Comforter.") It is almost expedient that Christ should depart, so that this closer companion, also named "Spirit of Truth" (viz. "troth") and "Holy Ghost," should come to abide with men.

Three kinds of congruence between this analogue and the poem may be considered: the propriety of showing the Comforter as a fawn, the similarities of theme, and similarities bearing on the action as a whole. Concerning the issue of propriety, I can only say that the third Person is traditionally a dove, and that the Church Fathers often associate the third Person with charity, or pure creature-feeling, rather than with power (the first Person) or wisdom (the second Person). To the nymph the fawn is simply a creature that loves her, and she reciprocates its love. When she says, "I cannot be/Unkind, t'a Beast that loveth me," Marvell renders her attitude succinctly, that it would be "un-kind" (unnatural, uncreaturely) to be "un-kind." To see the fawn as an allegorical emblem for the Comforter at least respects the fact that the poem deals with the possibility of consolation. The fawn might have been, for a Protestant, a playful yet not unfitting image of the humble Spirit that prefers "th' upright heart and pure." The change from dove to fawn could have been imposed by the very mode of allegory, since the dove is, strictly speaking, not an allegory but a symbol of the third Person. Marvell, moreover, as his poem "On Mr. Milton's Paradise Lost" shows, is wary of the direct treatment of religious subjects. The classical image of Lesbia mourning her sparrow, or the archetypal images of child with bird and virgin with unicorn, may also have served to bring the subject to its deeply veiled and affective form. The change from dove to fawn is, however, strong and unusual enough to compel explanation or put the allegory in doubt.

A second, still insufficient congruence is that of theme. Keeping the story of the Comforter in mind, we note that the fawn is a memento given at a time when the nymph suspects nothing, and with a hint (not understood by her) that it will take Sylvio's place:

> Unconstant *Sylvio,* when yet
> I had not found him counterfeit,
> One morning (I remember well)
> Ty'd in this silver Chain and Bell,
> Gave it to me: nay and I know
> What he said then; I'me sure I do.
> Said He, look how your Huntsman here
> Hath taught a Faun to hunt his *Dear.*
> (25–32)

Here the fawn is clearly identified as Sylvio's surrogate. One huntsman will be replaced by another. The fawn, moreover, is to Sylvio as the Comforter is to Christ, insofar as the latter appears "unconstant" compared to this more faithful household spirit. Without her lover the soul must find a way to redeem the time (cf. lines 37 ff.), and it is helped to do so by a subtle comforter who gradually wins her heart.

But against the fawn's wooing—at once a respect of time and nature— is set the irruptive disrespect of the troopers. For these troopers we find no immediate clue in the scripture story, though they could be carried over from another part of the scripture. Is is also not obvious why Sylvio must be shown as huntsman as well as lover. Adding our previous query, why dove is changed to fawn, the divergencies yield a pattern. They point to the imaginative realm of the spiritual chase. The story of the Comforter is conflated with this most common of Christian and Romance motifs, whose imagery harmonizes with that of Song of Songs. The conflation, which helps to engender a richly detailed allegory, expresses with extraordinary neatness a spiritual chase that kills the spirit—the spirit being the Comforter, the residual and restitutive providence working patiently through church or nature until the Second Coming.

The theme of the chase enters the poem from the beginning. The troopers' pursuit of the fawn is sharply if elliptically distinguished from the way the fawn hunts the nymph, an action which occupies by contrast the major part of the poem. The fawn is subtle: it both entices the nymph and teaches her the futility of chase. It intimates that the Spirit must seek and woo the soul, rather than vice versa:

> Among the beds of Lillyes, I
> Have sought of oft, where it should lye;
> Yet could not, till it self would rise,
> Find it, although before mine Eyes.
>
> (77-80)

The "wanton" troopers, however—the adjective *wanton* recalling Shakespeare's "As flies to wanton boys, so are we to the gods"—engage on a willful, crude, and untimely act. Their activism paradoxically forfeits what they perhaps wished to gain.

> Though they should wash their guilty hands
> In this warm life blood, which doth part
> From thine, and wounded me to the Heart,
> Yet could they not be clean: their Stain
> Is dy'd in such a Purple Grain.
> There is not such another in
> The World, to offer for their Sin.
>
> (18-24)

The blood they shed, unlike Christ's, has not purifying virtue because the fawn's migration to Elisium means the migration of the Comforter, our remaining source of *temporal* hope. The fawn's departure may be compared to the Ascension of the young girl's soul in Donne's *Anniversaries*. With it goes the world's "balm," the comfortable hope binding a soul to its station here below. The nymph's very haste to die reveals that she too has relinquished the hope of nature being allied to grace.

I would recall, at this point, that the theme of the spiritual chase and that of the Comforter are closely related. The idea of a Comforter enters the

Gospels when Christ foresees a conflict between apocalyptic expectation and secular time. What attitude should his disciples take toward things temporal during his "desertion" and before the end of days? The end may be near, yet there remains a space of time not redeemed by the divine presence. One can hardly blame the expectant soul for showing impatience—it has waited sixteen centuries. Its dilemma, at once moral and political, a dilemma Protestantism sharpened, is whether to accept the temporizing character of the church. It is not difficult to see the troopers as the spirit of activism wishing to speed redemption or ruin—in short, to force the issue—by an act directed in a sense against time itself. The poem, of course, does not allow us to say more about their deed than that it is epochal, like the slaying of the albatross in "The Ancient Mariner." But to say this is enough: when their act is compared to the respect for time and nature shown by their victim, we are apprised of two opposite attitudes toward temporality.

It is interesting that the chase after the spirit affects even the nymph. Though her wish to die has, like everything in the poem, a psychological justness, she too is *hastening the end.* The excess of love speeding her toward death:

> O do not run too fast: for I
> Will but bespeak they Grave, and dye
> (line 109 f.)

perhaps resembles, on another plane, the haste of the troopers. It is not unusual in Marvell's world:

> Thus, though we cannot make our Sun
> Stand still, yet we will make him run.
> ("To His Coy Mistress")

> And Flow'rs, and Grass, and I and all,
> Will in one common Ruine fall.
> ("The Mower's Song")

Such a chase out of or beyond nature stands directly against the fawn's example, its slow metamorphosis. The fawn prefigured a redemption with nature, not from it. The comfort it gave was that even the smallest thing in nature is worthy of love. Thus there are two similar violations depicted in Marvell's poem. Like wantonness, great spiritual love removes the soul from the sphere of redemptive patience.

Marvell goes very far in depicting the fawn as an exemplar of loving patience which effects the redemption of nature with man, of all in all.

Because of the fawn, nymph and garden merge. With the strong images of Song of Songs in the background ("I am the rose of Sharon, and the lily of the vallies"), the nymph comes close to being identified with the garden in which the fawn grazes; and when the fawn prints roses on her lips it suggests her metamorphosis, one parallel to its own. The pun in the strangely emphasized lines:

> Said He, look how your Huntsman here
> Hath taught a Faun to hunt his *Dear*
>
> (31-2)

marks this ultimate blending in a playfully prophetic way. The nymph, hunted by the fawn, approaches fawn nature. The distinction of kind is dissolved, and the statue the nymph imagines at the poem's end also draws her and the fawn into a single, if artificial, body—into an "artifice of eternity."

With this we have an allegory that respects the poem. The fawn, in its widest significance, wooing the soul to hope in a love redemption inclusive of nature, is a *Panunculus,* a little Pan; it foreshadows the reintegration or restitution of all things (see Rom. 8:32 and Acts 3:21). Thus the pastoral trappings (Sylvio, nymph, fawn) are not patina. The poet needs a world in which metamorphosis is possible—where a nymph is a nymph, able to assume both a human and an elemental shape, while her pet is equally amphibious. This is the world of Pan, the reconciler of man and nature—in Marvell's conception, the reconciler of all things, even of Pagan and Christian. For in the poem hardly a sentiment or phrase must be taken as Christian. The poet is himself a Pan who has created through the accepted magic of poetry a middle-world pointing to the ultimate reconciliation of Pagan and Christian. His consciousness, like the nymph's love, stands ideally beyond the division into sacred and profane.

Ideally, for there remains the opening and crucial event, the blood fact which thrusts us into the midst of, and itself on, this happy world. I want to comment, finally, on its brevity. It stands against everything the pastoral stands for by a brutal shorthand. As such it threatens not only the realm of the nymph but also that of *musing* generally. The event is the intrusion of a historical into a pastoral world. Perhaps even more: is not history here set fatally against poetry? The problematic situation of the poet begins to emerge.

Before Marvell, the opposition between history and poetry is more conciliable. A poet, following Virgil's example, begins with pastoral or "oaten reeds" and graduates to epic or "trumpets sterne." Not that pastoral is completely aloof from history, from politics in the largest sense. The pressure of the greater world is there for those who can recognize it. Virgil always sings of "arms and the man," even in his pastoral world which is no less precarious or competitive than the world of the *Georgics* or of the *Aeneid*. There are things, crucial things, to be gained or lost in all the worlds. But with Spenser the realm of the pastoral expands so much that we never reach epic as such. *The Faerie Queene* is pastoral which has swallowed both epic and romance. Whatever the reason for this, it is clear from the shape of Spenser's career—which begins with a translation of those strange emblem sonnets in Van der Noot's *Theater for Worldings*—that the opposition now is less between pastoral and epic than between pastoral and apocalypse. Van der Noot's *Theater,* a kind of visionary peep show, sets up a pastoral image (a stately ship, a fair hind, a pure spring of water) only to show its destruction—the ship sunk, the hind hunted to death, the spring defiled. This medieval, or now Calvinistic, excerise can but lead to a passionate cry to be delivered from the body of this death, or to a justifying and compensatory revelation—we are duly given both. Although Spenser's part in the *Theater for Worldings* may have been marginal, his mature poetry develops as an attempt to overcome this crude kind of hiatus or vacillation between levels of truth. His allegories are a marvellous blend of pastoral, historical, and apocalyptic—an imaginative, fluid, and shifty continuum. The *Faerie Queene* is a maze that cannot be threaded except by a kind of relay technique: one interpretation being suspended in favor of another just as, on the level of plot, an action may be suspended in mid-career. Spenser pays a price, however, for this essentially humble emphasis on the depth and deviousness of the progress from pastoral innocence to ultimate truth. His poetry is patently a conceit, a magnanimous yet artificial construct. It suggests that only as *poesis* can poetry mediate between pastoral appearances, historical darkness, and apocalyptic revelation.

Poetry's mediating virtue is still, for Marvell, the great and necessary virtue, but no longer a sufficient one. The new, perhaps desperate faith of his age in the *sortes* of history—its desire for a clean break and a clear commencement of the kingdom of God on earth—militates against an ethic of compromise which poets had learned from their long endeavor to reconcile classical forms and Christian sentiments. The opening of Marvell's "Horatian Ode,"

> The forward Youth that would appear
> Must now forsake his *Muses* dear

drives a wedge between acting and musing as clearly as "The Nymph's

Complaint." It does so even as violently as that poem because Cromwell,

> like the three fork'd Lightning, first
> Breaking the Clouds where it was nurst,
> Did thorough his own Side
> His fiery way divide.

Cromwell's first act is that "bloody" stroke which in Marvell's poetry threatens so often the pastoral consciousness and expresses the necessity for civilization to proceed by and through schism. There is the stroke that separates
church from church, and now sect from sect; the stroke that separates
province from province; and the stroke that separates the head (the king)
from the body. What can poetry do in this situation? It gathers to itself at
the opposite pole the vision of lost and original unity, yet cannot be more
(because separated by history from history) than a perennial monument of
tears. Marvell's poem ends with an image of itself, an evocation of exquisitely
fashioned grief.

The irremediable disjoining of—in particular—profane and sacred, or
history and providence, is expressed most directly by the "Horatian Ode."
Cromwell's rejection of the slowly grinding divine mills, his espousal of an
actively urged salvation, violates, like the Troopers, a nature identified as
providential time. A "bleeding Head" is once again and ironically the
prerequisite for the body politic's wholeness. Marvell acknowledges this
wound inflicted on the "great Work of Time." Yet he lives at the heart of
the dilemma and refuses to hasten the end. He does not, like the nymph,
forsake hope in temporal salvation because of a single unnatural act. There
is no doubt, however, that Cromwell's mode of redemption is hazardous. The
new order is forced to unify by the sword, by division, by a rape of time.

At this point the obvious classical analogue to Marvell's story of nymph
and fawn becomes relevant. I refer to the slaying of Sylvia's stag in the seventh
book of the *Aeneid*. Here also there is a wanton intrusion of history-bearers
into a pastoral world. Marvell shares the Virgilian regret for a transcended
world closer to nature's rhythm. But that world is indistinguishable now
from the state of mind that can evoke it, a state of mind which has no future
and enshrines itself in idylls and precious relics. For despite Spenser's great
example, the forsaking of the Muses has continued. Having ravaged many
a blissful bower, the Renaissance hero will not spare the bower of poetry
itself. In "The Nymph" Spenserian allegory laments itself in the pagan form
of the brief elegy. The death of nymph and fawn denotes too deep a schism
in human affairs for pastoral allegory to assuage.

BARBARA   K.   LEWALSKI

Thomas Traherne: Naked Truth, Transparent Words, and the Renunciation of Metaphor

Traherne included extracts from Donne's sermons in his *Church's Year-Book*, as well as the whole of Herbert's poem, "To all Angels and Saints." Moreover, Traherne's poems, rediscovered in 1896 after falling into oblivion for more than two centuries, were first ascribed to Vaughan. Yet despite these links, both Traherne's theology and his part appear to set him apart from the major strain of seventeenth-century Protestant poetry and poetics.

His most striking departure from the Protestant consensus is his ecstatic celebration of infant innocence, which all but denies original sin as an hereditary taint, ascribing its effects chiefly to corruption by the world as the infant matures. His Neoplatonic conception of man's dignity and unlimited spiritual potential (often echoing Pico, Hermes Trismegistus, Theophilus Gale, and the Cambridge Platonists) is grounded upon the conviction that man's will is free and that he may always choose to live within the spiritual rather than the mundane order. Also Neoplatonic (and some feel, mystical) is Traherne's celebration of vision as the means whereby Christians may experience even now the bliss of eternity. In all this, Traherne seems to abandon the fundamental Protestant paradigm of the spiritual life with its Pauline classifications and its metaphors of struggle and pilgrimage. He seems also to avoid the Protestant emphasis upon providential history, which tends to assimilate individual Christian lives to typological patterns. Instead, as Stanley Stewart has noted, Traherne's pervasive imagery of cir-

From *Protestant Poetics and the Seventeenth-Century Religious Lyric.* ©1979 by Princeton University Press.

cularity breaks through linear time categories, associating infant innocence and regenerate vision with the sanctity and bliss enjoyed in the heavenly kingdom.

Traherne's poetry is also quite different form that of Donne, Herbert, and Vaughan. Except for *The Thanksgivings* it hardly qualifies as devotional poetry: instead of prayers or hymnic praises to God or mediations upon scripture, the creatures, or the sinful self, Traherne's lyrics are chiefly analyses and celebrations of the speaker's glorious condition, privileges, and joys. In addition, Traherne's distrust of language and figures seems much more radical than the doubts and hesitations voiced by other Protestant religious lyrists about poetic ornament. His poetics disparages metaphor by obscuring naked truth, and, although his poetry does not wholly eliminate tropes, the language is often curiously flat, with little development or exploitation of figures.

Yet for all of this, the fundamental elements of the Protestant poetics shape Traherne's poetry, and contribute largely to its often considerable power. It is usually valued below his prose, especially the dense, profound, tonally complex, and often strikingly beautiful *Centuries of Meditation*. At the same time studies of Traherne's markedly original thought tend to treat both modes together, as interchangeable vehicles of expression. By contrast, my concern with religious lyric requires attention to Traherne's poems in their own terms—to see what kind of poetic statement they make, by what poetic means, and how successfully. Stanley Steward has in part redressed the customary depreciation of Traherne's poetry promoted by new critical preferences for densely metaphorical, as opposed to more abstract, poetic language. But there is need to study Traherne's use and adaptation of the concepts and concerns of Protestant poetics in his various poems, with special attention to the rather different poetic methods employed in his . . . poetic sequences. . . .

Although the poetic texture is richer, fewer lyric kinds are represented in the Dobell than in the "Infant-Ey" sequence. There are no hymns (though one or two stanzas in "The Estate" and "Desire" rise to hymnic praise). There are no prayers, except for the final lines of "Thoughts (IV)." And there are no meditations on specific personal experiences become emblems, in the manner of "Shadows in the Water." Nor is there such a prodigal variety of stanzaic forms as in the "Infant-Ey" sequence but, rather, some meaningful recurrence of verse forms keyed to particular meditative styles. There are several long poems in heroic couplets often employing and usually beginning with epigrammatic maxims or axioms which associate them with the Biblical genre of Proverbs. These poems—"Dumnesse," "Silence," "Nature," "Thoughts (III)," "Thoughts (IV)"—tend to be logical, ordered analyses of rather complex arguments or abstract concepts. A larger number of poems are in regular lyric stanzas. Those in four- or-five-line stanzas— "The Instruction," "Ease," "Another," "The Rapture"—are simple songs or lessons, lyric expressions of a single impulse or emotion. Several others in regular stanzas of six, seven, or eight lines—"The Salutation," "The Vision," "Amendment"—are rather more elaborate in tone and argument. The rest, in long, intricately patterned stanzas with irregular line-lengths and highly complex rhyme schemes, are dithyrambic, ode-like: "The Preparative," "My Spirit," "Fullnesse," "The Anticipation," "The Recovery," "Love," "Thoughts (I)," "Thoughts (II)," "Desire," "Goodnesse." Traherne, it seems, has distinguished his basic meditative kinds by developing a formal analogy to the old rhetorical scheme of low, middle, and high styles.

His meditative sequence on man's felicity is ordered in three stages, each of which has two parts. The first stage, as [John] Wallace has noted, is a kind of preparation: the speaker recalls the experience of his innocent infant state and then derives from that experience a program and method for meditation. In the first four poems, the speaker recalls the infant felicity he once knew, as a basis for understanding the true human condition. But only the opening poem, "The Salutation," undertakes to render the infant's response directly, with the speaker personating the child in the moment of discovering and rejoicing in his limbs and senses and the world around him: "Welcom ye Treasures which I now receiv. / . . . Into this Eden so Divine and fair, / So Wide and Bright, I com his Son and Heir" (lines 12, 35–36). Yet even in this poem the naive response is filtered through the mature speaker's mind, as the diction of stanza four with its reference to "Organized Joynts, and Azure Veins" indicates, providing thereby a double perspective on the experience. The next poems, in the past tense, are clearly the mature speaker's recollections. "Wonder" records his response to the shining glory of all the creation and his sense that the world and its people are all his own: "How like an Angel come I down! / How Bright are all Things here! / When first among his Works I did appear" (lines 1–3). "Eden" defined that bliss as a "learned and a Happy Ignorance" (line 1) of all the vanities and errors and baubles of men, so that like Adam he saw only "The Glorious Wonders of the DEITIE" (line 49) "Innocence" identifies the chief bliss of that time as the absence of sin and guilt; skirting the question of whether evil comes through custom rather than nature, or whether God "by Miracle" removed the guilt of his original sin early, the speaker claims only that he did in fact recapitulate the Adamic innocence: "I was an Adam there, / A little Adam in a Sphere" (lines 51–52). As Wallace notes, these poems present something like a traditional meditative composition of place—with the significant difference that the normative scheme and pattern of perfection is taken from his own life rather than Christ's, in a radical extension of that application to the self so characteristic of Protestant meditation, typology, and sermons. The speaker concludes this initial phase with a formal resolution to undertake a species of reverse pilgrimage: "I must becom a Child again."

The next poems consider the means to that end, meditation, and again infancy provides the model. In "The Preparative" the speaker recalls his soul's earliest moment of consciousness, when it was as yet unaware of its bodily habitation, and still enjoyed unlimited vision of all things as "A Living Endless Ey, / Far wider then the Skie" (lines 12–13). This conception of his soul as "A Meditating Inward Ey" (line 27) dictates a meditative program of withdrawing from the world and the flesh so as to become again a serene and pure mind—"My Soul retire, / Get free, and so thou shalt even all Admire" (lines 69–70). "The Vision" concludes this preparatory stage by identifying the purpose of the flight-meditation: "Flight is but the Preparative: The Sight / Is Deep and Infinit" (lines 1–2). The speaker's goal is to learn to see the fountain of bliss, God, and more especially to recognize himself as the end or purpose of that bliss, and the recipient of all God's treasures.

The first meditative topic, infant felicity, is explored in two parts, the first of which, beginning with "The Rapture" and concluding with "Silence," analyzes the kind of seeing characteristic of infancy. Reversing the Ignation method, Traherne's meditations often begin with a stirring of the affections, and then proceed to analysis. In "The Rapture" the speaker, even as he retains his adult consciousness, personates the infant marveling at his own greatness and querying its source, even as Adam might have done:

> O how Divine
> Am I! To all this Sacred Wealth,
> This Life and Health,
> Who raisd? Who mine
> Did make the same? What Hand Divine!
> (16–20)

Then, in the analytic mode, "The Improvement" forcefully and logically argues the proposition, "Tis more to recollect, then make"—that is God's wisdom, power, and love are better displayed in the speaker's re-collection of all things as his own possessions, than they were in the initial creation.

He recalls also that his "Infant Sence" perceived God's attributes by instinct and effect, rather than (as now) by understanding (lines 67–70). In "The Approach" he marvels at God's initial advances—"He in our Childhood with us walks, / And with our Thoughts Mysteriously he talks" (lines 7–8)— but wonders still more at God's assaulting, wooing, and converting his adult heart, so that he now sees "with New and Open Eys" (line 25). The next two poems present the wordless, speechless condition of the child as guide to the meditator, for the child's dumbness and deafness enabled him "with Cleerer Eys / To see all Creatures full of Deities; Especially Ones self" ("Dumnesse," lines 39–41).

The shift to the second aspect of this topic, the kind of felicity won through the infant vision, is indicated by another rhapsody stirring the affections. "My Spirit" celebrates the speaker's amazed, ecstatic recognition of the infant seer-self as literally Godlike—simple, a "perfect Act" of seeing (line 26), his mind encompassing all places and things. Subsequent poems, from "The Apprehension," to "The Design," analyze this condition and its applicability to the speaker now. In "The Apprehension" he perceives that this intuition constituted "my whole felicitie" (line 7), and in "Fullnesse" he recognizes in that awareness the "Fountain" or "Spring" of present bliss and understanding (line 15). In "Nature" the speaker finds that nature's instantaneous teachings about the beauties of earth and sky reveal God's love to be the fountain and himself to be the recipient of all created good—a perception which understanding may preserve. "Ease" (in simple four-line stanzas contrasting sharply with the complex argument just concluded) expands lyrically upon the theme, "How easily doth Nature teach the Soul" (line 1). "Speed" testifies again to the instantaneousness of the infant's perception of the glories of creation, of his possession of all things, and of his own divine state. Finally, "The Designe" relates these insights to the *topos*, "Truth the daughter of Eternity," personifying that truth which was made lovely to him in infancy.

The second meditative topic looks beyond infant experience as model and guide, to consider the felicity proper to the adult Christian. This topic is also explored in two parts, but in this case the progression is from the nature of the felicity to the faculty by which it is attained. The first part, beginning with "The Person" and ending with "Love," analyzes the mature Christian's felicity in terms of his place in the divine economy, as the end of all God's works and desires and the source of all the praises and thanks-givings returned to God. "The Person" celebrates the body and all its functions, senses, and powers—not the infant or the Adamic body but the body the speaker now possesses and prizes. The speaker proposes now to add to what he at first perceived intuitively of the body's glory by creating "A richer Blazon . . . then first I found" (lines 2-3); this poetic blazon will be radically unmetaphorical, with all ornament removed so as to display the body's naked beauty. The poem ends with a catalogue of the body's glorious parts—"My Tongue, my Eys, / My Cheeks, my Lips, my Ears, my Hands, my Feet"—as "Themes" and "Organs" of divine praise (lines 60-64). In "The Estate" the mature speaker claims all the splendors of the world as his estate, possessed and enjoyed by means of the body's faculties and senses; the poem rises to a high pitch of emotion by the mimesis of the speaker's excited voice counting over all his wealth:

> We plough the very Skies, as well
> As Earth, the Spacious Seas
> Are ours; the Stars all Gems excell.
> The air was made to pleas
> The Souls of Men; Devouring fire
> Doth feed and Quicken Mans Desire.
> The Sun it self doth in its Glory Shine,
> And Gold and Silver out of very Mire,
> And Pearls and Rubies out of Earth refine,
> While Herbs and Flowers aspire
> To touch and make our feet Divine.
> (57-67)

The next group of poems is more abstract, exploring in ever more complex terms the interconnections among God, the world, and man, which constitute the basis for man's felicity and enable his praises. By a series of analogues from the natural order—the sponge must take up water before expressing it, the wine jug must receive wine before pouring it forth, the tenant must receive land before he can raise corn or pay rent—"The Circulation" argues the proposition that man must receive gifts and blessedness before he can give praise: "He must a King, before a Priest becom" (line 22). Receiving is a matter of seeing rightly the gifts which are always there: "*Tis Blindness Makes us Dumb. /* Had we but those Celestial Eys, / . . . *we should overflow / With Praises*" (lines 25-28). God seems at first to be exempt from this law of circulation, being the spring and ocean of all goods, but "Amendment" and "The Demonstration" revise this perception, affirming the greater value all things take on in God's eyes as they are enjoyed by, and evoke praises from, men. At the outset of "The Anticipation" the speaker is struck with amazement—"My Contemplation Dazles in the End / Of all I comprehend / And soars abov all Heights" (lines 1-3)—arising from the recognition of God as the ground of the whole circulation, the fountain, means, and end, a being with infinite desires and wants and joys. "The Recovery" urges man's profound responsibility for promoting God's felicity by his own "Gratitude, Thanksgiving, Prais" (line 55), and especially by offering "One Voluntary Act of Love":

> For God enjoyed is all his End.
> Himself he then doth Comprehend.
> When He is Blessed, Magnified,
> Extold, Exalted, Praisd, and Glorified
> Honord, Esteemd, Belovd, Enjoyd,
> Admired, Sanctified, Obeyd,
> That is receivd. For He
> Doth place his Whole Felicitie
> In that, who is despised and defied
> Undeified almost if once denied.
>
> (11-20)

This section culminates in "Love," an ecstatic paean itself providing that voluntary act of love. The poem conveys feeling and experience approaching if not attaining to mystical rapture. Beginning in a high rhetorical strain, the speaker seeks for analogues for God's gifts and God's love in Jove's golden rain showered on Danae, and Jove's elevation of Ganymede to his own banquet table. These are virtually the only mythological allusions in Traherne's lyrics, and even here the speaker soon gives over his recourse to the usual resources of poetic eloquence. Only a simple list of sanctioned Biblical metaphors can adequately suggest the love binding God and man:

> But these (tho great) are all
> Too short and small,
> Too Weak and feeble Pictures to Express
> The true Mysterious Depths of Blessedness.
> I am his Image, and his Friend.
> His Son, Bride, Glory, Temple, End.
>
> (35-40)

The second part of this topic explores the faculties by which the speaker as a mature Christian knows his glorious condition: the infant's *eye* was an organ of intuitive vision, to which the adult speaker's *thoughts* are the counterpart. "Thoughts (I)" is a long series of apostrophes describing and analyzing thoughts: they are "brisk Divine and Living Things," "Engines of Felicitie," a means to possess all joys (lines 1-6, 13). Their special quality is their omnipresence and eternity; ranging through space and time, they make past and future joys present, and in this they surpass even the Infant Eye, being the "Sweetest, last and most Substantial Treasures" (line 20). "Thoughts (II)" identifies a thought as the quintessence and fruit of all God's works and also the highest work of man, the temple of praise built by David. "Thoughts (III)" urges the divinity of thought:

> Thoughts are the Things wherwith even God is Crownd,
> And as the Soul without thems useless found,
> So are all other Creatures too. A Thought
> Is even the very Cream of all he wrought.
>
> A Thought can Cloathe it self with all the Treasures
> Of GOD, and be the Greatest of his Pleasures.
> It all his Laws, and Glorious Works, and Ways,
> And Attributs, and Counsels; all his Praise
> It can conceiv, and Imitate, and give:
> It is the only Being that doth live.
>
> (15–18, 49–54)

"Desire" begins as a thanksgiving to God for the "restlesse longing Heavenly Avarice" (line 8) which led the speaker to find an unknown paradise above the skies. "Thoughts (IV)" argues that, since thoughts may at any time be present at God's throne and see "The New Jerusalem, the Palaces,/ The Thrones and feasts, the Regions of the Skie, / The Joys and Treasures of the DEITIE" (lines 10–12), they are then the means by which "we in heav'n may be / Even here on Earth did we but rightly see" (lines 35–36). Through thoughts, God's omnipresence enters us, setting us above with the Seraphim. Thoughts, then, are Traherne's means for locating in the individual speaker (even as Donne locates in Elizabeth Drury) both infant innocence and heavenly glory; the speaker's thoughts recapitulate the one and foreshadow the other, making both present. As Richard Jordan notes, Traherne holds that the Christian living his life in the world lives at the same time in eternity. The conclusion of this poem (which might seem to be an apt conclusion to the sequence) is a brief prayer to God for grace to live in accordance with the terms just defined:

> O give me Grace to see thy face, and be
> A constant Mirror of Eternitie.
> Let my pure Soul, transformed to a Thought,
> Attend upon thy Throne, and as it ought

Spend all its Time in feeding on thy Lov,
And never from thy Sacred presence mov.
So shall my Conversation ever be
In Heaven, and I O Lord my GOD with Thee!
(95-102)

· But this is not the end. Having discovered himself to be closely conjoined with God in the circulations of thought, the speaker, in the final poem ("Goodnesse") joins with others in further circulations. Like God he finds his chief bliss in "The Bliss of other Men" (line 1), and like God he basks in the beams reflected from other men's faces. Moreover, he finds his own full fruition in other men's harvests—"The Soft and Swelling Grapes that on their Vines" ripen (line 49), and the praises produced by the "Swelling Grapes" of their lips:

Their Lips are soft and Swelling Grapes, their Tongues
A Quire of Blessed and Harmonious Songs.
    Their Bosoms fraught with Love
    Are Heaven all Heavens above
And being Images of GOD, they are
The Highest Joys his Goodness did prepare.
(65-70)

Traherne is characteristically Protestant in this return from contemplation to action, from right principles to active charity, from heavenly bliss to life in the world. To be sure, the world for Traherne is no vale of tears and sin but is itself enclosed within eternity for those whose right principles enable them so to view it. Yet Traherne's Christian elect must confront a challenge not altogether unlike that confronting the more traditionally conceived Protestant *miles Christianus* or *peregrinatus:* he must in a fallen world replete with sin and misery win through to, and hold fast to, spiritual vision—those "good thoughts" which alone reveal to man his true condition of felicity.

The dominant tropes in this as in the "Infant-Ey" sequence are light, sphere, and temple: they are first associated with the child's felicity and then, in altered terms, with the man's. The dominant symbol or synecdoche for the child and his special intuitive vision is (as before) the eye. The presentation of the speaker as child, and as disembodied eye, is often reminiscent in a general way of emblem plates and books, though the poems do not conform very closely to the details of specific emblems.

In these metaphorical terms, the child is first aware of a light conveying to him "a World of true Delight"; he enjoys "The anchient Light of Eden," and was "A little Adam in a Sphere." And even before he became aware of his own senses and of the world they conveyed to him, he was aware of his soul as "an *Inward Sphere of Light,* / Or an Interminable Orb of *Sight* / . . . all Sight, or Ey." God's wisdom, power, and goodness reflected in his works delight the child's eye which is "The Sphere / Of all Things," yet the mature speaker intimates his possession of an "eye" which can see farther than the child's: "But Oh! the vigor of mine Infant Sence / Drives me too far: I had not yet the Eye / The Apprehension, or Intelligence / Of Things so very Great Divine and High." Speechless, dwelling within a "World of Light," the child's eyes bring the spiritual meaning of the universe into the "Temple" of his mind, in which ceremony the earth serves as priest:

> Before which time a Pulpit in my Mind,
> A Temple, and a Teacher I did find,
> With a large Text to comment on. No Ear,
> But Eys them selvs were all the Hearers there.
> And evry Stone, and Evry Star a Tongue,
> And evry gale of Wind a Curious Song.
> The Heavens were an Orakle, and spake
> *Divinity:* The Earth did undertake
> The office of a Priest; and I being Dum
> (Nothing besides was dum;) All things did com
> With Voices and Instructions.
>   ("Dumnesse," 57–67)

In "Silence" the speaker sees the infant spirit as a sphere encompassing both God and the world: "The World was more in me, then I in it. / The King of Glory in my Soul did sit. / . . . For so my Spirit was an Endless Sphere" (lines 81–82, 85). Expanding on that last image, "My Spirit" ecstatically celebrates the child's soul as "all Ey, all Act, all Sight" like the Deity, imaging and so embodying all things as "A Strange Mysterious Sphere," "A Strange Extended Orb of Joy," which is, like God, center and circumference of everything (lines 29, 76, 86). Modulating to the present tense in an apostrophe to that child-soul which is at once sphere, eye, and temple, he intimates that the soul's nature and capacities remain unchanged in the mature speaker:

> O Wondrous Self! O Sphere of Light,
>   O Sphere of Joy most fair;
> O Act, O Power infinit;

O Subtile, and unbounded Air!
O Living Orb of Sight!
Thou which within me art, yet Me! Thou Ey,
And temple of his Whole Infinitie!
O what a World art Thou! a World within!
All Things appear,
All Objects are
Alive in thee! Supersubstancial, Rare
Abov them selvs, and nigh of Kin
To those pure Things we find
In his Great Mind.

(103-16)

In the section concerned with adult felicity the key metaphors—light, sphere, and temple—are associated with thought (rather than with the eye) as the quintessence of the human spirit. In "The Circulation" the soul's participation in a cosmic spherical process is indicated: the source of the soul's bliss is the reflection of the "fair Ideas" from the sky in the "Spotless Mirror" of the mind (lines 1,3), and the soul cooperates in the eternal circulation of gifts and praises exchanged between God and Man, whereby both are at once fountain, stream, and end of all things. Vision is now a matter of gaining the "Celestial Eys" to recognize these circulations and contribute the praises which make up man's part—"*Tis Blindness Makes us Dum*" (lines 24, 25). But as "The Demonstration" shows and its title implies, celestrial eyes are a function more of thought than of sight: eyes are susceptible to "Miste," and the highest things—such as these principles of circulation—are "only capable of being *Known*" (lines 2, 3). Such knowledge however finally dissolves in light—"My Contemplation Dazles in the End / Of all I comprehend" ("The Anticipation," lines 1, 2). The "Thoughts" poems assume and argue the dominance of thought over sight. In "Thoughts (I)" thoughts are identified as "Engines of Felicitie" seated in the spirit: serving as a mirror to reflect all things, they thereby contain them and so endow the soul "with Life and Sight," whereby it comprehends eternity, time, and space (lines 6, 50). Thoughts, though unseen, are thus, paradoxically, supreme. In "Thoughts (II)" a thought is identified as the quintessence and fruit of all God's works and also the ultimate human creation: "That Temple David did intend, / Was but a Thought, and yet it did transcend / King Solomons" (lines 25-27). As such it is a world (sphere) which far surpasses the world created by God: "It is a Spiritual World within. / A Living World, and nearer far of Kin / To God, then that which first he made" (lines 43-45). "Thoughts (III)" represents thoughts (when good) as the offspring of God, spheres which bear "the Image of their father's face" (line 31); as the greatest, most transcendent, and most divine of beings they make the soul infinite and omnipresent as God is:

> The Best of Thoughts is yet a thing unknown,
> But when tis Perfect it is like his Own:
> Intelligible, Endless, yet a Sphere
> Substantial too: In which all Things appear.
> All Worlds, all Excellences, Sences, Graces,
> Joys, Pleasures, Creatures, and the Angels Faces.
>   (67-72)

Finally, "Thoughts (IV)" presents God's eternity as a "true Light" enclosing us, and God's omnipresence as an "Endless Sphere, / Wherin all Worlds as his Delights appear" (lines 41, 29-30), identifying thought as the vehicle for living even now in God's eternity and omnipresence. Moreover, as the soul by thought dwells above with God, so God by his eternity and omnipresence dwells in the "pure Soul, transformed to a Thought" (line 97):

> It enters in, and doth a Temple find,
> Or make a Living one within the Mind.
> That while Gods Omnipresence in us lies,
> His Treasures might be all before our Eys:
> For Minds and Souls intent upon them here,
> Do with the Seraphims abov appear:
> And are like Spheres of Bliss, by Lov and Sight,
> By Joy, Thanksgiving, Prais, made infinite.
>   (87-94)

The final spheres the speaker enjoys and possesses are seemingly more commonplace but even more wonderful—the "grapes" of other men's harvests and other men's lips employed in praises ("Goodnesse").

As their title suggests, Traherne's *Thanksgivings* are in the hymnic mode. We have seen that the two meditative sequences [the Dobell and the "Infant-Ey"] contain little in the mode of prayer or praise: the Dobell sequence calls for and argues the necessity for man's praises in the total divine economy, but does not actually produce them. The apostrophes and celebrations in both of these sequences are directed to the glorious self. But Traherne's *Thanksgivings* is a book of divine praises and thanksgivings, modeled upon and indeed incorporating large segments from the Book of Psalms. Such assimilation is akin to Traherne's characteristic inclusion of lengthy extracts from other men's writings in his *Church's Year-Book* and *Meditations on the Six Days of the Creation,* but his purpose and aesthetic accomplishment here are very different. The *Thanksgivings* is an achieved poetic work, not a collection of extracts nor a series of meditations upon Biblical texts: in them various Biblical voices, and especially David's are fused with Traherne's own. Traherne does not merely paraphrase or imitate the Psalmist, nor does he, like Herbert, seek to become a New Covenant psalmist, recasting the Psalmist's role in his own antitypical terms. Rather, he assimilates the Psalmist's voice to his own, so that the Davidic type becomes part of the antitype he himself presents. This strategy has produced poems which are set forth as hymns of thanksgiving, closely modeled upon the rhythms and cadences of the psalms and the prophetic books. However, Traherne's hymns are not lyrical; they are indeed hardly poetry in the usual sense. Rather, they are long prose-poems or free-verse rhapsodies, in a mixture of styles but in an overall tone of sublime exaltation. Curiously enough, the poetics defined in these praises is not unlike that set forth in the other sequences, but here the Psalmist is claimed as the model for Traherne's consistently-held ideal of sublime plainness:

> *All Tropes are Clouds; Truth doth it self excel,*
> *Whatever Heights, Hyperboles can tell.*

> O that I were as *David,* the sweet Singer of Israel!
> In meeter Psalms to set forth thy Praises.
> ("Thanksgivings for the Body," 339-42)

Though the *Thanksgivings* contain extracts from and allusions to some other Biblical books, for all but the last of them the Psalms provide the pervasive ground tone. "Thanksgivings for the Body" is probably the most complex, conjoining the greatest variety of modes of discourse. The poem begins with a verbatim extract from Psalms 103:1-5, introducing the pattern of long, free-verse lines of sonorous praise: "Bless the Lord, O my Soul: and all that is within me bless his holy name." A short passage in the poet's own "psalmic" but more personal voice follows, proclaiming his intention to praise: "O Lord who are clothed with Majesty, / My desire is, to praise thee. / With the holy Angels and Archangels / To glorifie thee" (lines 10-13). Another extract (Psalm 139:14-18) follows, ringing out again the Psalmist's lofty praises: "I will praise thee, for I am fearfully and wonderfully made, marvellous are thy works" (lines 20-21). Then, for a long passage, the speaker's analytic voice takes over, making large use of syntactical parallelism, repetitive schemes, and Ramistical outlines to divine, enumerate, list,

and categorize the elements and aspects of the body he praises. The following
passage is typical of this mode:

> O blessed be thy glorious Name!
> That thou has made it,
>   A Treasury of Wonders,
>   Fit for its several Ages;
>   For Dissections,
>   For Sculptures in Brass,
>   For Draughts in Anatomy,
>   For the Contemplation of the Sages.
>   Whose inward parts,
>   Enshrined in thy Libraries,
>   The Amazement of the Learned,
>   The Admiration of Kings and Queens,
>   Are ⎰ The Joy of Angels;
>   The Organs of my Soul.
>   The Wonder of Cherubims.
>   (59–73)

Or this, in a more schematic and cryptic vein of analysis:

> Even for our earthly bodies, hast thou created all things.
>   ⎰ Visible.
>   All things ⎱ Material.
>   ⎱ Sensible.
>   Animals,
>   Vegetables,
>   Minerals,
>   Bodies celestial,
>   Bodies terrestrial,
>   The four Elements,
>   Volatile Spirits,
>   Trees, Herbs, and Flowers,
>   The Influences of Heaven,
>   Clouds, Vapors, Wind,
>   Dew, Rain, Hail, and Snow,
>   Light and Darkness, Night and Day,
>   The Seasons of the Year.
>   (242–58)

This analytic mode is punctuated throughout by allusions to and extracts from the psalms of praise, and (occasionally) from other Biblical books. Such passages are sometimes quoted verbatim, but are more often adapted so as to blend unobtrusively with the syntax and rhythms of the speaker's voice. The poem also has two extended passages of personal meditation in a smooth and elegant middle style (iambic pentameter couplets) which falls somewhere between the plain (curt) style of the analytic sections and the rhapsodic psalmic passages. The final lines of the work are virtually a melange of psalm extracts, culminating with extracts from Canticles (4:9-11, 6:12-13, 8:2, 8:1) which present in the love exchanges of the Bride and Bridegroom the highest pitch of exaltation of the body and the senses. The work concludes with a prose prayer petitioning and thanking God for the power to praise him.

The remaining Thanksgivings—"for the Soul," "for the Glory of God's Works," "for the Blessedness of God's Ways," "for the Blessedness of his LAWS," "for the Beauty of his Providence," "for the Wisdom of his WORD," "for God's Attributes"—are somewhat simpler in structure in that they have nothing resembling the couplet passages included in the "Thanksgivings for the Body," and only the "Thanksgivings for the Soul" ends (like the former poem) with a prose prayer. Otherwise, they exhibit the same mix of modes—psalm extracts, rhapsodic passages imitative of the Psalms, schematic analytic passages, brief Biblical allusions and quotations chiefly but not exclusively from the Psalms—all assimilated without identification or distinction into the poet's complex voice. The subjects of praise dictate the manner of development and the choice of Biblical material. In "Thanksgivings for the Soul" Traherne invokes his favorite eye and temple tropes for the soul:

> For the Glory of my Soul:
> Which out of Nothing thou has builded,
> To be a Temple unto God.
> A living Temple of thine Omnipresence.
> An understanding Eye.
> A Temple of Eternity.
> A Temple of thy Wisdom, Blessedness, and Glory.
>   (16-22)

The "Thanksgivings for the Glory of God's Works" draws most heavily upon the psalms praising the creatures, including man—Psalm 8, 65, 103, 104, and the Mosaic blessings in Deuteronomy 33:13-16. The "Thanksgivings for . . . his LAWS" is a kind of descant upon extracts and passages from that long, artful celebration of the Law, Psalm 119.

The final poem, "A Thanksgiving and Prayer for the NATION," is cast, as its title signifies, in a more complex mode. With this poem, the *Thanksgivings,* like the meditative sequences, conclude by reaching out to other men, as the speaker defines his role in relation to others. As he has been a psalmist incorporating the stance and voice of David in giving praises to God, so now he becomes a prophet adopting and adapting the words and manner of the major prophets in speaking to God, about and for God's people:

> O Lord spare thy people;
>> Spare thy people, O my God!
> Those Jewels in thy Cabinet, those Persons on thy Stage,
> that fill the World with wonderful Actions.
>
> Make me a $\begin{cases} Moses, \\ Nehemiah, \\ Ezra, David \end{cases}$ to thee & them.
>
> (47-53)

The Biblical extracts in this work are from the major prophets—Moses (Deut. 9), Isaiah, Jeremiah, David's psalms of meditation, and especially Lamentations. Indeed, at one juncture, Traherne not only echoes particular passages in Lamentations but takes on the persona, developed in chapters one and two of that book, of the city as bereaved widow weeping for her desolation and that of her children:

> Tread not underfoot thy might men,
>> In the midst of me,
>> Crush not my young men.
> Carry not my Virgins away Captive O Lord.
> They respect not the persons of Priests or Elders.
> Let not the breath of our Nostrils be taken in their pits;
>> Nor our Princes suffer the reproach of Servants. Nor our
> Fathers be abused; nor our Bodies lie as Dung upon the Ground;
> nor our Wives be ravished: nor our Children slain in the top of
> every Street.
>
> In the days of her affliction, all the pleasant things that my
> people had of old, would come into mind;
>> Increase my Melancholy,
> And shew me the filth of her skirts in those.
>
> (153-76)

Traherne's three verse sequences are conceptually fascinating, as daring attempts to link together intricate philosophical argument and rhapsodic emotional response; moreover, they show conscious experimentation in a variety of genres and styles and verse forms. With Traherne, the Protestant poetics of the religious lyric develops in one clearly defined direction out from the center occupied by Herbert and Vaughan. Traherne is as conscious a theorist as Herbert about the poet's responsibility to praise God and about the issue of appropriate plainness for the religious lyric; he also experiments as readily, though in different ways, with Biblical models and genres and with the appropriation of Biblical personae as quasi-typological figures for himself as poet. Moreover, his poetic sequences derive their special power from that personal testimony and self-probing which is the dominant characteristic of the Protestant line: in Traherne's poems this power inheres in a complex persona who registers urgently and vibrantly a wide spectrum of spiritual emotions and experiences.

But Traherne's religious lyrics are less successful as poems than those of Donne, Herbert, and Vaughan—in part perhaps because his vision of the Protestant aesthetic involved approaching language as a transparent medium pointing to essences rather than as a densely and complexly suggestive poetic matrix. Accordingly, he draws upon Biblical models and genres and personae, Biblical metaphors and typological symbolism in rather direct and conceptual ways, whereas the other poets discussed here were able to use these elements as stimuli for their own creative responses and as a treasury of language, symbolism, and association which could give a special charge to their own words. To say this is to recognize that although Traherne's achievement in the religious lyric is considerable, his mind and sensibility are those of a philosopher even more than a poet, and that he has moved the religious lyric and its poetics some distance in the direction of philosophical abstraction.

Chronology

1572	John Donne born.
1584	Donne matriculates at Hart Hall, Oxford.
1591	Robert Herrick born.
1592	Donne admitted to Lincoln's Inn.
1593	George Herbert born.
1596	Donne sails with Essex in the English expedition to Cadiz.
1597	Donne sails on the Azores Expedition.
ca. 1598	Donne becomes secretary to Sir Thomas Egerton.
1601	Donne marries Ann More, secretly, and is imprisoned by her father, Sir George More, the following year and dismissed from his post with Egerton.
1605	Herbert attends Westminster School.
1609	Herbert enters Trinity College, Cambridge.
1610	Donne publishes *Pseudo-Martyr*.
1611	Donne publishes *Ignatius His Conclave* and *The First Anniversarie*.
1612	Donne publishes *The Second Anniversarie*. Herbert publishes two memorial poems, in Latin, on the death of Prince Henry.
ca. 1612	Richard Crashaw born.

1613	Herrick enters St. John's College, Cambridge; receives B.A. in 1617, M.A. in 1620.
1615	Donne ordained as deacon and priest at St. Paul's Cathedral; appointed royal chaplain.
1617	Donne's wife Ann dies.
1618	Herbert appointed reader in rhetoric at Cambridge.
1620	Herbert elected public orator at Cambridge.
1621	Henry Vaughan born. Andrew Marvell born. Donne elected Dean of St. Paul's.
1623	Donne composes *Devotions Upon Emergent Occasions*. Herrick ordained as deacon and priest of the Church of England.
1623-27	Herrick lives in London, associating with Jonson and other poets.
1631	Donne delivers *Death's Duel,* his last sermon; dies on March 31. Crashaw enters Pembroke College, Cambridge; receives B.A. in 1634, M.A. in 1638.
1633	Herbert dies; *The Temple* published posthumously. Donne's first collected edition of poems published. Marvell matriculates at Trinity College, Cambridge.
1635	Crashaw ordained as a priest in the Anglican Church.
1637	Thomas Traherne born.
1638	Vaughan studies at Jesus College, Oxford.
1639	Marvell receives B.A. from Cambridge.
1640	Vaughan in London studying law.
ca. 1642	Marvell travels abroad in Holland, France, Italy, and Spain.
1643	Crashaw flees from Cambridge before Cromwell's forces; he lives in exile on the continent.
1645	Crashaw converts to Catholicism. Vaughan serves in the Royalist army.

1646   Vaughan publishes *Poems, with the Tenth Satyre of Juvenal.*
        While in Rome, Crashaw's *Steps to the Temple* and *The Delights of the Muses* are published in London.

1648   Herrick publishes *Hesperides.*

1649   Crashaw dies.

1650   Vaughan publishes the first part of *Silex Scintillans.*
        Marvell writes "Tom May's Death" and "An Horatian Ode."

1652   Traherne enters Brasenose College, Oxford; receives B.A. in 1656.
        Marvell dedicates "Upon the Hill and Grove at Bill-borow" and "Upon Appleton House" to Thomas, Lord Fairfax.
        Crashaw's *Carmen Deo Nostro* published posthumously in Paris.

1655   Vaughan publishes the second part of *Silex Scintillans.*
        Marvell publishes "The First Anniversary of Government Under His Highness the Lord Protector."

1657   Marvell appointed Latin secretary.

1659   Marvell elected to a seat in Parliament for Hull, which he holds until 1678.

1660   Traherne ordained as deacon and priest.
        Marvell works to release Milton from prison.

ca. 1666–70   Traherne composes *Centuries of Meditations.*

1667   Marvell writes "Last Instructions to a Painter"; "Clarindon's House-Warming."

1669   Traherne receives Doctor of Divinity from Brasenose College, Oxford.

1672   Marvell publishes *The Rehearsal Transpros'd.*

1673   Traherne publishes *Roman Forgeries* anonymously.

1674   Herrick dies.
        Traherne dies.

1678   Marvell dies.

1681   Marvell's *Miscellaneous Poems* published.

1695   Vaughan dies.

Contributors

HAROLD BLOOM, Sterling Professor of the Humanities at Yale University, is the author of *The Anxiety of Influence, Poetry and Repression,* and many other volumes of literary criticism. His forthcoming study, *Freud: Transference and Authority,* attempts a full-scale reading of all of Freud's major writings. A MacArthur Prize Fellow, he is general editor of five series of literary criticism published by Chelsea House.

JOHN FRECCERO is Rosina Pierotti Professor of Italian Literature at Stanford University and is best known for his various articles on Dante.

JOHN HOLLANDER is Professor of English at Yale University. His books include *The Untuning of the Sky* and *The Figure of Echo.*

WILLIAM KERRIGAN is Professor of English at the University of Virginia. His books include *The Prophetic Milton* and *The Scared Complex: On the Psychogenesis of "Paradise Lost."*

CLAUDIA BRODSKY is Assistant Professor of Comparative Literature at Princeton University, and has published essays on Goethe and seventeenth-century literature.

THOMAS R. WHITAKER is Professor of English at Yale University and the author of *Swan and Shadow: Yeats's Dialogue with History* and *William Carlos Williams.*

STANLEY E. FISH is Professor of English at The Johns Hopkins University. His books include *Surprised by Sin: The Reader in "Paradise Lost"* and *Self-Consuming Artifacts.*

HELEN VENDLER is Professor of English at Boston University and visiting Professor at Harvard University. She is the author of *Yeats's "Vision" and the Later Plays* and *On Extended Wings: Wallace Stevens's Longer Poems.*

A. R. CIRILLO teaches English at Northwestern University and is the author of articles on Milton and on English Renaissance poetry.

LOUIS MARTZ is Sterling Professor of English Emeritus at Yale University. His numerous books include *The Poetry of Meditation* and *The Paradise Within.*

RUTH NEVO is Professor of English Literature at the Hebrew University of Jerusalem. She is the author of *Comic Transformations in Shakespeare* and *The Dial of Virtue.*

HARRY BERGER, JR. is Professor of English at the University of California, Santa Cruz. He is the author of *The Allegorical Temper* and many essays on Spenser and the Renaissance.

GEOFFREY HARTMAN is Karl Young Professor of English and Comparative Literature at Yale University. His books include *Wordsworth's Poetry* and *The Fate of Reading.*

BARBARA K. LEWALSKI is Professor of English at Harvard University. She is the author of *Milton's Brief Epic: The Genre, Meaning, and Art of "Paradise Lost"* and *Donne's "Anniversaries" and the Poetry of Praise.*

Bibliography

JOHN DONNE

Aers, David, Bob Hodges, and Gunther Kress. *Literature, Language, and Society in England, 1580–1680.* Dublin: Gill and MacMillan, 1981.

Allen, Don Cameron. "Dean Donne Sets His Text." *ELH* 10 (1943): 208–29.

———. "The Double Journey of John Donne." In *A Tribute to George Coffin Taylor,* edited by Arnold Williams, 83–99. Chapel Hill: University of North Carolina Press, 1952.

Andreasen, N. J. C. *John Donne: Conservative Revolutionary.* Princeton: Princeton University Press, 1967.

Anselment, Raymond A. " 'Ascensio Mendax, Descensio Crudelis': The Image of Babel in the *Anniversaries." ELH* 38 (1971): 188–205.

Armstrong, Alan. "The Apprenticeship of John Donne: Ovid and the *Elegies." ELH* 44 (1977): 419–42.

Bennet, Joan. *Five Metaphysical Poets.* Cambridge: Cambridge University Press, 1963.

Benson, Donald R. "Platonism and Neoclassic Metaphor: Dryden's *Eleonora* and Donne's *Anniversaries." Studies in Philology* 68 (1971): 340–56.

Carrithers, Gale. *Donne at Sermons.* Albany: State University of New York Press, 1972.

Cathcart, D. *Doubting Conscience: Donne and the Poetry of Moral Argument.* Ann Arbor: University of Michigan Press, 1975.

Chambers, A. B. " 'Good Friday, 1613. Riding Westward': The Poem and the Tradition." *ELH* 28 (1961): 31–53.

Colie, Rosalie. *Paradoxica Epidemica: The Renaissance Tradition of Paradox.* Princeton: Princeton University Press, 1966.

Elliot, Emory. "The Narrative and Allusive Unity of Donne's *Satyres."*

Journal of English and Germanic Philology 75 (1976): 105-16.

Empson, William. "Donne and the Rhetorical Tradition." *Kenyon Review* 11 (1949): 571-87.

Fiore, P. A., ed. *Just So Much Honor.* University Park: Pennsylvania State University Press, 1972.

Fowler, Alastair. *Triumphal Forms.* Cambridge: Cambridge University Press, 1970.

Fox, Ruth A. "Donne's *Anniversaries* and the Art of Living." *ELH* 38 (1971): 528-41.

Gardner, Helen. "The Argument about the *Ecstasy*." In *Elizabethan and Jacobean Studies Presented to F. P. Wilson,* edited by H. Davies and H. Gardner. Oxford: Clarendon Press, 1959.

Guss, Donald L. *John Donne, Petrarchist: Italianate Conceits and Love Theory in the "Songs and Sonets."* Detroit: Wayne State University Press, 1966.

Hardison, O. B., Jr. *The Enduring Moment: A Study of the Idea of Praise in Renaissance Literary Theory and Practice.* Chapel Hill: University of North Carolina Press, 1962.

Henrickson, Bruce. "The Unity of Reason and Faith in John Donne's Sermons." *Papers on Language and Literature* 11 (1975): 18-30.

Hughes, Richard E. *The Progress of the Soul: The Interior Career of John Donne.* New York: Morrow, 1968.

Hunt, Clay. *Donne's Poetry.* New Haven: Yale University Press, 1954.

Lauritsen, John R. "Donne's *Satyres*: The Drama of Self-Discovery." *Studies in English Literature* 16 (1976): 117-30.

Leishman, J. B. *The Monarch of Wit: An Analytical and Comparative Study of the Poetry of John Donne.* London: Hutchinson, 1951.

Levine, Jay Arnold. "'The Dissolution': Donne's Twofold Elegy." *ELH* 28 (1961): 301-15.

Love, Harold. "The Argument of Donne's *First Anniversary*." *Modern Philology* 64 (1966): 125-31.

Manley, Frank, ed. *John Donne:* The Anniversaries. Baltimore: The Johns Hopkins University Press, 1963.

Martz, Louis. *The Poetry of Meditation.* New Haven: Yale University Press, 1954.

Maud, Ralph N. "Donne's *First Anniversary*." *Boston University Studies in English* 2 (1956): 218-25.

Mazzaro, Jerome. *Tranformations in the Renaissance Lyric.* Ithaca: Cornell University Press, 1970.

Miller, Clarence H. "Donne's 'A Nocturnall Upon S. Lucies Day' and the

Nocturne of Matins." *Studies in English Literature* 6 (1966), 77–86.

Miner, Earl Roy. *The Metaphysical Mode from Donne to Cowley.* Princeton: Princeton University Press, 1969.

Mueller, William R. *John Donne, Preacher.* Princeton: Princeton University Press, 1962.

Nellist, B. F. "Donne's 'Storm' and 'Calm' and the Descriptive Tradition." *Modern Language Review* 59 (1964), 511–5.

Pepperdene, Margaret W., ed. *That Subtle Wreath: Lectures Presented at Quartercentenary Celebration of the Birth of John Donne.* Atlanta: Agnes Scott College, 1973.

Praz, Mario. *The Flaming Heart.* New York: Doubleday, 1958.

Rooney, William J. " 'The Canonization': The Language of Paradox Reconsidered." *ELH* 23 (1956): 36–47.

Roston, Murray. *The Soul of Wit: A Study of John Donne.* Oxford: Clarendon Press, 1974.

Sackton, Alexander. "Donne and the Privacy of Verse." *Studies in English Literature* 7 (1967): 67–82.

Sanders, Wilbur. *John Donne's Poetry.* Cambridge: Cambridge University Press, 1971.

Sicherman, Carol M. "The Mocking Voices of Donne and Marvell." *Bucknell Review* 17 (1969): 38–40.

Sleight, Richard. "John Donne: 'A Nocturnall Upon S. Lucies Day, Being The Shortest Day'." In *Interpretations,* edited by John Wain. London: Routledge and Kegan Paul, 1955.

Sloan, Thomas O. "The Rhetoric in the Poetry of John Donne." *Studies in English Literature* 3 (1963): 31–44.

Smith A. J. *John Donne: The Songs and Sonnets.* London: Arnold, 1964.

——, ed. *John Donne: Essays in Celebration.* London: Methuen, 1972.

Smith, James. "Metaphysical Poetry." In *Determinations,* edited by F. R. Leavis. London: Folcroft Press, 1934.

Spencer, Theodore, ed. *A Garland for John Donne.* Cambridge, Mass.: Harvard University Press, 1931.

Stein, Arnold. *John Donne's Lyrics: The Eloquence of Action.* Minneapolis: University of Minnesota Press, 1962.

Stanwood, P. G. " 'Essential Joye' in Donne's *Anniversaries.*" *Texas Studies in Literature and Language* 13 (1971): 227–38.

Tuve, Rosemond. *Elizabethan and Metaphysical Imagery.* Chicago: The University of Chicago Press, 1947.

Webber, Joan. *Contrary Music: The Prose Style of John Donne.* Madison: University of Wisconsin Press, 1963.

Williamson, George. "The Design of Donne's *Anniversaries.*" *Modern Philology* 60 (1963): 183-91.

———. "The Convention of 'The Exstasie'." In *Seventeenth Century Contexts.* London: Faber and Faber, 1960.

ROBERT HERRICK

Allen, Don Cameron. "Good Friday: Rex Tragicus, or Christ Going to His Crosse." In *Image and Meaning: Metaphoric Traditions in the Renaissance*" 138-51. Baltimore: The Johns Hopkins University Press, 1968.

Asals, Heather. "King Solomon in the Land of the *Hesperides.*" *Texas Studies in Literature and Language* 18 (1976): 362-80.

Berman, Ronald. "Herrick's Secular Poetry." *English Studies* 52 (1971): 20-30.

Braden, Gordon. *The Classics and English Renaissance Poetry: Three Case Studies.* New Haven: Yale University Press, 1978.

Briggs, Katherine M. *The Anatomy of Puck: An Examination of Fairy Beliefs Among Shakespeare's Contemporaries and Successors.* London: Routledge and Kegan Paul, 1959.

Brooks, Cleanth. "What Does Poetry Communicate?" In *The Well Wrought Urn.* New York: Harcourt Brace Jovanovich, 1947.

Capwell, Richard L. "Herrick and the Aesthetic Principle of Variety and Contrast." *South Atlantic Quarterly* 71 (1972): 488-95

Chambers, A. B. "Herrick and the Trans-Shifting of Time." *Studies in Philology* 72 (1975): 85-114.

———. "Herrick, Corinna, Canticles, and Catullus." *Studies in Philology* 74 (1977): 216-27.

Deming, Robert H. *Ceremony and Art: Robert Herrick's Poetry.* The Hague and Paris: Mouton, 1974.

DeNeef, A. Leigh. *"This Poetik Liturgie": Robert Herrick's Ceremonial Mode.* Durham, N.C.: Duke University Press, 1974.

Gertzman, Jay. "Robert Herrick's Recreative Pastoral." *Genre* 7 (1974): 183-95.

Godshalk, William Leigh. "Art and Nature: Herrick and History." *Essays in Criticism* 17 (1967): 121-4.

Holmer, Joan Ozark. "Religious Satire in Herrick's *The Faerie Temple: or, Oberons Chappell.*" *Renaissance and Reformation* 17 (1981): 40-57.

Jenkins, Paul R. "Rethinking What Moderation Means to Robert Herrick." *ELH* 39 (1972): 49-65.

Kimmey, John L. "Order and Form in Herrick's *Hesperides.*" *Journal of English and Germanic Philology* 70 (1971): 255-68.

———. "Robert Herrick's Persona." *Studies in Philology* 67 (1970): 221-36.

Malpezzi, Frances P. "The Feast of Circumcision: The Return to Sacred Time in Herrick's *Noble Numbers.*" *Notre Dame English Journal* 14 (1981): 29-40.

Marcus, Leah Sinanoglou." Herrick's *Noble Numbers* and the Politics of Playfulness." *English Literary Renaissance* 7 (1977): 108-26.

———. "Herrick's *Hesperides* and the 'Proclamation Made for May'." *Studies in Philology* 76 (1979): 49-74.

Miller, Edmund. "Sensual Imagery in the Devotional Poetry of Robert Herrick." *Christianity and Literature* 28, no. 2 (1979): 24-33.

Miner, Earl Roy. *The Cavalier Mode from Jonson to Cotton.* Princeton: Princeton University Press, 1971.

Patrick, J. Max, and Roger Rollin, eds., *Trust to Good Verses: Herrick Tercentenary Essays.* Pittsburgh: University of Pittsburgh Press, 1978.

Reed, Mark L. "Herrick among the Maypoles: Dean Prior and the *Hesperides.*" *Studies in English Literature* 5 (1965): 133-50.

Schleiner, Louise. "Herrick's Songs and the Character of *Hesperides.*" *English Literary Renaissance* 6 (1976): 77-91.

Schwenger, Peter. "Herrick's Fairy State." *ELH* 46 (1979): 35-55.

Strakman, Miriam. "*Noble Numbers* and the Poetry of Devotion." In *Reason and the Imagination: Studies in the History of Ideas 1600-1800,* edited by J. A. Mazzeo. New York: Doubleday, 1962.

Summers, Joseph H. *The Heirs of Donne and Jonson.* New York: Oxford University Press, 1970.

Toliver, Harold. "Herrick's Books of Realms and Moments." *ELH* 49 (1982): 429-48.

Warren, Austin. "Herrick Revisited." *Michigan Quarterly Review* 15 (1976): 245-67.

Woodward, Daniel H. "Herrick's Oberon Poems." *Journal of English and Germanic Philology* 64 (1965): 270-84.

GEORGE HERBERT

Allen, Don Cameron. "George Herbert, 'The Rose'." In *Image and Meaning: Metaphoric Traditions in Renaissance Poetry,* 102-14. Baltimore: The Johns Hopkins University Press, 1968.

Asals, Heather, *Equivocal Predication: George Herbert's Way to God.* Toronto: University of Toronto Press, 1981.

Bell, Ilona. " 'Setting Foot into Divinity': George Herbert and the English Reformation, " *Modern Language Quarterly* 38 (1977): 219-41.

Benet, Diana. *Secretary of Praise: The Poetic Vocation of George Herbert.* Columbia, Mo.: University of Missouri Press, 1984.

Bloch, Chana. "George Herbert and the Bible: A Reading of 'Love (III)'." *English Literary Renaissance* 8 (1978): 329-40.

Blunden, Edmund. "George Herbert's Latin Poems." *Essays and Studies* 19 (1923): 29-39

Bowers, Fredson. "Herbert's Sequential Imagery: 'The Temper'." *Modern Philology* 59 (1962): 202-13.

Carnes, Valerie. "The Unity of George Herbert's *The Temple*: A Reconsideration." *ELH* 35 (1968): 505-26.

Carpenter, Margaret. "From Herbert to Marvell: Poetics in 'A Wreath' and 'The Coronet'." *Journal of English and Germanic Philology* 69 (1970): 50-62.

Clark, Ira. " 'Lord, in Thee the Beauty Lies in the Discovery': 'Love Unknown' and Reading Herbert." *ELH* 39 (1972): 560-84.

Clements, A. L. "Theme, Tone, and Tradition in George Herbert." *English Literary Renaissance* 3 (1973): 264-83.

Colie, Rosalie. *Paradoxia Epidemica: The Renaissance Tradition of Paradox.* Princeton: Princeton University Press, 1966.

Coolidge, John S. *The Pauline Renaissance in England: Puritanism and the Bible.* Oxford: Clarendon Press, 1970.

Eliot, T. S. *George Herbert.* London: Longmans, Green and Co., 1962.

Elsky, Martin. "George Herbert's Pattern Poems and the Materiality of Language: A New Approach to Renaissance Hieroglyphics." *ELH* 50 (1983): 245-60.

Empson, William. *Seven Types of Ambiguity.* New York: New Directions, 1955.

Endicott, Annabel M. "The Structure of George Herbert's *Temple*: A Reconsideration." *University of Toronto Quarterly* 34 (1965): 226-37.

―――. " 'The Soul in Paraphrase': George Herbert's 'Library'." *Renaissance News* 19 (1966): 14-16.

Fisch, Harold. *Jerusalem and Albion: The Hebraic Factor in Seventeenth-Century Literature.* New York: Schocken Books, 1964.

Fish, Stanley E. *The Living Temple: George Herbert and Catechizing.* Berkeley and Los Angeles: University of California Press, 1978.

Freeman, Rosemary. *English Emblem Books.* London: Chatto & Windus, 1948.

Freer, Coburn. *Music for a King: George Herbert's Style and the Metrical Psalms.* Baltimore: The Johns Hopkins University Press, 1972.

Gallagher, Michael P. "Rhetoric, Style, and George Herbert." *ELH* 37 (1970): 495–516.

Grant, Patrick. *The Transformation of Sin: Studies in Donne, Herbert, Vaughan, and Traherne.* Amherst: University of Massachusetts Press, 1974.

Halewood, William H. *The Poetry of Grace: Reformation Themes and Structures in English Seventeenth-Century Poetry.* New Haven: Yale University Press, 1970.

Hart, Jeffrey. "Herbert's 'The Collar' Re-read" in *Seventeenth-Century Poetry: Modern Essays in Criticism,* edited by W. R. Keast, 248–56. New York: Oxford University Press, 1971.

Hollander, John. *The Untuning of the Sky: Ideas of Music in English Poetry 1500–1700.* Princeton: Princeton University Press, 1961.

Johnson, Lee Ann. "The Relationship of 'The Church Militant' to *The Temple.*" *Studies in Philology* 67 (1971): 200–6.

Jones, Nicholas R. "Tests and Contests: Two Languages in George Herbert's Poetry." *Studies in Philology* 79 (1982): 162–76.

Kelliher, W. Hilton. "The Latin Poetry of George Herbert." In *The Latin Poetry of English Poets,* edited by J. W. Binns, 26–57. London: Routledge & Kegan Paul, 1974.

Klause, John L. "George Herbert's *Kenosis* and the Whole Truth." In *Allegory, Myth, and Symbol,* edited by Martin W. Bloomfield, 209–25. Cambridge, Mass.: Harvard University Press, 1981.

Knieger, Bernard. "The Purchase-Sale: Patterns of Business Imagery in the Poetry of George Herbert." *Studies in English Literature* 6 (1966): 11–24.

Kronenfeld, Judy Z. "Herbert's 'A Wreath' and Devotional Aesthetics: Imperfect Efforts Redeemed by Grace." *ELH* 48 (1981): 290–309.

Levang, Dwight. "George Herbert's 'The Church Militant' and the Chances of History." *Philological Quarterly* 36 (1957): 265–68.

McCanles, Michael. *Dialectical Criticism and Renaissance Literature* Berkeley and Los Angeles: University of California Press, 1975.

McLaughlin, Elizabeth, and Gail Thomas. "Communion in *The Temple.*" *Studies in English Literature* 15 (1975): 110–24.

Mahood, M. M. "Something Understood: The Nature of Herbert's Wit." In *Metaphysical Poetry,* 123–48. Stratford Upon Avon Studies 11. London: Edward Arnold, 1970.

Merrill, Thomas F. "Sacred Parody and the Grammar of Devotion." *Criticism* 23 (1981): 195-210.

Mills, Jerry Leath. "Recent Studies in Herbert." *English Literary Renaissance* 6 (1976): 105-18.

Miner, Earl Roy. *The Metaphysical Mode from Donne to Cowley.* Princeton: Princeton University Press, 1969.

Montgomery, Rupert. "The Province of Allegory in George Herbert's Verse." *Texas Studies in Literature and Language* 1 (1960): 457-72.

Nardo, Anna K. "Play, Literary Criticism, and the Poetry of George Herbert." In *Play and Culture*, edited by Helen B. Schwartzman, 30-38. West Point, N.Y.: Leisure, 1980.

Ostriker, Alicia. "Song and Speech in the Metrics of George Herbert." *PMLA* 80 (1965): 62-69.

Rickey, Mary Ellen. *Utmost Art: Complexity in the Verse of George Herbert.* Lexington, Ky.: University of Kentucky Press, 1966.

Roberts, John R., ed. *Essential Articles for the Study of George Herbert's Poetry.* Hamden, Conn.: Archon Books, 1979.

Rubey, Daniel. "The Poet and the Christian Community: Herbert's Affliction Poems and the Structure of *The Temple*." *Studies in English Literature* 20 (1980): 105-23.

Sanders, Wilbur. " 'Childhood Is Health': The Divine Poetry of George Herbert." *Melbourne Critical Review* 5 (1962): 3-15.

Sherwood, Terry G. "Tasting and Telling Sweetness in George Herbert's Poetry." *English Literary Renaissance* 12 (1982): 319-40.

Stewart, Stanley. "Time and *The Temple*." *Studies in English Literature* 6 (1966): 97-110.

Strier, Richard. *Love Known: Theology and Experience in George Herbert's Poetry.* Chicago: The University of Chicago Press, 1983.

Summers, Claude J., and Ted-Larry Pebworth, eds. *"Too Rich to Clothe the Sunne*: Essays on George Herbert." Pittsburgh: University of Pittsburgh Press, 1980.

Tuve, Rosemond. *A Reading of George Herbert.* Chicago: The University of Chicago Press, 1952.

Walker, John. "The Architectonics of George Herbert's *The Temple*." *ELH* 29 (1962): 289-305.

RICHARD CRASHAW

Adams, Robert M. "Taste and Bad Taste in Metaphysical Poetry: Richard

Crashaw and Dylan Thomas." *Hudson Review* 8 (1955): 60–77.

Bertonasco, Marc F. *Crashaw and the Baroque.* University, Ala.: University of Alabama Press, 1971.

Chambers, Leland. "In Defense of 'The Weeper'." *Papers on Language and Literature* 3 (1967): 11–21.

Collmer, Robert G. "Crashaw's 'Death More Misticall and High'." *Journal of English and Germanic Philology* 55 (1956): 373–80.

Hollander, John. *The Untuning of the Sky: Ideas of Music in English Poetry, 1500–1700.* Princeton: Princeton University Press, 1961.

McCanles, Michael. "The Rhetoric of the Sublime in Crashaw's Poetry." In *The Rhetoric of Renaissance Poetry,* edited by Thomas O. Sloan and Raymond B. Waddington, 189–211. Berkeley and Los Angeles: University of California Press, 1974.

Manning, Stephen. "The Meaning of 'The Weeper'." *ELH* 22 (1955): 34–47.

Martz, Louis. *The Wit of Love.* Notre Dame: University of Notre Dame Press, 1969.

Miner, Earl Roy. *The Metaphysical Mode from Donne to Cowley.* Princeton: Princeton University Press, 1969.

Neill, Kerby. "Structure and Symbol in Crashaw's 'Hymn in the Nativity'." *PMLA* 63 (1948): 101–13.

Peter, John. "Crashaw and 'The Weeper'." *Scrutiny* 19 (1953): 258–73.

Praz, Mario. "The Flaming Heart: Richard Crashaw and the Baroque." In *The Flaming Heart.* New York: Doubleday, 1958.

Raspa, Anthony. "Crashaw and the Jesuit Poetic." *University of Toronto Quarterly* 36 (1966): 37–54.

Schwenger, Peter. "Crashaw's Perspectivist Metaphor." *Comparative Literature* 28 (1976): 65–74.

Strier, Richard. "Crashaw's Other Voice." *Studies in English Literature* 9 (1969): 135–51.

Wallerstein, Ruth. *Richard Crashaw: A Study in Style and Poetic Development.* Madison: University of Wisconsin Press, 1935.

Warren, Austin. *Richard Crashaw: A Study in Baroque Sensibility.* University, La.: Louisiana State University Press, 1939.

Williams, George Walton. *Image and Symbol in the Sacred Poetry of Richard Crashaw.* Columbia, S.C.: University of South Carolina Press, 1963.

Young, R. R. *Richard Crashaw and the Spanish Golden Age.* New Haven: Yale University Press, 1982.

HENRY VAUGHAN

Allen, Don Cameron. "Vaughan's 'Cock Crowing' and the Tradition." *ELH* 21 (1954): 94-106.

Bradford, Melvin E. "Henry Vaughan's 'The Night': A Consideration of Metaphor and Meditation." *Ariel: A Review of Literature* 1 (1968): 209-22.

Brooks, Cleanth. "Henry Vaughan: Quietism and Mysticism." In *Essays Presented in Honor of Esmond Linworth Marilla*, edited by Thomas Kirby and William John Olive, 3-26. Baton Rouge: Louisiana State University Press, 1970.

Chambers, Leland H. "Henry Vaughan's Allusive Technique: Biblical Allusion in 'The Night'." *Modern Language Quarterly* 27 (1966): 371-87.

――――. "Vaughan's 'The World': The Limits of Extrinsic Criticism." *Studies in English Literature* 8 (1968): 137-50.

Farnham, Fern. "The Imagery of Henry Vaughan's 'The Night'." *Philological Quarterly* 38 (1959): 425-35.

Grant, Patrick. *The Transformation of Sin: Studies in Donne, Herbert, Vaughan, and Traherne.* Amherst: University of Massachusetts Press, 1974.

Kermode, Frank. "The Private Imagery of Henry Vaughan." *Review of English Studies* 1 (1950): 206-25.

Malpezzi, Frances M. "An Approach to Vaughan's 'Isaac's Marriage'." *English Language Notes* 14 (1976): 112-17.

Marcus, Leah Sinanoglou. "Vaughan, Wordsworth, Coleridge, and the *Encomioun Asini*." *ELH* 42 (1974): 224-41.

Murrin, Michael. *The Veil of Allegory.* Chicago: The University of Chicago Press, 1969.

Olson, Paul. "Vaughan's 'The World': The Pattern of Meaning and the Tradition." *Comparative Literature* 13 (1961): 26-32.

Pollock, John. "The Divided Consciousness of Henry Vaughn." *Papers on Language and Literature* 10 (1974): 422-42.

Post, Jonathan F. S. *Henry Vaughan: The Unfolding Vision.* Princeton: Princeton University Press, 1982.

Rickey, Mary Ellen. "Vaughan, *The Temple* and Poetic Form." *Studies in Philology* 59 (1962): 162-70.

Rudrum, A. W. "The Influence of Alchemy in the Poems of Henry Vaughan." *Philological Quarterly* 49 (1970): 469-80.

――――. "An Aspect of Vaughan's Hermeticism: The Doctrine of Cosmic

Sympathy." *Studies in English Literature* 14 (1974): 129-38.

Sandler, Florence. "The Ascent of Spirit: Henry Vaughan on the Atonement." *Journal of English and Germanic Philology* 73 (1974): 209-26.

Shawcross, John T. "Vaughan's 'Amoret' Poems: A Jonsonian Sequence." In *Classic and Cavalier: Essays on Jonson and the Sons of Ben,* edited by Claude J. Summers and Ted-Larry Pebworth. Pittsburgh: University of Pittsburgh Press, 1982.

Simmonds, James D. *Masques of God: Form and Theme in the Poetry of Henry Vaughan.* Pittsburgh: University of Pittsburgh Press, 1972.

Summers, Claude J., and Ted-Larry Pebworth. "Vaughan's Temple in Nature and the Context of Regeneration." *Journal of English and Germanic Philology* 74 (1975): 351-60.

Wyly, Thomas J. "Vaughan's 'Regeneration' Reconsidered." *Philological Quarterly* 55 (1976): 340-53.

ANDREW MARVELL

Allen, Don Cameron. *Image and Meaning: Metaphoric Traditions in Renaissance Poetry,* 93-153. Baltimore: The Johns Hopkins University Press, 1960.

Asp, Carolyn. "Marvell's Nymph: Unravished Bride of Quietness." *Papers on Language and Literature* 14 (1978): 394-405.

Berek, Peter. "The Voices of Marvell's Lyrics." *Modern Language Quarterly* 32 (1971): 143-57.

Berger, Harry, Jr. "Marvell's 'Garden': Still Another Interpretation." *Modern Language Quarterly* 28 (1967): 290-309.

———. "Andrew Marvell: The Poem as Green World." *Forum for Modern Language Studies* 3 (1967): 290-310.

Berthoff, Ann Evans. *The Resolved Soul: A Study of Marvell's Major Poems.* Princeton: Princeton University Press, 1970.

Bradbrook, M. C., and M. G. Lloyd Thomas. *Andrew Marvell.* Cambridge: Cambridge University Press, 1940.

Brett, R. L. "Andrew Marvell: The Voice of His Age." *The Critical Quarterly* 20 (1978): 5-17.

———, ed. *Andrew Marvell: Essays on the Tercentenary of His Death.* Oxford: Oxford University Press, 1979.

Brooks, Cleanth. "Criticism and Literary History: Marvell's 'Horatian Ode'." *Sewanee Review* 55 (1947): 199-222.

———. "Andrew Marvell: Puritan Authority with Classical Grace." In

Poetic Traditions of the English Renaissance, edited by Maynard Mack and George deForest Lord, 219-28. New Haven: Yale University Press, 1982.

Carpenter, Margaret. "From Herbert to Marvell: Poetics in 'A Wreath' and 'The Coronet'." *Journal of English and Germanic Philology* 69 (1970): 50-62.

Colie, Rosalie. *My Echoing Song: Andrew Marvell's Poetry of Criticism.* Princeton: Princeton University Press, 1970.

Cullen, Patrick. *Spenser, Marvell and Renaissance Pastoral.* Cambridge, Mass.: Harvard University Press, 1970.

Eliot, T. S. "Andrew Marvell." In *Selected Essays.* London: Faber and Faber, 1932.

Erickson, Lee. "Marvell's 'Upon Appleton House' and the Fairfax Family." *English Literary Renaissance* 9 (1979): 158-68.

Evett, David. "'Paradices Only Map': The *Topos* of the *Locus Amoenus* and the Structure of Marvell's 'Upon Appleton House'." *PMLA* 85 (1970): 504-13.

Fitzdale, Jay. "Irony in Marvell's 'Bermudas'." *ELH* 42 (1974): 203-13.

Friedenriech, Kenneth, ed. *Tercentenary Essays in Honor of Andrew Marvell.* Hamden, Conn.: Archon Books, 1977.

Godshalk, William Leigh. "Marvell's 'Garden' and the Theologians." *Studies in Philology* 66 (1969): 50-62.

Goldberg, Jonathan. "Marvell's Nymph and the Echo of Voice." *Glyph* 8 (1981): 19-39.

Gray, Allan. "The Surface of Marvell's 'Upon Appleton House'." *English Literary Renaissance* 9 (1979): 169-82.

Guild, Nicholas. "Marvell's 'The Nymph Complaining for the Death of Her Faun'." *Modern Language Quarterly* 29 (1968): 385-94.

Hartman, Geoffrey. "Marvell, St. Paul and the Body of Hope." In *Beyond Formalism: Literary Essays 1958-1970.* New Haven: Yale University Press, 1970.

Herron, Dale. "Marvell's 'Garden' and the Landscape of Poetry." *Journal of English and Germanic Philology* 73 (1974): 328-37.

Hinz, Evelyn J., and John J. Tuenissen. "What Is the Nymph Complaining For?" *ELH* 45 (1978): 410-28.

Kermode, Frank. "The Argument of Marvell's 'Garden'." *Essays in Criticism* 1 (1952): 225-41.

———. "Marvell Transpros'd." *Encounter* 27 (1966): 77-84.

Larkin, Philip. "The Changing Face of Andrew Marvell." *English Literary Renaissance* 9 (1979): 149-57.

Legouis, Pierre. *Andrew Marvell, Poet, Puritan, Patriot.* Oxford: Clarendon Press, 1965.

Lord, George deForest. "From Contemplation to Action: Marvell's Poetic Career." *Philologic Quarterly* 46 (1967): 207-24.

Martz, Louis. *The Wit of Love.* Notre Dame: University of Notre Dame Press, 1969.

Miner, Earl Roy. *The Metaphysical Mode from Donne to Cowley.* Princeton: Princeton University Press, 1969.

Norford, Don Parry. "Marvell and the Arts of Contemplation and Action." *ELH* 41 (1974): 50-73.

Patrides, C. A., ed. *Approaches to Andrew Marvell: The York Tercentenary Essays.* London: Routledge & Kegan Paul, 1978.

Reedy, Gerard. " 'An Horatian Ode' and 'Tom May's Death'." *Studies in English Literature* 20 (1980): 136-51.

Richards, Judith. "Literary Criticism and the Historian." *Literature and History* 7 (1981): 25-47.

Schwenger, Peter. "'To Make His Saying True': Deceit in 'Appleton House'." *Studies in Philology* 77 (1980): 84-104.

Siemon, James E. "Generic Limits in Marvell's 'Garden'." *Papers on Language and Literature* 8 (1972): 261-72.

Spitzer, Leo. "Marvell's 'Nymph Complaining for the Death of Her Faun': Sources versus Meaning." *Modern Language Quarterly* 19 (1958): 231-43.

Summers, Joseph H. *The Heirs of Donne and Jonson.* New York: Oxford University Press, 1970.

Toliver, Harold. *Marvell's Ironic Vision.* New Haven: Yale University Press, 1965.

Warnke, Frank J. "Play and Metamorphosis in Marvell's Poetry." *Studies in English Literature* 5 (1965): 23-30.

THOMAS TRAHERNE

Botrall, Margaret. "Traherne's Praise of Creation." *Critical Quarterly* 1 (1959): 126-33.

Clements, A. L. *The Mystical Poetry of Thomas Traherne.* Cambridge, Mass.: Harvard University Press, 1969.

Dauber, Antoinette B. "Thomas Traherne and the Poetics of Object Relations." *Criticism* 23 (1981): 103-25.

Day, Malcolm. "Traherne and the Doctrine of Pre-Existence." *Studies in Philology* 64 (1968): 81-98.

———. " 'Naked Truth' and the Language of Thomas Traherne." *Studies in Philology* 68 (1971): 305-25.

Drake, Ben. "Thomas Traherne's Songs of Innocence." *Modern Language Quarterly* 31 (1970): 492-503.

Grant, Patrick. *The Transformation of Sin: Studies in Donne, Herbert, Vaughan, and Traherne.* Amherst: University of Massachusetts Press, 1974.

Hepburn, Ronald W. "Thomas Traherne: The Nature and Dignity of Imagination." *The Cambridge Journal* 6 (1953): 725-34.

Hunter, C. Stuart. "Thomas Traherne and Francis Bacon: In Definition of Traherne's Poetic." *The Humanities Association Review Bulletin* 27 (1976): 1-15.

Jordan, Richard. *The Temple of Eternity: Thomas Traherne's Philosophy of Time.* Port Washington: Kennikat, 1972.

Leishman, J. B. *The Metaphysical Poets: Donne, Herbert, Vaughan, Traherne.* Oxford: Clarendon Press, 1934.

Marks, Carol Louise. "Thomas Traherne and Cambridge Platonism." *PMLA* 81 (1966): 521-34.

Marshall, William H. "Thomas Traherne and the Doctrine of Original Sin." *MLN* 73 (1958): 161-65.

Sabine, Maureen. " 'Stranger to the Shining Skies': Traherne's Child and His Changing Attitudes to the World." *Ariel: A Review of English Literature* 11 (1980): 21-35.

Salter, Keith W. *Thomas Traherne: Mystic and Poet.* New York: Barnes and Noble, 1965.

Seelig, Sharon Cadman. *The Shadow of Eternity: Belief and Structure in Herbert, Vaughan, and Traherne.* Lexington, Ky.: University Press of Kentucky, 1981.

Selkin, Carl M. "The Language of Vision: Traherne's Cataloguing Style." *English Literary Renaissance* 6 (1976): 92-104.

Trimpey, John E. "An Analysis of Traherne's 'Thoughts (I)'." *Studies in Philology* 68 (1971): 88-104.

Uphaus, Robert. "Thomas Traherne: Perception as Process." *University of Windsor Review* 2 (1968): 19-27.

Wallace, John Malcolm. "Thomas Traherne and the Structure of Meditation." *ELH* 25 (1958): 79-89.

Acknowledgments

"Donne's Compass Image" (originally entitled "Donne's 'Valediction: Forbidding Mourning' ") by John Freccero from *ELH* 30, no. 4 (December 1963), ©1963 by The Johns Hopkins University Press. Reprinted by permission.

"Donne and the Limits of Lyric" by John Hollander from *Vision and Resonance: Two Senses of Poetic Form*, 2d ed., by John Hollander, ©1985 by Yale University. Reprinted by permission of Yale University Press.

"The Fearful Accommodations of John Donne" by William Kerrigan from *English Literary Renaissance* 4, no. 3 (Autumn 1974), ©1974 by *English Literary Renaissance*. Reprinted by permission.

"Donne: The Imaging of the Logical Conceit" by Claudia Brodsky from *ELH* 49, no. 4 (Winter 1982), ©1982 by The Johns Hopkins University Press. Reprinted by permission.

"Herrick and the Fruits of the Garden" by Thomas R. Whitaker from *ELH* 22, no. 1 (March 1955), ©1955 by The Johns Hopkins University Press. Reprinted by permission.

"Letting Go: The Dialectic of the Self in Herbert's Poetry" by Stanley E. Fish from *Self-Consuming Artifacts: The Experience of Seventeenth-Century Literature* by Stanley E. Fish, ©1972 by The Regents of the University of California. Reprinted by permission of The University of California Press.

"Alternatives: The Reinvented Poem" by Helen Vendler from *The Poetry of George Herbert* by Helen Vendler, ©1970, 1975 by The President and

Fellows of Harvard College. Reprinted by permission of Harvard University Press.

"Crashaw's 'Epiphany Hymn': The Dawn of Christian Time" by A. R. Cirillo from *Studies in Philology* 67, no. 1 (January 1970), ©1970 by The University of North Carolina Press. Reprinted by permission.

"Henry Vaughan" by Louis Martz from *The Paradise Within: Studies in Vaughan, Traherne, and Milton* by Louis Martz, ©1964 by Yale University. Reprinted by permission of Yale University Press.

"Marvell's 'Songs of Innocence and Experience' " by Ruth Nevo from *Studies in English Literature 1500–1900* 5, no. 1 (Winter 1965), ©1965 by William Marsh Rice University. Reprinted by permission.

"Marvell's 'Upon Appleton House': An Interpretation" by Harry Berger, Jr. from *Southern Review* (Australia) 1, no. 4 (1965), ©1965 by Harry Berger, Jr. Reprinted by permission.

" 'The Nymph Complaining for the Death of Her Faun': A Brief Allegory" by Geoffrey Hartman from *Beyond Formalism: Literary Essays 1958–1970* by Geoffrey Hartman, ©1970 by Yale University. Reprinted by permission of Yale University Press.

"Thomas Traherne: Naked Truth, Transparent Words, and the Renunciation of Metaphor" by Barbara K. Lewalski from *Protestant Poetics and the Seventeenth-Century Religious Lyric* by Barbara K. Lewalski, ©1979 by Princeton University Press. Reprinted by permission of Princeton University Press.

Index